Jacob Merrill Manning

Half Truths and the Truth

Lectures on the Origin and Development of Prevailing Forms of Unbelief

Jacob Merrill Manning

Half Truths and the Truth
Lectures on the Origin and Development of Prevailing Forms of Unbelief

ISBN/EAN: 9783337166441

Printed in Europe, USA, Canada, Australia, Japan

Cover: Foto ©ninafisch / pixelio.de

More available books at **www.hansebooks.com**

HALF TRUTHS AND THE TRUTH.

LECTURES

ON THE

ORIGIN AND DEVELOPMENT OF PREVAILING FORMS OF UNBELIEF,
CONSIDERED IN RELATION TO THE NATURE AND
CLAIMS OF THE CHRISTIAN SYSTEM.

BY

REV. J. M. MANNING, D.D.,

PASTOR OF THE OLD SOUTH CHURCH, BOSTON, AND LECTURER ON THE
RELATIONS OF CHRISTIANITY TO POPULAR INFIDELITY
AT ANDOVER THEOLOGICAL SEMINARY.

Other foundation can no man lay than that is laid, which
is Jesus Christ. 1 COR. iii. 11.

BOSTON:
LEE AND SHEPARD, PUBLISHERS.
NEW YORK:
LEE, SHEPARD AND DILLINGHAM.
1872.

CONTENTS.

INTRODUCTION.

Nature and spirit of the work. — Definition of the word "infidelity." — Charity; its limit. — Invidious use of the word. — Practical infidelity. — Sense in which the word is here used. — Etymological meaning. — To be used with discrimination at all times. — Should be boldly applied when deserved. — Two sources of infidelity. — Strictly but one source. — Effects of the Fall. — Two opposite mental tendencies. — Each tendency the source of a class of infidelities. — Scope of the present work. — Suggestions in advance. — Speculative and scientific theories not to be prejudged. — Error not always to be denounced. — Mistake respecting astronomy. — Treatment of geology. — Caution respecting Darwinism. — Fondness of clergymen for science. — Man's physical nature not a subject of revelation. — A true spirit of reform in the church. — Natural history of infidel reformers. — Infidelity welcomes those whom the church repels. — The church not innocent. — Should avoid a false position. — Duty of the pulpit. — Congregations must co-operate. — New England pulpit to be commended. — Effect of a weak pulpit. — Leading infidels. — How the exigency is to be met. — The spirit of Christ in his people our main reliance. — Duty of ministers. — The whole church must have the mind of Christ. — How the spirit of Christ is to be shown. — This spirit peculiar to Christianity. . . . . Pages 1—36

LECTURE I.

SPINOZA AND OTHER MASTERS.

A singular death-bed scene. — Spinoza's parents religious refugees. — His childhood. — His studies. — His defection. — His trial. — His conduct. — His excommunication. — A fugitive. — At school. — His love. — His purpose formed. — Reads Descartes. — Characteristics. — His poverty. — His

(v)

patience. — His tolerance. — His easy views of all events. — Vagueness of ancient writers. — The Alexandrine masters. — Plotinus. — Iamblichus. — Proclus. — Plato. — Aristotle. — Xenophanes the Eleatic. — Heraclitus. — Pythagoras. — Hylozoists and others. — The Orientals. — Egyptian speculation. — Primitive monotheism. — The Chinese. — The Greeks. — Testimony from Egypt. — Conclusion of Naville. — Origin of Fetichism. — The Totem of the Indians. — Spinoza our starting-point. — Vagueness before him. — Course of religious thought sketched. — Spinoza's system the receptacle. — Claims of Bruno. — Intellectual activity of the age favorable to Spinoza. — The Reformation. — Bacon. — The Pilgrim Fathers. — Richelieu and Cromwell. — The Dutch. — Locke. — Newton. — Triumphs of science. — Mathematics. — Astronomy. — Optics. — Literature of the seventeenth century. — Theology. — Religious writers. — Divine purpose. . . . . 37—73

LECTURE II.

THE NATURE AND GROUNDS OF PANTHEISM.

Definition of pantheism. — How it differs from theism and atheism. — Wherein atheism and pantheism agree. — Language of pantheists often ambiguous. — Many names for one thing. — Knowledge of Spinozism which the purpose of this work requires. — Descartes was Spinoza's guide. — This doubted. — Opinion of Saisset. — Parentage of Descartes. — Early purpose. — Criterion of truth. — Not original with Descartes. — Testimony as to Descartes' position. — Four main points in Cartesianism. — "I think, therefore I am." — Criticism of Gassendi and Huxley. — Descartes to be taken as he understood himself. — The Cartesian method. — Descartes' first step. — A foothold for Spinozism. — The recognition of Reid's doctrine of necessary truths would have saved Descartes. — The Cartesian argument for the divine existence favors Spinozism. — The argument for a God which now tends to prevail. — Descartes only seems to anticipate this. — How his argument legitimates pantheism. — The Cartesian method aids the tendency to pantheism. — The tendency further strengthened by his denial of second causes. — Spinoza's logic faultless. — The premises of pantheism untenable. — The central position of Spinozism. — The dogmatic result. — Three kinds of knowledge. — Some account of the Ethics. — Subject of the Second Part. — Of Part Third. — Of Part Fourth. — Of Part Fifth. — Of the First Part. — Definitions. — Axioms. — A demonstration. — Perfection of superstructure. — Two attributes of substance. — Bearing on question of immortality. — Fatalism. — The a priori philosophy not to be judged by Spinozism. — Malebranche. — Leibnitz. — The safeguard. . . . . 74—110

LECTURE III.

THE GERMAN SUCCESSION

A reaction. — Empiricism. — This movement to be passed over for the present. — Revival of Spinozism. — What is here attempted. — Relation of Leibnitz to the new movement. — The Leibnitz-Wolfian philosophy. — Kant's earlier views. — The need of a critic suggested by Hume. — Critique of the pure reason. — Relation of the reason to the understanding. — Space and time forms of the reason. — The categories of the understanding. — Ideas of the reason. — What they are. — Their subjective nature. — Where this critique leaves us. — Kant's plan broader than this sphere of the reason. — Another faculty. — Function of the practical reason. — Result not satisfactory. — Critique of the judgment. — The object not attained. — Three distinct tendencies in Kant. — Reinhold. — Jacobi. — His mystical tendency. — Argues against Kant's first critique. — The thinkers of his time not with him. — The interview with Lessing. — Character of Jacobi. — Hegel's criticism. — Fichte. — Thought-activity the only knowable thing. — The non-ego. — A product of the ego. — The alternative of atheism or pantheism. — Accused of atheism. — Becomes a pantheist. — Unlike Spinoza. — The true wisdom. — Fichte's pantheism considered defective. — Schelling. — Grand objection to Fichte. — Schellingian doctrine of knowledge. — How Schelling reaches the position of the pantheist. — His system described. — Agreement with Spinoza. — Three potences. — How they work in the evolution of spirit. — Distinction between nature and spirit. — How Schelling would account for Christianity. — The spirit of Schelling's system. — Short continuance of this school of pantheism. — Schelling and Edgar A. Poe. — Culminated in Hegel. — The best refutation of error its clear statement. — An anachronism. — Hegel. — The absolute idea. — Use of Kant's antinomies. — The logical movement. — Natural philosophy. — Philosophy of spirit. — Its theological result. — Hegel and Kant. — Consequences of the system. — Strauss. — Schleiermacher. — Net result. — Lesson of the survey now taken. — Testimony of Müller. 111—149

LECTURE IV.

THE PANTHEISTIC CHRISTOLOGY.

Philosophy and religion inseparable. — This more manifest in the a-priori philosophy. — Two uses of the word "religion." — When pantheism is a religion. — Religions to which pantheism may be applied. — Re-statement of

Hegelianism. — The absolute idea. — A triplicate process. — Compared with
Comte's "three states." — Illustrated in history of civilization. — In art. —
Progress and conservatism. — The absolute idea in religion. — Christianity a
form of the absolute idea. — Different views of Hegelianism. — The " right."
— The " left." — The " centre." — Strauss. — His Life of Jesus. — The idea
in religion alone important. — The question of historic truth trivial. — Essential Christianity. — How the idea produced the so-called record. — Criticism
deals with the non-essential. — Evidence that Strauss was a pantheist. — His
view of the Incarnation. — The origin of the Gospels. — Accepts Spinoza's
view of Christ. — Thinks his criticism true to the spirit of the narrative. —
The gospel record a piece of cloud scenery. — Advantage of this pantheistic
position. — The Paulists. — Evemerus. — His method revived by Lessing in
Wolfenbüttel fragments. — How used by Paulus. — Results of the theory. —
Regarded as a failure. — Eichhorn. — De Wette. — Strauss finds germs of his
theory in them. — Also in Origen and Philo. — Relation to other schools of
criticism. — Secret of popularity. — Three principles of interpretation. — The
position of Strauss. — The myth. — How he makes room for it. — The idea
produces the story. — What follows if the Gospels are post-apostolic. — Internal evidence against Strauss. — Also external evidence. — How he would
evade it. — The argument against him overwhelming. — Baur. — Differs from
Strauss. — How he accounts for the Gospels. — Traces of a conflict. — Pauline
party favored. — Peter overborne. — Paul triumphs. — The reasoning of Baur
not admissible. — No special refutation needed. — There were parties in the
early church. — Baur's treatment unfair. — An argument for inspiration. —
Renan. — Requires no special treatment. — Spirit of his criticism pantheistic.
— An irreverent comparison. — Free religion. — Its peculiarity. — May be
traced to Hegel. — Christianity triumphant. 150–182

LECTURE V.

THE CULTURE WHICH PANTHEISM LEGITIMATES.

A feature of modern thought. — Spontaneity. — Authority. — New theory untenable. — Relation to pantheism. — Goethe. — Why chosen. — Viewed only
in one aspect. — Relation to other thinkers of his age. — Ignorance of his
speculative views. — Early scepticism. — Proofs that he was a pantheist. —
Meets with Jacobi. — Wished to be known as a Spinozist. — Fatalism. — Divineness of nature. — Free necessity. — Tone of his writings. — The two
Goethes. — As a student of nature. — Works in which he shows to advantage.
— Shorter poems. — Iphigenia in Tauris. — Egmont. — Hermann and Dorothea. — Wherein his theory works evil. — Faust. — Goetz von Berlichingen.

— False theory of morals. — Popularity of Goetz. — Sorrows of Werther. — Its influence. — Origin of the work. — Complaints of his friends. — Wilhelm Meister. — The Fair Saint. — Philina. — Mignon. — Other characters. — Elective affinities. — Natalia and Wilhelm. — Goethe's theoretical views carried into his life. — His faults not to be passed over. — Had noble traits. — Was not a patriot. — Goethe not consistent with his theory of culture. — Would have been better as a man if more inconsistent. — Allowance to be made to art. — The obligations of the artist. — Christianity teaches the only adequate theory of human culture. . . . . 183—226

LECTURE VI.

PANTHEISM IN THE FORM OF HERO-WORSHIP.

The representative name. — Method of treatment. — Carlyle's position in English literature. — His style. — Ethical tendency. — A political reformer. — Was he a pantheist? — Not in the dogmatic sense. — Proofs of a pantheistic spirit. — His idea of history. — Of the individual. — Views of nature pantheistic. — His doctrine of necessity. — Of space and time. — Religious views. — Bibles. — Origin of worship. — Sincerity alone essential. — Accepts Goethe's definition of religion. — Result. — How his pantheism affects his political views. — Makes him revolutionary. — French Revolution. — Laws and compacts not the basis of true government. — Function of representative assemblies. — Hates democracy as much as constitutional monarchy. — Eulogy of the Pilgrims. — Mahometanism as good as Puritanism. — No love for free government in any case. — Scorn of moral and social reforms. — Origin of his contempt for democracies. — Negative side of his political creed. — His political and social creed positively stated. — Hero-worship. — This the basis of primitive governments. — Urged as the only real basis. — Great men a theophany. — Carlyle's ideal of a great man. — Plea for his theory of government. — The result of the theory is anarchy. — Hero-worship contrasted with Christianity. . . . . 227—267

LECTURE VII.

PANTHEISM IN THE FORM OF SELF-WORSHIP.

Individualism. — Represented by Emerson. — Method of treatment. — Contrasted with Carlyle. — His excellent temper. — Of purer tone than Goethe. — Monotony. — Nomenclature. — " Old Two-Face." — Comprehensive statements of pantheism. — All things are God. — History. — Literature. — God a gentleman. — Love. — Prayer. — What Emerson has to say of personality. — An ignis fatuus. — God impersonal. — But one conclusion possible. — Emerson's method. — Consciousness the way to all truth. — No mean egotism. — Definition of man. — The varieties of genius forms of the divine consciousness. — Teaches the pantheistic fatalism. — All things subject to fate. — No one can do otherwise than he does. — All life natural. — Emerson's use of words literal rather than rhetorical. — Even fate a mystery. — The objective world in the light of Emerson's philosophy. — History absorbed into the soul. — All literature the biography of each man. — A practical result. — Nature an evolution of the soul. — The world man externized. — Knowledge of nature but self knowledge. — Emerson's theory of nature that of every subjective idealist. — More specific injunctions. — Duty of self-reverence. — Self-reliance. — Self-assertion. — The moral law wholly subjective. — Duty of self-isolation. — To be wholly self-absorbed the highest blessedness. — "Men descend to meet." — Misanthropy. — Attitude towards the Bible and Christianity. — Insinuates that Christ was a pantheist. — Spirit of the two contrasted. — Emerson would unsettle all things. — No philanthropist. — Scorn of the masses. — No moral distinctions. — Better than his theory. — Inconsistency recommended. — The good man forced to be a hypocrite. — Transcendentalism not to be judged by Emerson. — Christian faith the grand safeguard. 268—316

LECTURE VIII.

THEISM WITH A PANTHEISTIC DRIFT.

Theodore Parker. — Disliked to be called an infidel. — Did not bow to Christ as the final authority in religion. — Affirms that Jesus was in error on many subjects. — Calls Christ and the Bible idols. — Unitarians denounced for retaining them. — What Parkerism finds in Christ. — The Old Testament long since outgrown. — His idea of religious progress. — The positive side of Parkerism. — Terms used to designate it. — Parker less original than he supposed. — Three factors of the absolute religion. — The sentiment. — The idea. — The conception. — The conception alone varies. — Origin of religions. — Their succession traced. — Parkerism to be superseded. — Theory of religious progress refuted by history. — Obscures the character of God. — Weakens our basis of hope for man. — The doctrine of redemption rational. — Parker not simply a theist. — Was he a pantheist? — A re-statement of the alternative of unbelief. — Parker could not be a positivist. — Pantheism may be mistaken for positivism. — Parker not a materialist. — Denies the possibility of atheism. — Denied that he was a pantheist. — But his definition is inadequate. — Acquits Spinoza. — Admits the thing while disowning the name. — More positive proofs of pantheism. — Held the Kantian philosophy. — His definition of God does not exclude pantheism. — All men theists. — Misrepresents pantheists. — Identifies God with the world. — With God subject and object are the same. — The fault of deism. — His view of immortality pantheistic. — God immanent in all things. — He is the substantiality of matter. — Men not responsible for the religion they hold. — Different religions a necessity of circumstances. — All the same at bottom. — An endless succession of religions. — The pantheistic fatalism. — Absolute toleration. — No second causes. — Creation and providence the same thing. — All action in nature God's action. — Held to the mathematical method. — God impersonal. — Makes personality the same as anthropomorphism. — God personal only in a rhetorical sense. — Our conception of God wholly subjective. — God is universal being. — Parker to be judged by his tendency. — The school of theism. — His real tendency held in check. — Character of his scholarship. — Relation to the Unitarians. — Some of his strongest supporters disowned his theology. — Early statements of his views most decided. — His most scriptural preaching best liked. — The fate of philosophy when bereft of faith in Christ. — The Rock of Ages.................. 317—361

LECTURE IX.

THE STRENGTH AND WEAKNESS OF PANTHEISM.

Recapitulation. — Authors excluded from this survey. — Refutation of pantheism. — This went along with the exposition. — The clear statement of error its best refutation. — Every pantheist has something peculiar to himself. — Wherein they agree. — Spinoza's method cannot reach ontology. — Same fault in Fichte and Emerson. — Function of consciousness mistaken. — Differs from the faculty of intuition. — What is granted for argument's sake. — The infinity of God said to involve pantheism. — This argument assumes what the pantheist has denied. — The essence of personality is free-will. — God the only perfect person. — The assertion that the mind can act only where it is. — Contradicted by our necessary beliefs. — Whatever else fails must insist on these. — The duty of mental science to these first truths. — The claim of comprehensiveness. — This claim cannot be made good. — Important truths which pantheism excludes. — Gives precedence to an inferior faculty. — All the faculties of the mind should be recognized. — Precedence due the moral faculty. — The emphasis of the soul demands this. — Every honest nature welcomes it. — The doctrine of the divine immanency said to be a source of power. — Proves too much. — The real power not limited to this doctrine. — Bryant. — Thomson. — These have as much poetical vantage-ground as Emerson. — Source of immorality in literature. — Joaquin Miller. — Good men exposed to peril. — The doctrine of the divine immanency a weakness of pantheism. — The argument from great men. — Pantheism cannot claim these. — Transcendentalism can. — They have escaped the perils of that philosophy. — Metaphysics in education. — Better than physical science. — Opinion of Hamilton. — Scientific eras barren of literature. — The vaunted honors stolen. — Purity of life in the teacher not a test of his doctrine. — The ethical criterion. — Christianity above patronage. — How men may become pantheists. — Times in which pantheism may be popular. — Legitimates disorder. — Our exposure to the peril. — Our defence. — Something better than pantheism offers. — Conclusion. — A feeling of relief. — Richter's dream. — Pantheism cannot reach what is best in us. — The prayer of Schiller's father surpasses anything in Goethe. — Power of the twenty-third Psalm. 362—398

INTRODUCTION.

My purpose, in the lectures which follow, is to treat of popular infidelity, — its sources, its development, and its relation to what is known as the Biblical or Christian system. This work is not undertaken in a controversial or partisan spirit. I am no dogmatist or polemic, though my point of view, to which much patient study has led me, is the supernaturalism of Jesus of Nazareth. It seemed needful to say this at the outset, owing to the acrimonious and denunciatory style in which, for the most part, the questions between Christianity and its assailants have been hitherto debated. The natural presumption, in view of the past, is, that whoever appears on this field has only entered into the strifes of other zealots; that he comes as a warrior thirsting for victims, and in no sense as an inquirer. The terms which this ancient debate has bequeathed to us, and to some of which a certain odium still adheres, cannot be now laid aside. They have such a currency, in the language of the day, that no candid person will charge it to bigotry or unfairness, but purely to the necessity of the case, that they continue to be used. It will be seen, in the title which I have chosen for this work, that I regard many forms of infidelity as half truths, at least in their origin. Believing that the human intellect naturally craves truth, I shall not easily be persuaded that any body of doctrines, which has been put forth by earnest thinkers, is unmixed error; nor shall I fail, so far as the nature of my undertaking will permit, to point out the merits of writers whom, as to their main tenets, I may feel bound to condemn. Some of those writers manifest, at times, a calm spirit of inquiry which their critics would do well to emulate. It is not only lawful, but often greatly for our advantage, to learn from those with whom we disagree. Truth has not as yet revealed itself wholly to any finite mind; and the remark of Him who was the Truth, about the beam in the eye which sees the mote in a brother's eye, is not altogether inapplicable to those who are defending scriptural doctrine against the assaults of infidelity.

Definition of the word "infidelity." The word "infidelity" is so loosely used by the writers and speakers of our time, that one might almost despair of being able to define it. And yet, owing to this great variety of usage, there seems all the more need, if we would understand each other in what is to follow, that its meaning should be brought within some tolerably well settled limits. We certainly *Charity,* ought, in simple justice, to distinguish between systems of infidelity and the persons who confess themselves more or less in accord with those systems. In no way, perhaps, is it more easy to overstep the bounds of charity, than in identifying individuals with theories which they cannot make up their minds to reject utterly, or for which they express a partial sympathy. The intercourse of life puts us in contact with many men and women holding theoretically to what is called infidelity in the language of the schools, yet our personal acquaintance with whom convinces us that to call them "infidels" would be the grossest injustice. We are constantly running against infidelities, yet are forced to own that there is an amazing scarcity of infidels. This may be accounted for in part by the odium attaching to the word, which causes most persons to dread it, and to resent the application of it to themselves. Therefore our charity should have a limit. Though many are raised above their theoretical unbeliefs by a natural and acquired goodness, yet there are those whom the word "infidel" alone can properly describe to us; nor should we hesitate thus to distinguish such, wherever we find them. And its limit.

The invidious use of this term in theological controversy must strike all fair minds as the extreme of meanness and cowardly unmanliness. It always injures the cause in whose behalf it is employed. When not a confession of weakness, it is a blunder. All are repelled by it, save those whom prejudice or rude passion has blinded; nor does it influence even these, except for the time being. Though the poisoned arrow with which a prostrate antagonist seeks to wound his conqueror, though the desperate cry by which he summons to his rescue the pack of ignorant and noisy zealots, yet it ever fails to deliver him, while at the same time it makes his defeat doubly disgraceful. Invidious use of the word.

We often have occasion to use the phrase "practical infidelity." These words, whether used in the pulpit or religious literature, point especially Practical infidelity to those persons in the Christian church who practise the forms of a godly life while destitute of its power. They lack sincerity in their confessions and worship. Amid all their attention to the formalities of religion, their rigid orthodoxy of opinion, and punctilious regard for what is outward and ceremonial, there is in them an evil heart of unbelief. Inwardly, and so far as witnessing for Christ before men goes, they are full of heresy and alienation from the truth. The fruits which they produce in their lives are no better than if they made no pretence of believing the doctrines which Christ taught. This is the infidelity which God visits with his special abhorrence. It was the great sin of the Jews, bringing upon them a worse fate than overtook Sodom and Gomorrah. The gospel, with its doctrine of the new birth and freedom from external rites, was given to rescue man, if possible, from this demon of doubt, which is so apt to creep into the heart of the formal religionist.

Sense in which the word is now used.

But the use of the word "infidelity" does not, in any of the cases now noticed, touch the subject-matter which I propose to treat. We are concerned with the unbelief which has become an intellectual theory; to the support of which logic and argument are summoned; which assails the Christian system, affects to be in some real sense its rival, and seeks, by dint of philosophical reasoning, to displace it. I should say that any person who does not recognize the authority of Christ as final on all questions of religious faith, is, in the judgment of the largest charity, an infidel. Even Professor Newman, the radical religionist, is candid enough to say, "It is evident that we must either quite disown the

Gospels, or admit that Christ regarded men as impious who did not bow before him as an authoritative teacher." Strictly speaking, an infidel is one who has apostatized. This is according to the etymology of the word. [Etymological meaning.] The first Christians used it, I suspect, as those in later times certainly did, to designate one who, after attaching himself to Christ, had become unfaithful, or had forsaken him. A distinction is thus made between the infidel and such as have never believed on Christ's name. He is a far baser person than the pagan, who, having no knowledge of Christ, nor at any time confessing him as Lord, cannot be charged with unfaithfulness to him. But we need not use the term in this harsh sense. Though the infidel of to-day is one who dwells where Christ is preached, and who therefore may have fallen away from the Christian faith into his present state of unbelief, yet his heart does not plead guilty to the charge of treachery. He may have a conviction of honesty, and the approval of conscience, in what he has done. All this we are ready to grant him; nor do we, in applying to him a term which usage has made current, mean anything beyond what he is ready to acknowledge; namely, that he has rejected Christ as the supreme authority in matters of religious faith. Such, I take it, is the most legitimate application of the word at present. I do not propose to employ it, save in this perfectly fair and honorable method.

If the word "infidelity" be odious to-day, the odium is in the character of those who have been its advocates. To be an infidel is no more a shame now, than to be crucified was a shame in the time of Christ. But Christ and his followers have made the cross glorious. If infidels cannot thus transfigure their reproach, this but proves the absurdity of their claims. Those who set up no claim in opposition to Christ, who acknowledge him as the supreme authority in religion, who accept his word as that by which any religious doctrine is to be judged, are improperly called infidels. It is an abuse of language, as well as contrary to the "new commandment" in the gospel, when the various Christian bodies thus brand each other. Some of those bodies may seem to us to teach fatal error, and we may conscientiously refuse to have fellowship with them; but so long as they make Christ their Master, we have no good right to call them infidels. To misinterpret the divine Teacher's words is not the same thing as denying his authority. Men may differ widely as to what Christ taught, — so widely as to be unable to dwell together in ecclesiastical fraternity, — and yet be equally earnest in maintaining that Christ is Lord. Where this supremacy is not accorded, however; where any one has rejected Christ, after full opportunity to know him; and not only that, but has framed this his denial into a positive creed, and is seeking to establish it as true by what he regards as rational argument, — there we should recognize infidelity, in the proper sense of the term. He has investigated and reflected, till he has come to certain conclusions; and those conclusions are entirely subversive of Christianity as an authoritative religion. This their logical effect he sees, and not only makes no effort to avoid it, but stoutly insists upon it. What the treatises are, which come within this definition, I do not now under-

[marginal notes: To be carefully used, even in its milder sense. Should be boldly applied, where deserved.]

INTRODUCTION. 7

take to say. The catalogue of modern infidelities need not be given. Any list which I might draw up would be regarded by some as incomplete; while others might accuse it of injustice, saying that it included speculations worthy of better company. It is enough to have given a criterion, — entirely fair, I think all must admit, — by which we may each determine the religious bearing of any book or utterance that meets us. Whatever claims pre-eminence over Christ, or denies to him the supremacy in matters of religious faith, or lays down propositions known to be subversive of his authority, is an infidelity. In that view of it, although associated with much that we admire, and even approve, it deserves no quarter at our hands. As the disciples of Christ, believing that he spoke the absolute truth, and concerned for the well-being of men as truly as for his honor, we are bound to unmask the intruder, and battle against it under its proper designation.

As to the sources of these various infidelities which are around us, and throughout the Christian world, one need feel less hesitation in speaking. *Two sources of infidelity.* They seem to me to be reducible to *two* sources — Pantheism, represented by Spinoza, and Positivism, represented by Comte. Some may be inclined to add a third source, namely, Deism. But this is hardly more than a dependent form of infidelity. It rests on no steady foundation of its own, but is always falling away into either Pantheism or Positivism, where it is not happily exalted into Christianity.

But even this statement may be simplified; *Strictly but one source.* for, in the last analysis, all forms of religious

error may be brought to a single source — the separation of man from God. It was in the garden of Eden that these poisonous waters, still polluting the earth, took their rise. When man fell from his Maker's embrace, then immediately infidelity began. It is evident, since man came forth from God, that his faculties must have acted abnormally, leading him astray constantly in all his searches after truth, as soon as he had separated himself from God. This may seem to be a sweeping remark; for it might be said that many persons, into whose thoughts the idea of a God almost never enters, have yet been successful students of nature, of history, of the human mind; have shown excellent judgment in matters of business, and in all that concerns the welfare of the state. But this latter remark seems to me to need qualification, rather than the other. If we look at human conduct comprehensively, — if we consider it in all its relations, and follow it on to its remoter issues, — we shall find that it is never thoroughly wise while acting independently of God. The statesman does not plan what is best for the state, the reformer mingles much of evil with his good, and the most successful man of business fails in certain important respects while not inspired and kept by a divine influence. In no partial sense, but in the broadest sense, it is true that "the fear of the Lord is the beginning of wisdom." We cannot separate material interests from spiritual, or temporal from eternal. Profitableness and ungodliness, wisdom and atheism, are never joined together. The human mind acts abnormally on all subjects, mistaking error for truth, and confounding success with failure, as soon as it has departed from God.

Effects of the Fall.

The finite is safe only in the embrace of the infinite. "Were God, and man's relation to God, to become the central and informing soul of all knowledge and all studies," says Dr. John Young, of Edinburgh, "then philosophy would spring into new life, and become at once more ennobling and more profound; science would become more luminous and more quickening; literature would catch a new glow and flush from the breath of heaven, and be more enkindling and more beauteous; art would be radiant with a sweeter, a holier, and a diviner grace. It is the most fatal of all mistakes to judge that the loving sense of God, in the soul, is one which we may have or want, indifferently. It is an absolute necessity to our being. Religion is not a separate department of human knowledge — a branch, like other branches of human inquiry. It is rather the all-encompassing atmosphere, in which, whatever be our studies or works, we can alone truly breathe and live; the one inspiring influence, which alone puts a soul into our efforts, and gives them a divine meaning. Religion is the sum of the whole inner nature, intellectual, moral and spiritual, without which all is sterile, cold, and dark."[1]

But this primal source of infidelity, of all errors in religion, whether modern or ancient, transcends the purpose of our present inquiry. We are concerned with the two heads — Pantheism and Positivism — into which it has become divided. The human mind, being separate from God, wanders; and it wanders in two different paths, or by two opposite methods, according to certain inherent tendencies. Coleridge has

Two opposite mental tendencies.

[1] 'Light and Life of Men' (London and New York, 1866), pp. 495, 496.

remarked that all men are born either Aristotelians or Platonists. Perhaps it would be stating the case more intelligibly to some, to say that all men are born either Baconians or Cartesians. All who think are a-posteriori or a-priori thinkers. They either make the outer world of sense and experience, or the inner world of consciousness, their starting-point; reason from effects to causes, or from causes to effects. Emerson expresses this fact by saying, "Mankind have ever been divided into two sects, materialists and idealists; the first class founding on experience, the second on consciousness; the first class beginning to think from the data of the senses; the second class perceive that the senses are not final, and say, the senses give us representations of things, but what are the things themselves they cannot tell. The materialist insists on facts, on history, on the force of circumstances, and the animal wants of man; the idealist on the power of thought and of will, on inspiration, on miracle, on individual culture."[1] This language overstates the distinction in some particulars, though the brilliant essayist was right as to the existence and universality of the fact. It may be doubted whether any thinker ever does, or ever can, pursue one of these methods to the exclusion of the other; but they are sufficiently distinct to mark two conflicting schools of thought, to indicate two radically different intellectual tendencies in men. "Not of choice," says Dr. Young, "but in consequence of a real necessity, occasioned by their individual structure, men are materialistic or spiritualistic, logical or philosophical, argumentative or intuitional, the one and the other alike being

[1] Miscellanies (Boston, 1858), pp. 320, 321.

simply the effect of original mental conformation. They limit themselves to the range of the understanding, and to what can be submitted to its processes and decisions; or they love to ascend to the region of the supersensual, and covet intensely the higher revelations of a disciplined faith. The two orders are ever ranged on opposites, in theology, in philosophy, and in real life. Respecting the origin of the universe, the question of a First Cause, the being and character of God, the introduction of evil into the universe, the nature of volition, the final destiny of man, they are always essentially divided, and are rightly distinguished as empiricists and transcendentalists."[1]

Now, both these tendencies, which would ever proceed aright and harmoniously in union with God, being without that inspiration and guidance, are constantly going astray. Thus it is that each tendency becomes the source, or creates the centre and root, of a distinct class of infidelities. If the mental tendency be transcendental, it ultimates itself in Pantheism; if it be empirical, it ultimates itself in Positivism. Such I conceive to be, in each case, the genesis of the two opposite sources of modern infidelity. All religious errors, which are subversive of Christianity in their aim, have either no claim on our notice, do not even deserve to be refuted, or may be traced to one of these two fountains. Between these two extremes the irreligious mind of the race has been ever swinging, — wearily swinging, with a pendulous motion, while the hand on the dial has marked the steady advance of the kingdom of Christ. Whenever the prevailing philosophy of the world has been transcen-

Each tendency the source of a class of infidelities.

[1] Light and Life of Men, p. 102.

dental, the prevailing infidelity has been pantheistic; and when that philosophy has been empirical, the infidelity has had in it more or less of positivism. Ancient Buddhism is associated with the philosophy of the senses, Brahmanism with that of consciousness. Descartes gave the a-priori method to Europe, and out of that method sprang Spinozism; Bacon and Locke gave the a-posteriori, which was pushed forward into sensationalism. Kant taught a spiritual philosophy, and Hegel was, in some real sense, his successor; the prevailing philosophy of the present time is materialistic, and Comtism is the infidelity which claims its protection. In Germany, where thinking has had more to do with ideas than with facts, pantheism has had a prodigious growth; in France, where the study of what is outward prevails, positivism finds its home and stronghold. Infidelity has existed all along through the history of our race, ever since man first departed from God; and it will continue to exist, in every nation and age, till men are restored to God in Christ. In ages and countries where thought is chiefly concerned with the material and outward, the forms of infidelity will have their ground in positivism; in those times and places where truth is sought chiefly in consciousness, pantheism will be the informing spirit of unbelief. One or the other of these two yokes of bondage men will wear, until delivered into the glorious liberty of the children of God.

Scope of the present work. A full and adequate treatment of the topics contemplated in these lectures would include, therefore,

I. A CRITICAL HISTORY OF PANTHEISM, WITH A REFUTATION OF IT UPON PHILOSOPHICAL GROUNDS;

INTRODUCTION. 13

II. A Similar History of Positivism, with a like refutation; and

III. A Statement of the manner in which Christianity meets that human want which they are forever flattering only to delude.

This whole vast field is more than I can hope to explore, in the series of lectures which here follows. It will be enough, and more than I dare promise, if even tolerable justice be done to the first main department namely, Pantheism. And inasmuch as there is a wide field of examination to go over, requiring us to eliminate and define the errors which may be classed under this head, thus at length preparing the way for argument against them; considering, I say, that we must wait so long without formally replying, while the authors on trial are allowed to speak for themselves in large part, I deem it proper, in the remainder of this Introduction, to make a few suggestions of general import, as to the most effective methods of meeting and forestalling any forms of religious error. Suggestions in advance.

1. In the first place, the defenders of the Christian system should not be too ready to condemn, as a form of infidelity, every new speculation, or scientific theory, which may happen to be put forth. This premature judgment may be reversed by a later and more intelligent verdict. The friends of Christianity will then be convicted of hindering the cause they sought to forward; of ignorantly putting forth their hand to steady the sacred ark where it was in no danger. The new theory or speculation may be yet in its infancy, crude, Speculative and scientific theories not to be prejudged.

broached in the tentative rather than the dogmatic form. If alarmists within the church would be at pains to know the author personally, they might find him a devout and reverent thinker, as much concerned for the honor of Christianity as themselves. Perhaps he has carefully considered the very points at which they stumble, and sees a way of justifying them to his Christian faith which has not occurred to his critics. Why should they stultify themselves by raising a false alarm? Very likely he only puts his views into the form of an inquiry at first, and leaves them at the tribunal of reason and common sense. Why need we, in our concern for the Bible, rush upon them frantically, or blow our trumpets for a warning, before those theories have won a sure foothold, even in the scientific or philosophical world? When they have passed over that frontier, coming safely out of every struggle, and surviving every attack on their proper ground, then it will be early enough for us to conclude whether or not our batteries should open upon them. Multitudes of them are overthrown and trodden down, while running the gantlet wholly outside of our domain; and if here and there one escapes, surviving the opposition of rival theories, and overcoming the severest scientific criticism, this fact should be taken as presumptive evidence that it comes to us, not as an enemy, but as a friend; for truth cannot be the foe of truth.

Error not always to be denounced. Even where we detect grave signs of error, it may be wiser to seek fellowship than to withdraw it. It was Judaism that said, "Get thee out of thy country, and from thy kindred;" Christianity says, "Go ye into the world." Perhaps Luther was wrong in thinking that the Reformers could do most for their cause by staying in the Papal church. Perhaps they are mistaken who think that the churches of New England lost ground by withdrawing from Arianism in Dr. Channing's time. But as long as the honor of Christ will permit, we should avoid driving any new error into an open declaration of war. It may be no more than the pet delusion of a few individuals, and, at the worst, will live only while they live, if let alone. By assailing it we provoke it to take positive ground; at once put its advocates out of the reach of our Christian influence; enable it to raise against us the cry of persecution, which will be sure to bring crowds of curious and sympathetic people to its support; and thus a party may be organized, through which its influence will be vastly widened, and prolonged far beyond the term of its natural life. A broad wisdom, gleaned from the fields of history and experience, admonishes us to brand no man as a teacher of infidelity, till absolutely compelled to by our loyalty to Christ. Whoever does not insist on being the enemy of Revealed Religion, should be esteemed its friend.

Great harm was done to the cause of Christ, when his church condemned, as of infidel tendency, some of the earlier astronomical discoveries. *Mistake respecting Astronomy.* We are amazed now, that the fathers of the church should make themselves a tribunal to judge the Copernican theory, and that they should proceed to condemn it, declaring it to be a damnable heresy. Not that Copernicus himself was thus condemned. Being one of the devoutest men of his times, living amidst powerful friends who wisely guarded his reputation, and not publishing his great discovery till just as he died, he escaped ecclesiastical censure. It was reserved for Galileo, his follower in the next century, to bear the Papal condemnation; by which his name has been lifted up, as an everlasting warning to theologians, not to make their own ignorance a throne of judgment, from which to hurl anathemas at the novelties of science and philosophy.

Treatment of Geology. Yet that warning has not been always heeded. The blunder of those Romish doctors was repeated as late as the present century, when the theories of geologists began to challenge attention. How many students of the new science were thus repelled, from what they mistook as the narrowness and bigotry of Christianity, until they became open opposers of the church and its teachings, we shall know only in the day of the revelation of all things. It is not these denunciatory champions, who seem to be born with the scent of religious error in their nostrils, that Christianity needs. They do much harm to her sacred cause. Such men as Thomas Chalmers are the rather our examples. When the ministers of Scotland were beginning to raise their hue and cry against geology, he exclaimed, "This is a false alarm. The writings of Moses do not fix the antiquity of the globe. If they fix anything at all, it is only the antiquity of the species." These great words produced a revolution, and prevented a revolution. They were caught up, and shouted throughout the United Kingdom, till geologists saw they had no cause to rebel against the church, and the church saw she had no occasion for denouncing geology. It was this noble stand which made Chalmers the champion, at once, of both the new science and Christianity. From that time forth geology was mainly a Christian science in Great Britain; whereas, but for that grand utterance and leadership, it would, from all that now appears, have speedily fallen into infidel hands.

At the present day there is a controversy, going on in the scientific world, respecting which the friends of Christianity need to beware. I refer to the Darwinian theory of the origin of species through natural selection, which argues that all the animal races now on the earth have been developed out of one central mass of life; and its opposing theory, held by Agassiz among others, according to which there are many such centres, so distinct in the near past that even the races of men could not all have descended from a single pair. The nature of this controversy, and its attitude towards certain portions of the Bible, are thus stated by Professor Huxley: "The hypotheses respecting the origin of species which profess to stand on a scientific basis, and, as such, alone demand serious attention, are of two kinds. The one, the 'special creation' hypothesis, presumes every species to have originated from one or more stocks, these not being the result of the modification of any other form of living matter, or arising by natural agencies, but being produced, as such, by a supernatural creative act. The other, the so-called 'transmutation' hypothesis, considers that all existing species are the result of the modification of pre-existing species, and those of their predecessors, by agencies similar to those which, at the present day, produce varieties and races, and therefore in an altogether natural way; and it is a probable, though not a necessary consequence of this hypothesis, that all living beings have

Caution respecting Darwinism.

arisen from a single stock. The doctrine of special creation owes its existence very largely to the supposed necessity of making science accord with the Hebrew cosmogony; but it is curious to observe that, as the doctrine is at present maintained by men of science, it is as hopelessly inconsistent with the Hebrew view as any other hypothesis." [1] The relative merits of the two theories, as judged by our scriptural standards, are certainly well stated in the closing words of this paragraph, though Huxley is inexcusably reckless in assuming that he knows precisely what the Hebrew view, as he calls it, was. It is plain that those who adhere to the common interpretation of the first of Genesis must reject both these theories. When they applaud Agassiz for some hard blow given to Darwin, they ought not to forget that Agassiz is no champion of theirs, but quite as hostile to them as his opponent. And are we yet sure that either of them is hostile to the inspired record, so much as to what translators and interpreters have made that record say? One or the other of the two theories may be destined to prevail; and we can afford to wait undisturbed, while the battle goes forward in the outer court of science, not taking up our weapons till either "special creation," or "transmutation," having been declared victor there, shall assail the sanctuary of our religious faith. Why should we excommunicate zoology, even after its own friends are at peace, so long as it is sure that our sacred philology has yet a great deal to learn? If it becomes the settled creed of the scientific world, as few anticipate, I suspect, that the races of men sprang from

---

[1] Lay Sermons and Addresses (Appleton & Co., New York, 1871), pp. 279, 280.

several distinct origins, the laws of language may be trusted to show us that no word of the Bible, claiming to come from God, contradicts that creed. And on the other hand, if some improved form of Darwinism becomes established, as is now extremely probable, the task of the Bible interpreter will be comparatively easy. I have no expectation that this Development theory will be proved true, as it is held and applied by some of its advocates. But if it foreshadows a natural truth, respecting the origin of the human race, which may yet be brought out by scientific research, we have every reason to believe that that truth, whatever it is, will not contradict, but establish the words of God. We should not too hastily assail it, even though it may have seemed thus far to be against us; remembering — as Coleridge so nobly says — that an error is sometimes the shadow of a great truth yet below the horizon. Let us not bequeath to the future a fresh instance of theological blundering, compelling those after us to look back on our treatment of zoology with as much shame as we now look back on the ado made about geology and astronomy.

It has been too much the fashion to charge upon the clergy this prejudice against science which I now deprecate. In one view of the case there could hardly be a greater injustice. Whatever may have been true in the past, no class of men are now more tolerant of scientific theories, or give them more respectful attention. Suspicion is not the rule, but the exception, and rarely appears, save in those least enlightened. Every new truth in science is another pillar of theology. It can

Fondness of Clergymen for Science.

be shown that even the persecutions of Galileo were not due to the clergy so much as to the jealousy of certain other philosophers; and a full knowledge of all the facts would no doubt prove, in similar cases, that wrong has been done in representing Christian ministers as hostile to scientific pursuits. They show an interest in such studies which naturalists have been slow to reciprocate. They have done more than any other class to familiarize the public with the best science of the times. And I am happy, in making these statements, to find that no less a personage than Professor Tyndall is ready to confirm them. What he says of the clergy of England, and especially of the clergy of London, is still more emphatically true of the better part of the profession in America. "They have nerve enough," says Tyndall, addressing his brother scientists, "to listen to the strongest views which any among us would care to utter; and they invite, if they do not challenge, men of the most decided opinions to state and stand by those opinions in the open court. No theory upsets them. Let the most destructive hypothesis be stated only in the language current among gentlemen, and they look it in the face. They forego alike the thunders of heaven and the terrors of the other place; smiting the theory, if they do not like it, with honest secular strength." Such I believe to be the feeling of the best Christian ministers, at least in the present age. By continuing to cherish this spirit they will be kept from the mistakes of former times — the mistakes of a few men, not always clergymen, which have been made in such circumstances, and so thrust forward, that the whole church has had to bear the odium.

It is altogether unworthy of Christians at this day, be they clergymen or laymen, to be disturbed about the progress of science, or to attempt to discredit it with denunciation and sneers. {Man's physical nature not the special subject of Revelation.} In regard to Darwinism, what force can stale jests about ancestral apes and tadpoles have, from those who confess to being, in their mortal make, brothers of the worm? All in us that can perish was taken out of the same ground from which they came forth; is no less dust than the reptile we bruise with our heel, and to the dust it shall return. We sow not that body that shall be. There is a natural body, and there is a spiritual body. Who knows but the researches of zoology may yet so enlighten our criticism and exegesis, that we can fearlessly say, speaking of that natural body, The writings of Moses do not fix the antiquity of man; if they fix anything, it is only the time when, by the inbreathing of the spirit of God, he became an immortal and morally responsible being? Then the discovery of lake-dwellings in Europe, and of human remains in ancient caves and geological formations, such as have been adduced by Lyell and others, will cease to hold any hostile attitude towards the Christian revelation. Certainly we shall not give up anything by taking the simple ground that the Scriptures were not meant to teach zoology, — to give us the natural history of a race which is crushed before the moth. Certainly we shall keep all that is essential to the integrity of our faith, by simply maintaining that the divine oracles are concerned with that spirit, made in the image of God, which is his child, and which, through disobedience, has fallen away from his fatherly embrace. Herein are the true glory and eternal peril of man. What science has to do with is vanity; it wastes away with the grass and flowers, and the places which *Man's spiritual nature above science.* knew it shall know it no more. That divine likeness it was, not this frail tenement, which died in Adam; which has lain dead in trespasses and sins, all through the long generations; which is made alive in Christ, and which, living and believing in him, shall never die. We need have no fear of zoology while it stays within the range of natural law; we may but immortalize our own ignorance, and degrade our cause, by assaulting it in the name of Revelation; it can never reach the truth of a spiritual creation, to which our consciousness testifies, and which is the citadel of the Christian faith; and, by not disowning it, but throwing around it the warm atmosphere of a brotherly interest and charity, we may save both it and ourselves.

A spirit of reform prevents infidelity. 2. In the second place, we may meet or forestall many religious errors of our times by owning all true charities and reforms about us as branches of the one great work committed to the Christian church. The rise and progress of not a few infidel tendencies, all along in Christian history, may be easily traced. There is, in almost every instance, a natural history of the revolt, which bears a striking lesson for us. Certain philanthropical movements have begun in the church, or under its immediate notice. Where else did they ever begin? The leading membership, perhaps also the ministry, watched *Natural history of infidel reforms.* the new development with a disturbed feeling. It jostled opinions they had long held, — so long as for that reason to believe them true. The rising charity or reform found its more ready advocates among the inconspicuous and less refined of the brethren. Might not those who seemed to be somewhat lose their prestige, and become followers or only equals where they had been wont to lead, if they gave place to the innovation? That control which they had enjoyed till it seemed to them a natural right, depended on keeping all things as they were. There might be a Christian spirit in some of these philanthropists, it was admitted; possibly they were of that open-minded, unprejudiced class of men who, even in the time of Christ, welcomed truths which the learned would not receive. But they gradually acquired a habit of forwardness in the church, wholly out of keeping with their former modesty; and they had a blunt way of stating new views, out of season oftener than in season, which neither pleased delicate ears, nor became the place where all should be done decently and in order. Under this strong temptation the damaging step was taken. That new enterprise, the child of Christian impulse, was voted a mischievous intruder; was disowned, frowned upon, requested to take itself out of the way. The attempt was made to soothe the feelings of those who had thus been wounded, by assuring them that no doubt they were right in their motives. They were only a little too fast. It would be wiser in them to wait God's time, or till society should be ripe for their enterprise. This, however, so far from quenching the flame, was but adding fresh fuel to it. For, these aggrieved brethren justly argued, how is society ripened for any reform save by constant hearing of it? or how does God make known his time, if not by laying a necessity on the hearts of his people? Such are the evil devices by which, in instances sadly numerous, the church has alienated her own children, and, like the god in pagan mythology, sought to devour them.

Infidelity welcomes those whom the church repels.

But while the church has been displaying this centrifugal force within herself, there have risen, on the border-land between her and the world, certain rallying-points for these same discarded philanthropies. There the disowned and ostracised brethren meet, tell the story of their persecutions at home, and form new alliances for the common advantage and safety. Shrewd observers, men of ability and ambition, who are seeking a constituency, and who bear the church no love, here begin to take up the injured cause. These leaders, going too far in their tirades against Christianity, repel the more devout or timid of their new followers, who flee back into the church from what they regard as a half-way house to infidelity. But though returning themselves, they do not bring with them the cause for which they went out. That stays among those with whom they found temporary refuge. Such is the way, briefly told, in which we are often furnished with that strange and monstrous spectacle, the work of the church ostensibly going forward under infidel auspices; Christ's enemies, apparently, saving him from his friends. If the good man had not been asleep, the spoiler had not broken up his house. People look on the outward appearance; and the church has not avoided the appearance of evil, while these unbelievers seem to be carrying out the Saviour's express commands.

The church not innocent.

Thus it is that the infidelity which might have been forestalled, springs forth and thrives. We must confess, in looking over the history of the church, that Christians have many times abandoned their own arsenals to their foes. Christianity has furnished to infidels the weapons with which they have assailed Christianity. The enemy, watching for occasion against our cause, did not fail to strike when the occasion was given. Identifying the Bible with those who professed to be builded together on it, he could readily make it abhorrent to undiscriminating minds. Did churchmen find arguments in the Bible in favor of systems of injustice? Did they quote its words on the side of slavery, as favoring the indulgence of appetite in strong drinks, against efforts of woman to improve her condition? This was just the opportunity which the wary adversary sought. He took their interpretation of the Book for the Book itself. Their commentary on divine truth was the war-club with which he assailed that truth.

We who are Christian believers ought not to allow ourselves to be thus driven into a false position. *Should avoid a false position.* It is better to stay in the church, and bear much opposition from our own brethren, than yield up the sword of truth into the hands of the enemy. All real charities are the children of Christianity. Where they are we have a right to be, and ought to be. We may be suspected, avoided, and threatened for a time, by those who make their own traditions the sole criterion of truth, but if we save these charities from falling into infidel hands, — if we keep them safely housed, folded within the fold of the Good Shepherd, breathing there a more congenial atmosphere than they can find without, — our reward shall not be always wanting. Then religious error will have no chance to clothe itself in the garments of truth. We shall keep those garments where they belong. Then infidelity will not be able to steal from us that charm which gives it its power. Then Christianity will not repel, but attract, those who are enlisted in any cause of good will to men. Then it will be seen with a clearness which none can gainsay, will shine forth with a brightness from which infidelity shall flee confounded, that faith in Christ, and the fellowship of his gospel, are the way to all that is loving, or just, or kind between man and man. The church has only to be true to her divine Founder, walking in his own blessed footsteps of beneficence, and occupying all the ground that is hers by the terms of her great commission, and infidelity, shut out upon the bleak and barren rock where it was born, will soon starve or freeze to death.

Duty of the pulpit. 3. In the third place, those who are called to preach the gospel can do much to prevent the growth of religious error, by compelling thoughtful persons to respect them as men of culture and power. I offer this remark partly as a balance to what has just been said. Whatever Christian ministers may do on the plane of common charity, they should strive to perform their especial work with a masterly hand. Hard study and thinking, which, after all, are the true secret of intellectual power, must nerve them daily, or their grasp on the better class of minds will be neither strong nor permanent. If Paul had wished to teach Timothy how to save men from infidelity, he could have written nothing better than the charge, "Let no man despise thee." It should be said, however, that the power of the pulpit, in this respect, does *Congregations must co-operate.* not rest altogether with the ministry. Congregations are largely responsible. Not all of them will bear, without restiveness, such a style of preaching as would satisfy more thoughtful listeners. Instead of making the preacher feel that he must exert himself to write up to their capacity, they are constantly tempting, and almost dragging him down to a lower level. They pack the house of God with a miscellaneous crowd, who come, not to be instructed, not to grapple with themes which tax the attention and reason, that their moral nature may be profoundly and healthfully aroused, but who must be amused, and superficially excited in such a way as shall incline them to come again. The preacher's office is thus made a kind of advertising agency, in the interest of those who own the pews and pay the parish expenses. He cannot be a growing man, in any worthy sense; nor is he allowed to practise, but must neglect, and gradually forget, those deeper investigations of truth which alone win the respect of the intelligent, and which all men need to have pressed on their attention, whether they think so or not. There should be an atmosphere of intellectual vigor around the minister, which shall not only stimulate him, but compel the sluggish and ill-disciplined among his hearers to exert their latent powers. Thus alone can the weak be made strong, or the strong who are of the opposite party have any chance to be convinced. On this score, thanks to a faithful ministry and their earnest flocks, we find much to honor in the Puritan pulpit of New England. Wendell Phillips, the distinguished popular orator, once confessed to a friend that Dr. Lyman Beecher taught him how to argue. Infidels went to hear Nathaniel Emmons preach, not because they liked his doctrines, but because, in the

<small>New England pulpit to be commended.</small>

handling of them, he showed himself to be a master. Preachers of this stamp were wont to reason till their hearers trembled. Nor were those hearers repelled; but, delighting in sermons which taxed their powers of thought, they were drawn, as by a spell, to the ever fresh displays of intellectual strength. Such preaching made its adversaries ashamed, drew a charmed circle about those who took pleasure in profound thinking and sound logic. They had no inducement to wander off after the teachers of scepticism. Their religious doubts were not a matter on which they set any great value, but, at the best, only secondary. What they craved, and must have, as what alone almost all doubters are ever earnest about, was mental food and quickening. They were not restive, nor was their sceptical bias strengthened. The germs of infidelity in them could not grow, having nothing to feed upon, while they were held by this magic power of argument. Though they came to scoff, not unfrequently they left to pray, being awed into a respect which deepened to godly sorrow, faith, and repentance not to be repented of. A

Effect of a weak pulpit. jejune, slipshod style of thinking in the pulpit, though careless heads like it, and fill the newspapers with praises of it, can never win these higher victories. The same stale thoughts, however variously the changes be rung on them, and though they be set off with an odd text, many scraps of poetry, and humorous allusions, will not go down, Sabbath after Sabbath, with really sensible men. The multitude of those who desire simply to be put on good terms with themselves, may increase; but another class, serious-minded though inclined to doubt, will scatter away into solitude, or where there is some appearance of intellectual life. "These crudities and extravagances," say they, "are not what we come to the house of God for. Empty buckets, forever going into the well and fetching nothing up, do not meet our case. Whatever interest we may have in religious discussions, our time is valuable; nor do we wish to put ourselves too much under the influence of such an intellectual standard, avoiding weak preachers just as we do weak books, lest our own standard of style and thought should be unconsciously lowered." Thus it is that some of the best minds, in search of a high culture, though doubtful respecting the Christian faith, are repelled till they quit the church to go where their minds shall at least get some sort of nutriment.

Men thus repelled fall an easy prey to the higher forms of infidelity. They often become leading propagators of religious error. Or if kept from this by some absorbing pursuit, their withdrawal from Christian relations tells against the truth, and serves to point the sneer of the open opposer. We are not to be servile imitators of those who triumphed in a past age. Very likely the style of preaching which prevailed then would be unsuited to the present times. We, whom Christ is now calling to give the gospel to men, should serve our own age as the faithful of other days served theirs. We need to be like them chiefly in knowing the habits of mind, the literature, the science, the theology amidst which we live; need to understand the present spirit and tone of all thinking, and catch the enthusiasm of our great forerunners, so as to meet error effectually and wield the truth with power. Therefore, beyond any collateral good which he may seek to accom-

Leading infidels.

How the exigency is to be met.

plish, the preacher should strive to make men respect him in his sacred office. The overshadowing fact in his ministry should be, not that he is active in the charities and philanthropies of his time, but that he brings home to men's hearts, with an honest strength which they cannot resist, the gospel of the Son of God. This must be his grand business, and no popular demand must hinder him from consecrating to it all his energies. Pastors of churches can show their sympathy with reforms without becoming pack-horses for all the societies which propose to aid or relieve somebody or something. They can show a tender interest in every parishioner, a good will towards the public enterprises of the day, love for their friends, a kind regard for the sick, the sorrowing, the poor of the outlying districts, without becoming ministerial vagabonds. Let some one else do the canvassing for needy colleges and theological schools, for churches unable to pay their debts, and mission societies whose treasuries are empty. It is not reason, said the apostles at the time of Pentecost, that Christ's ministers should leave the word of God, and serve tables. Deacons are appointed to the offices of parochial charity — a fact which must be emphasized, and made to cover as much ground as possible, or what chance can ministers have, in an age of great mental activity, to magnify their calling? They should be free to act upon their own deep conviction that they are nothing while they are not preachers of the gospel. This is the necessity which the Spirit, if he ever called them to their work, laid on them at the beginning. And woe unto them if they preach not the gospel; if they do not so preach it as to make it respected; so as to silence the gainsayer; so as to hold sturdy thinkers firmly to the truth, giving them no occasion to wander from it, till they shall be convinced that it is the only bread which they can eat and never hunger.

4. In the fourth place, Christ's followers may do much to prevent the rise and spread of infidelity, by proving to men that their discipleship is not prompted by selfishness or self-seeking, but is purely a filling up of the blessed ministry to others which Christ began. Let it appear to the unbelieving that we are in nothing their beneficiaries, but in all things their benefactors. Christ said, "I am among you as one that serveth;" and again, "I came not to be ministered unto, but to minister." God reigns over the universe because he is love; it is being the servant of all, as no other can be, that makes him Lord of all. In such royal and godlike service, according to the capacity given us, is the hiding of our strength — the main secret of any ability we may hope for to make the truth mightier than error. "Do good, hoping for nothing again," is the sublime precept, " and ye shall be like your Father in heaven." *The spirit of Christ in his people our main reliance.*

As regards the ministry, though we who preach the gospel may live of the gospel, yet we should, like Paul, suffer loss rather than have our glorying made void. . We should preach as debtors to all men, and not as those who look for a reward. It should be our boast that we have no hire but souls; that the slight provision which we receive for present needs is not of the nature of pay, so much as an expression of gratitude on the part of those who contribute it; that our entire ministry is a witness to all men that we seek not theirs, but them. If left to *Duty of ministers.*

suffer for this world's comforts, it is better to remember Him who had not where to lay his head, the Good Shepherd who gave his life for the sheep, than to be suspected of any mercenary motive. When those who reap our spiritual things do not let us reap their temporal things, it is wiser to rebuke them manfully, or depart out of their city shaking the dust from our feet, if the privation can be no longer endured, than to be all the time breathing a spirit of complaint. That brooding discontent, if indulged, will gradually infect our whole ministry; and then the power and glory of our office will be gone. Rather than sink down into this state of mind, than have the sense of unrequited service grow to be a chronic disease, it would become us, like Christ and the apostles if need be, not to enter on our ministry till we have made provision for our temporal support; to be able to cultivate a farm, deliver lectures, practise some handicraft, or have other means of supplying our few temporal wants, which shall stand us in stead when they that are taught forget to "communicate with" him that teacheth. It becomes the ministers of Christ to avoid, in all possible ways, the imputation that they are hirelings; that their pastorates are simply their "livings;" that they follow their profession, just as all worldly men labor, for the sake of temporal wages. They must compel men to own that their ministry is indeed a discipleship of Him who, though rich, became poor that others through his poverty might be rich; that it is peculiarly and sublimely a labor of love; that this is its distinctive trait, wherein no other calling or pursuit, in all the world, can be compared with it.

But this devotion on the part of those who preach the

gospel is not enough. It may be made weak through the unfaithfulness of the great body of church-members. There have been ministers remarkable for their spirit of self-sacrifice in every age. Their spirit of devotion was shorn of its power, however, because it was seen to be an exception to the general life of the church. Whatever is exceptional, among persons of the same class and profession, is apt to be regarded as abnormal. The average life of the whole body is taken as the index of its real spirit. On this ground it is that infidels ascribe the zeal of such Christians as Henry Martyn, David Brainerd, and Harlan Page, to religious fanaticism. They see in it, not a proof of the transforming power of the gospel, but a sign of mental disorder. On the same ground the martyr-spirit of the apostles is attributed to natural enthusiasm, awakened by the undue excitement of the religious imagination, and the life and death of Christ are said only to prove that he was the greatest of religious enthusiasts. This objection can be effectually answered only by a spirit of devotion pervading the church. There is a supernatural element in the Christian life, — a love of sacrifice and self-denial in doing good, — which cannot be accounted for by mere natural causes. But this element must appear in the great body of Christians, thus forcing men to see that it is in no case abnormal or exceptional, but a uniform result of faith in Christ Jesus, or the few good works, which are done will not lead them to glorify our heavenly Father. There can be no question, reasoning from the nature of the human mind as well as from history, that when the laity and clergy are one in this thing, every mouth of the gainsayers

The whole church must co-operate.

will be stopped. All men will be forced to recognize the things which are not seen, and which are eternal, in order to account for the phenomena which the life of the church will present. This general union, in filling up what is behind of Christ's sufferings, will make it impossible for the world not to confess that he proceeded and came forth from the Father.

Almost all our reliance, in meeting the doubts which scientific or speculative thinking may from time to time generate, must be on this leaven of sincerity and devotion to good works in the mass of Christ's followers; a power which we shall get only as we have Christ formed within us, and as we put on Christ day by day, so that the life which we live in the flesh shall be the life of God manifested through us. To reveal him is the sublime office of all those who make up the one visible church. If we cherish a friendly feeling towards the science and philosophy of our time, that favor should be for this supreme object. If we give our godspeed to every genuine charity, that sympathy should be for one and the same purpose. If we preach the doctrines of the gospel thoroughly and with all our might, that faithfulness should have no less an end than to declare the Father's name. All our studying, all our toiling, all our self-sacrificing should be to show forth the excellency of Him who has called us; to make men see that the gospel, reproduced in the lives of Christians, is the wisdom and power of God; to prove, by the all-loving spirit which animates us, that any form of unbelief which seeks to displace Christianity is a thief and a robber. Let the Christ-like spirit of all who believe, compel men to

How the spirit of Christ is to be shown.

see that infidelity is an imposture which bodes them only evil; that if admitted amongst them it would put cursing for blessing, darkness for light, corrupting selfishness for holy and heavenly charity. If we choose to be identified with one school of theology rather than another, it should be clear to all that that preference grows out of a higher consecration. Not as partisans, but the better to seek and save the lost, should we strive to organize the truths of the gospel into a compact doctrinal system. Why need we care what human name is stamped on our weapons, or from whose armory they came, if so be that they are of celestial temper, and we find them mighty through God to the pulling down of strongholds? And any denominational likes or dislikes which we may happen to have, should grow out of the same high aim as our other differences. They should be our instrumentalities, not our ends; chosen not for their own sake, but as the harness in which we can work most easily and effectually for Christ. In this view the variety of Christian denominations is a great advantage to the universal church. They are to be rejoiced in, so long as they do not usurp the place of the objects of the gospel, since they enable every believer, whatever his natural peculiarities, to find some place of service which shall be congenial to him. David can have his sling and stones, and Saul's mighty men their heavy armor; and thus Israel shall not divide, but greatly increase his strength against the hosts of the Philistines. Whether it be a question of theology, or of ecclesiastical polity, all should be free to choose under Christ, with the utmost charity and confidence towards each other. Souls hungering for the peace of God will be drawn to us by seeing that we have no party zeal, — no wish to build up this or that branch of the church for its own sake, or at the expense of some other branch,— but make it our supreme concern, through whatever special fellowship we may choose to be in, to save and bless mankind.

<small>This spirit peculiar to Christianity.</small> Nothing but Christianity has ever given to the world such a service as this. There were faint foreshadowings of it in ancient times, and in some pagan lands men have shown a capacity for it, within certain narrow lines; but to find another Jesus of Nazareth, or another such mission of love as he founded, would be as impossible as to put another sun in the heavens. That kingdom of love and suffering, through the weakness of those to whom it has been committed, may at times have seemed untrue to its lofty tone and standard; and thus doors may have been opened for the incoming of religious error; yet under its broader aspects, and as judged by its acknowledged spirit, it has proved itself to be, all along through the Christian ages, the light and the life of men. And if we take up this kingdom in our turn, and carry it forward in the all-sacrificing spirit of the Lamb of God, any unbeliefs that may be lowering about us will swiftly disappear. It is the advancing sun that makes the snow and ice melt, the light shining in beauty that causes the darkness to flee away. Men will recoil from the arts of the infidel, in the presence of a church thus in earnest; and will hasten from him to be under its covert, instinctively choosing life rather than death, that which quickens rather than that which chills and dwarfs their noblest powers. They will turn to it as the imprisoned plant turns to the window; they will flock to it as birds fly from winter to a warmer and brighter clime.

PANTHEISM.

LECTURE I.

SPINOZA AND OTHER MASTERS.

ON the 22d day of February, 1677, in a small hired chamber at the Hague, while the owners of the humble dwelling were at church, it being Sunday, a physician, having seen the tenant of that lonely room heave his last breath, and hastening to depart, took to himself a little money and a silver-handled knife, which lay on the table near the dead man's body, fearing that he might receive no other fee for his medical services.[1] The man whose lifeless remains were thus deserted, to await the return of his simple host and hostess, was Benedict Spinoza. Not wishing to withhold from him any honor which is justly his due, but choosing that he should be over-praised rather than disparaged, I am willing to accept as historically true, all that his most ardent disciples or friends have said of him. The eulogistic account of Mr. Lewes, in his Biographical History of Philosophy,[2] shall be given,

A singular death bed scene.

---

[1] Accounts of the death of Spinoza, as of various events in his life, do not agree. Willis (Life, Correspondence and Ethics of Spinoza, London, 1870) differs from Lewes, whom I have chiefly consulted. Colerus, pastor of the Lutheran church at the Hague, who greatly admired Spinoza, and took pains to gather up all the local memories of him, is their principal authority; though they do not hesitate to question his veracity (especially Willis) when it conflicts with their own prejudices.

[2] Appleton & Co., New York, 1857, pp. 456-469.

so far as my space will permit, with no tittle of abatement from its full meaning.

Spinoza's parents religious refugees. According to this writer, Spinoza died at the meridian of his manhood, being but forty-four years and three months old. He was of Jewish parentage, and his father and mother resided in Amsterdam at the time of his birth. They had but recently come to this city of free Holland, escaping thither from their home in Portugal, where intolerance of the Jews would not suffer them to live. Their flight, it thus seems, was nearly in the same age, and for the same reasons, as that of the Pilgrim Fathers from England. They sought an asylum from religious oppression. This is a circumstance which should be noted, in sketching the life of Spinoza. If he had known Christianity as anything but a persecuting power, he might, upon renouncing Judaism, have embraced something better, possibly, than the dream which he himself dreamed in his solitude. But for this hereditary prejudice and hatred, which we all can understand, he might have made the choice of a Paul or a Neander. He seems, however, when he forsook the national faith, to have seen no alternative but to invent a religion of his own.

His childhood. Benedict, or Baruch, as he was called before he forsook the religion of his people, is described as a remarkably active boy, though lacking in physical robustness; fond of playing, with his sisters Miriam and Rebecca, about the squares and wharfs of the city. He was remarkable for his "bright, quick, and penetrative" eyes; and for his dark hair, which floated in "luxuriant curls over his neck and shoulders." His father is represented as a successful merchant, who hoped that this only son would choose the same occupation. But a passion for study which showed itself very early, together with a slender constitution, daily growing more slender through devotion to books and meditation, induced the parent to change his purpose. The beloved son, *His studies.* already "sicklied o'er with the pale cast of thought," was allowed to enter upon a course of the higher Hebrew learning. He gave himself to his studies with the greatest enthusiasm, and with astonishing success; so that when he was only fourteen years old, hardly a doctor or rabbi, in the whole country, surpassed him in amount and accuracy of knowledge. Very high hopes were entertained of him, among adherents to the Jewish faith. His teacher, Saul Levi Morteira, a zealous Israelite, looked on him with feelings of pride and admiration. We may easily judge, therefore, how great were the disappointment and alarm of his friends, when they found him pushing his inquiries beyond the limits of the Old Testament and the Talmud, scattering the arguments of the rabbis with his nimble logic, and proposing to them a multitude of very plain questions which they saw it to be for their interest not to attempt to answer. *His defection.* Two young men, nearly of his own age, are mentioned as courting his intimacy at this time,[1] and urging him to divulge his opinions, under a pretence of discipleship; though, as he suspected, with the purpose of betraying him to the Jewish elders. He was so reticent to these young men respecting his new views, that whatever they may have at first designed, they took offence at his reserve, and reported him as one who was secretly undermining the ancient faith. Straightway he

---

[1] Willis, pp. 31, 32.

was summoned before the leaders of the synagogue, whose minds were already beginning to turn against him. This peremptory demand made him feel, no doubt, the great inconsistency of his people, in refusing him the freedom of opinion which they had gone into exile to secure. He appeared, however, in answer to the requirement; and that, too, so promptly and willingly as to raise strong hopes, among his relatives and friends, that he would deny or retract the opinions which had been charged against him. Yet in all this he was consistent with himself. Though he would not have his sentiments drawn out of him and stated in court by others, he shrank not from the opportunity thus to state them with his own voice and in his own language. He therefore eagerly obeyed the summons. He gave a frank account of his heresies to the proper tribunal. His bearing was so easy, and without apparent concern for himself, in the presence of his judges, as to amount to a kind of "gay carelessness," says one writer. He refused to take back what he had now asserted openly, unless he should be convinced of his error by sound argument. He defiantly but coolly confronted the accusers who appeared against him; and when his judges threatened him with excommunication for his obstinacy, though he answered them respectfully, there was something in his voice and manner which betrayed a deep contempt for both their office and themselves. His old teacher Morteira, grieved that his brilliant pupil should be lost to Israel, pleaded and kindly remonstrated; but these failing, he, too, joined in the attempt to overawe the heretic. But threats had no power to intimidate the youthful thinker. From whatever

His trial.

His conduct.

source coming, so long as he saw no reason in them they only awakened his proud disdain. His was one of those natures, often found in feeble bodies, which are incapable of fear. The more he was threatened the less disposed was he to be terrified; and when it was finally resolved to cut him off from the Jewish church, in the awful manner which the rules of the synagogue prescribed, it is said that he anticipated the sentence by publicly declaring himself no longer a Jew in faith. That sentence, read forth at night in the synagogue, amid doleful wailings, and under lights which went out one by one _{His excommunication.} till they left the congregation in utter darkness, was as follows: "With the judgment of the angels, and the sentence of the saints, we anathematize, execrate, curse, and cast out Baruch de Spinoza, the whole of the sacred community assenting, in presence of the sacred books with the six hundred and thirteen precepts written therein, pronouncing against him the anathema wherewith Joshua anathematized Jericho, the malediction wherewith Elisha cursed the children, and all the maledictions written in the book of the law. Let him be accursed by day, and accursed by night; let him be accursed in his lying down, and accursed in his rising up, accursed in going out, and accursed in coming in. May the Lord never more pardon or acknowledge him; may the wrath and displeasure of the Lord burn henceforth against this man, load him with all the curses written in the book of the law, and raze out his name from under the sky; may the Lord sever him for evil from all the tribes of Israel, weight him with all the maledictions of the firmament contained in the book of the law, and may all ye who are obedient to the Lord your God be saved this day." [1]

A fugitive.

It may be proper to add that the health of Spinoza did not fail, as soon as this dreadful ceremony was over; and that he lived nearly twenty years after it, quite as long as his poor body ever promised to last, during which years he seems to have fully carried out his one great purpose. But that malediction, like similar ones from the Head of the Romish church at different times, was not altogether an idle thunderbolt. So greatly enraged were his old associates and friends at his withdrawal from them previous to this sentence, thus showing an open contempt not only for their worship but for their power to curse him, that his life was not safe. Forgetting the words of the frightful sentence, which forbade them to come "within four cubits' length" of him, they waylaid him, with evil intent, in his nightly walks; and on one occasion, at least, the assassin's knife would have entered his neck, had he not dexterously avoided its thrust. Regard for his personal safety now compelled him to keep away from his former haunts. His own kindred even sought him but to do him harm. For the sake of their good standing with the synagogue, no doubt with true Hebrew vengeance also, they had publicly disowned him, and wrathfully denounced him. He wandered about in places where he was not known, unable to tell what death might befall him any moment; and though scorning it, yet menaced by the cloud of curses which hung over him. But he was not at all moved from his deeper plans, during the years that he led this uncertain life. He went

[1] Willis, pp. 34, 35.

straightway to a physician in Amsterdam, Van den Ende
by name, who was a tutor in the Latin tongue.
This language was the key to the philosophy of _{At school.}
the time, and the medium of intercourse among learned
men. The Hebrew religion had forbidden Spinoza, as it
did all Israelites, to know this language; yet he seems
to have already had considerable acquaintance with it,
nevertheless. His object, in seeking Van den Ende, may
have been to perfect himself in this, and in the Greek
tongue; and also, as Willis thinks, to earn a pittance by
aiding his tutor with other pupils. Another fact associated
with this school greatly interests us, since it is one of the
few proofs we have that there was to Spinoza's nature a
deeply tender and susceptible side. Though almost nothing of an emotional nature can be found in his published
writings, I suspect that no man ever felt more keenly or
profoundly, on all those matters which most stir the human heart. It seems that his new professor had a daughter, as skilled as her sire in the speech of the Roman
maidens; and that to her tuition this young Benedict was
in some way assigned. However this may have
been, it is at least certain that he came, most _{His love.}
silently and deliciously, to be in love with his fair associate. Yet, with a true and knightly sense of honor, he
kept his affection secret, waiting for the time when his
prospects should be more settled. That time having
come, and the young lady having had full opportunity to
learn his character and peculiar religious views, he ventured to hint to her the state of his feelings and his hopes.
But he met no encouragement. Had he been a member
of the Papal church, a man of wealth, and a favorite in

gay society, she might not have objected. As it was, however, she preferred to cast in her lot with a young Hamburg merchant, who had the means of gratifying all her wishes for show and idle luxury. Spinoza was grieved to find that he had been offering his honorable heart to such vanity; he was astonished at himself, that he could have felt so much interest in so much selfishness and duplicity; and taking home the severe lesson, thankful that he had pressed his suit no farther, he turned away forever from love to philosophy. His susceptible nature seemed to be utterly driven in upon itself. Perhaps there never was a more absolute consecration to the search for truth, with the single fault that it was, at all events, to be a search made in his own strength; the trustworthiness of his individual intellect was not to be questioned. Disowned of kindred, his tenderness rebuffed in the first effort to speak it, he cheerfully accepted his lot; and he undertook the mighty riddle which was closing about him, with no faith in any wisdom but his own.

<small>His purpose formed.</small> All Spinoza now asked, whether of friend or foe, was to be permitted to live. And of this he was pretty sure while he kept out of the way; for his wants were very few, and he had learned the art of polishing lenses for optical instruments, by which he earned small sums of money from time to time. Leibnitz praised him for his skill in this art, writing, in a letter to the young truth-seeker, "Among the honorable things which fame has acquainted me with concerning you, I learn with no small interest that you are a clever optician." Spinoza was now, as he felt, fully able to provide for himself in the world. Independent and satisfied, determined to push his

inquiries boldly on all sides, he was careless of what any critic might say about him, and sure of supplying his few bodily needs from the earnings of spare hours. It was an instance of self-confidence hardly paralleled in the history of thinking, and which commands our admiration at least, when that student, only about twenty-five years old, departed from his native city scarcely knowing whither he went, and caring for nothing but to push the investigations of which he had taken hold. On the road between Amsterdam and Auwerkerke he found his first asylum, in a house which is said to be still standing, situated on what is called, in memory of the great thinker, Spinoza Lane.[1] From this retreat he went, after about five years, to reside in Rhynsburg; whence he again removed, some four years later, till finally he took lodgings in an obscure house at the Hague.

The fame of Descartes was at its zenith, during these years of Spinoza's life, the great idealist having been dead but a few years, and his enthusiastic disciples having installed his philosophy as a chief authority in the best schools of learning throughout Europe. To his works Spinoza at once turned, studying them with intense ardor, but subjecting every statement to the tests of his own consciousness and logic. Accepting the main premise, and the method of this master, he yet found much to disagree with in the structure of Cartesianism. The result of these studies was his first work, published at Amsterdam in 1663, entitled The Principles of the Philosophy of René des Cartes demonstrated by the geometrical method; to which are added

Read's Descartes.

[1] Willis.

Metaphysical Thoughts, by Benedict Spinoza.[1] The Thoughts, thus appended to his exposition of Descartes, contained the germs of his system of pantheism. His great work on Ethics, written subsequently, and not published till after his death, and in which we have the final embodiment of his philosophical views, grew out of this beginning. Such utterances, as we might readily infer, gave no little offence to the multitude of Cartesians; and their deep hostility was shown, at times, in ways more pointed than becoming. They abhorred the conclusions of Spinoza; and to see him grafting his system upon that of their adored master, was more than philosophy could bear. To add to their vexation they beheld the book of the new expounder and critic in the hands of almost every young student. Spinoza, though cast out from society, and exposed to death all the while, had yet succeeded in making for himself many admirers. All curious minds, whatever they might think of his religious leanings, were charmed by the boldness and novelty of his speculations.

Partly that he might the better command his time, and partly to be out of the way of his implacable foes, he withdrew at length into his little room at the Hague, where fifteen years later a consumption, the seeds of which he had inherited, put an end to his solitary life. Here he exhibited many traits of character which reveal the true philosopher and claim our honest admiration.

Characteristics. His unselfishness in common things was wonderful. An estate fell to him at his father's death, which his sisters denied his right to inherit, on account of his apostasy from the Hebrew faith. He there-

[1] Willis, p. 47.

fore first established his right in the civil courts, and then gave the whole estate to the sisters, to be divided between them. Self-possession and bravery were natural to him. On one occasion he was summoned away from his chamber by the great Condé, then in Holland with a French army. For this act he was suspected of some secret sympathy with the enemies of his country; and upon his return, an infuriated mob was speedily gathered about his lodgings. The owner of the house, dreading the ruin which threatened him, entreated Spinoza to take himself out of the way as quickly as possible. "Fear nothing," was the quiet reply; "I will go out and meet them." Accordingly, instead of running away and hiding, he did go out, greatly to the relief of his host; and the mob, overawed by his calm and fearless demeanor, stole away from him, afraid to touch a hair of his head. He scorned the least overreaching or unfair dealing. Being asked once to take the chair of philosophy at Heidelberg, he declined; for he knew that the theology there taught, if it did not give way, would soon bring him into open conflict with his associates. He would not even make converts to his own views at the expense of the orthodox party. Nor was he less independent than magnanimous. He would not put himself in the way of temptation, which might lead him to change his views, or become the tool of another man. He was offered a pension, if he would engage to dedicate his next work to Louis XIV. But he proudly refused, saying that he had "no intention of dedicating anything to that monarch." Such was the favor that sought him, and his way of meeting it; and that, too, while his poverty was all the time extreme. One day he would have no food but a dish of soup costing three halfpence, and a pot of beer worth three farthings. Another day he would be content with "a basin of gruel, with some butter and raisins, which cost him twopence halfpenny." "And," says pastor Colerus, who gathered these facts about Spinoza while occupying the same lodgings which had been the philosopher's, "although often invited to dinner, he preferred the scanty meal that he found at home, to dining sumptuously at the expense of another."[1]

His poverty.

It is said that in all his lifetime, after coming to years of discretion, he was never heard to murmur or complain. Silent, thoughtful, smiling, ever patient and ever toiling, he lived on in his solitary chamber. Nor was he too poor to indulge the kindliness of his nature now and then, by giving away something for the relief of the destitute. The mistress of the house in which he lodged was, together with her husband, a firm believer in the Christian religion; and when she came to him, as she repeatedly did, asking him to explain his religious views, so that she might know them and judge for herself, he mildly parried her request, urging her to be content with her present faith. "Your religion is a good religion," said he; "you have no occasion to look after another; neither need you doubt of your eternal welfare so as, along with your pious observances, you continue to lead a life of peace in charity with all."[2] It will be seen here that Spinoza, according to the doctrine of his Tractatus Theologico-Politicus, places religion in outward forms chiefly, which one may adopt or lay

His patience.

His tolerance.

[1] See Lewes. [2] Willis, p. 56.

aside at pleasure, his real character being a thing which they do not affect in any case. This extreme tolerance, and making man's eternal safety depend on the common moral virtues, is significant. It shows the small practical value which Spinoza attached to his own, or to any, conclusions of the intellect. All that is necessary in every case, as he seems to teach, is, that one's views be purely his own; not learned from any other person, but reached by an independent course of study. This, certainly, is a tolerance so large, that to see wherein it is not simply indifference to truth, must be hard for most minds. Imagine Jesus of Nazareth, at the well in Samaria, telling the woman who asked him about his religion, to be content with the faith in which she had been brought up! It is the tendency of a great truth, when one has embraced it, to make him a missionary. Just in proportion as he values it he feels bound to proclaim it, and to bring other men into it. We see this inspiration of truth nobly shown in the martyr, changed to a demon in the persecutor, manifested with heavenly beauty in Him who went about teaching among the villages of Galilee.

Does not this want of moral earnestness in Spinoza indicate that he studied and wrote not to instruct, so much as to please himself and puzzle mankind? The supposition that he found a certain secret enjoyment in confusing men's thoughts and bewildering them with his subtle paradoxes, would fall in with some of his easy views of all his well-known habits. "His only relaxations," events. says Mr. Lewes, "were his pipe, receiving visitors, chatting to the people of his house, and watching spiders fight. This last amusement would make the tears roll down his cheek with laughter." Willis, noticing the fact about the spiders, is anxious to prevent the suspicion of a wanton cruelty which it tends to awaken; and he suggests that it was not the battles, but the loves of the venomous insects, which so greatly amused the philosopher. The tradition that Spinoza kept a colony of spiders in his room, and that he fed them with flies, after the manner of the Roman theatre, where Christians were thrown to the lions, cannot be thus explained away. This pastime seems to have afforded quite as much pleasure as the other. Mr. Willis may discredit it, and Lewes pass it by silently; but a more sensitive writer has said, "I could never understand the mirth, the 'laughter' which Spinoza is said to have indulged in, when witnessing the contest between the spider and the fly. I can comprehend that so abstract a philosopher would have risen above our natural repugnance, and surveyed even calmly an instance of a general and a wise law of nature, — life surrendered to support other and generally higher life, — but why should the death of the poor fly have occasioned laughter?"[1] The disturbed author would have hardly started this query, had he duly considered what was the essence of Spinoza's doctrine. He should have known that the "abstract philosopher" was entirely consistent with his theory, in laughing at the struggles of the victim; for the grand lesson which his whole system impresses is, the right of power to triumph over weakness.

<small>Vagueness of ancient writers.</small> Thus lived and died Benedict Spinoza, the father of Modern Pantheism. Perhaps it would not be far out of the way to say that he was the

[1] Thorndale.

father of all pantheism, if we mean by that term only such systems, of the same nature as his, as have a logical completeness and have been clearly reported to us. The signs of agreement with him which we find in ancient thought are often more or less vague and uncertain. As there were reformers before the Reformation, so there may have been Spinozists before Spinoza. There is at least a pantheistic flavor, in some parts of ancient philosophy, which demands our attention; but the result, at the best, does not promise to be such as would repay an exhaustive treatment. There are, in the New Testament, words and phrases which a pantheist might use. Yet no candid scholar would affirm that pantheism is meant, where we read that "Christ is all and in all," that "whosoever is joined unto the Lord is one spirit," that "the Father dwelleth in us and we in him." If we use an exegesis which saves such passages as these from pantheism, which condemns nothing in the Fourth Gospel, nothing in the Epistles of Paul, nothing in the words of Christ himself, to that category, why not make a similar allowance in the study of uninspired writers? Indeed, there are modern writers, both of prose and poetry, who have spoken here and there in the forms of pantheism, yet whose words spoken in other places make it certain that the universe and God were not to them one and the same thing. Take, for instance, the lines of Pope, in his Essay on Man: —

> " All are but parts of one stupendous whole,
> Whose body nature is, and God the soul.
> That, changed through all, and yet in all the same,
> Great in the earth as in the ethereal frame.
> Warms in the sun, refreshes in the breeze,
> Glows in the stars, and blossoms in the trees,

> Lives through all life, extends through all extent,
> Spreads undivided, operates unspent,
> Breathes in our soul, informs our mortal part,
> As full, as perfect in a hair as heart;
> To him no high, no low, no great, no small;
> He fills, he bounds, connects, and equals all."

If such language as this may be corrected, in the light of other expressions by the same author, so as to leave him still a believer in the essential truths of Christianity, we certainly may suppose that at least some of the ancient authors, from whom pantheistic fragments only have come down, spoke other words, now lost, without which they cannot be fairly judged. I do not deny that some of them were clear and thorough-going pantheists; but the opinion of those best able to form a judgment in the case, has for years been inclining to the view, that not a little of what was once loosely called the pantheism of the ancients, was the more or less vague tradition of a primeval monotheism. In rejecting the many gods of paganism, and insisting on the divine unity, of which dim remembrances had been handed on to them, they may have used terms which we falsely regard as anticipating the theory of Spinoza.

The Alexandrian masters. One of the first movements in religious philosophy which here attracts our notice, is the Neo-Platonism of Alexandria. Perhaps we ought not to feel any hesitation in charging pantheism upon the teachers of that famous school. For we find them holding such language as this: "God is the only existence; he is the real existence, of which we, and other things, are but transitory phenomena." The greatest of the Alexandrine masters was Plotinus, who went to Rome, and founded a school there, where he had among

Plotinus.

his pupils the celebrated Porphyry. He died towards the close of the third century of our era. The following is from him: "How doth wisdom differ from that which is called nature? Verily in this manner, that wisdom is the first thing, but nature the least and lowest; for nature is but an imitation or image of wisdom, the last thing of the soul, which hath the lowest impress of wisdom shining upon it; as when a thick piece of wax is thoroughly impressed on a seal, that impress, which is clear and distinct in the superior superficies of it, will in the lower side be weak and obscure; and such is the stamp and signature of nature; compared with that of wisdom and understanding, nature is a thing which doth only do, but not know."[1] Thus did he seem to identify the essence of nature with that of intelligence; and this latter he appears to have held as one with the Godhead; for even in the agonies of death he exclaimed, "I am struggling to liberate the divinity within me." He wrote two books to prove that all being is one and the same; and the reason which he gave for not sacrificing to the gods was, that it became the gods, since he too was divine, to sacrifice to him. Views essentially the same as those of Plotinus, were taught by his successor Iamblichus at Alexandria; and as late as the year 529, at Athens, by Proclus and those who followed him in the school of that city. For a more full account of these masters and their philosophy than can be given here, the work of Butler may be consulted.[2] "It is the perpetual

Iamblichus.

Proclus.

[1] Cudworth's Intellectual System of the Universe, Vol. I., p. 240.
[2] Ancient philosophy, by William Archer Butler (Philadelphia, 1857), Vol. II., pp. 320–335.

lesson of Plotinus," says Butler, " that the object of reason is not, cannot be, external to reason ; that truth is not in the conformity of thoughts with things, but of thoughts with each other. Intelligence is at once the object conceived, the subject conceiving, and the act of conception. To rest on self is to commune with the universe." In his theory of knowledge, and of the world, which he held to be an efflux of the divine substance, the teaching of Plotinus is such as to give the impression that he anticipated the doctrine of Spinoza.

Plato.

This notice of the Alexandrine school brings us, by association, to Plato himself, from whom they claimed to derive the germs of their system. Butler says that Proclus "found in Plato all he wished to find ; " and that "the dreamy theories of Alexandria were not unnatural results of certain tendencies discoverable in the writings of Plato himself— tendencies for which his own well-balanced intellect, doubtless, provided sufficient counterpoise, but which too closely suited peculiar temperaments not to have been soon exalted into exclusive or predominant principles of speculation." [1] Plato seems to have tried to mediate between the empiricists of his day and pure rationalists of the Eleatic school ; yet the transcendental element in his writings is that which most powerfully affected his followers, and which was especially laid hold of by the Alexandrine teachers. They treated him " very much as Philo treated Moses ; " very much as some of the Christian fathers, trained at Alexandria, treated the New Testament writings. Whatever we find among the Neo-Platonists, therefore, we can trace back to Plato only

[1] Ancient Philosophy, Vol. II., p. 55.

in some such sense as the Alexandrine Jew might trace it to the writings of Moses, or the Neo-Platonic Christian to the words of Christ and the apostles.

Even in Aristotle there are statements which have a pantheistic look, though his genius was of the empirical cast. In his treatise on psychology, he seems to regard the soul as a principle pervading nature, which exists in the plants and animals no less than in the philosopher. Dr. South says he taught, "that there was one universal soul belonging to the whole species or race of mankind, and indeed to all things according to their capacity; which universal soul, by its respective existence in, and communication of itself to each particular man, did exert in him those noble acts of ratiocination and understanding proper to his nature; and those also in a different degree and measure of perfection, according as the different disposition of the organs of the body made it more or less fit to receive the communication of that universal soul; which soul only he held to be immortal, and that each particular man, both in respect of body and spirit, was mortal." We must perhaps accept this as monism; though, clearly enough, it anticipates the science of the Comtian school, rather than the metaphysics of Spinoza. Other expressions of Aristotle would indicate to us that it ought not to be interpreted too rigidly; and, even admitting that Dr. South caught the proper force of his words, they may have been simply his strong expression of dissent from the polytheism of the times.

Earlier than the age of Plato and Aristotle lived Xenophanes, the founder of the Eleatic school of philosophy. He, according to Grote, "conceived nature as one unchangeable and indivisible whole, spherical, animated, endued with reason, and penetrated by, or indeed identical with God : he denied the objective reality of all changes, or generation, or destruction, which he seems to have considered as only changes or modifications in the percipient, and perhaps different in one percipient and another." The Eleatics may have been pantheists ; yet we should bear in mind that this language is not theirs, so much as Grote's commentary on the teachings of their founder. The same may be remarked of Heraclitus, a pupil of Xenophanes, who was called "the weeping philosopher," and in whose teachings Hegel claimed to find the germs of Hegelianism. The decisive question in regard to him, as in regard to many others both before and after him, — a question impossible to answer, — is this : Had he any clear knowledge of the one living and true God ? If not, his utterances about the Divine Reason, and the One, are very probably pantheistic. But if he had such knowledge, those same utterances may indicate a more or less pure monotheism. Pythagoras, who lived in the fifth century before Christ, agreed apparently with the two thinkers last named ; though his method is peculiar. "Numbers," said he, "are the cause of the material existence of things." In the development of this theory of numbers, we find traces of what has been commonly held to be pantheism ; for he represents all things as the forthputtings of one eternal unit, held together by its underlying and pervasive power, and returning constantly by absorption into it. The doctrine of metempsychosis, which is associated with his name, seems to have grown out of this general theory,

Heraclitus.

Pythagoras.

as also perhaps the peculiar discipline which he established among his pupils. He was distinguished in his day for the honor he rendered to woman. His wife is said to have been as devoted as himself in the search for truth; and many of the noblest women of Greece were among his scholars, — in connection with which fact it should be remarked, however, that he required each one of his pupils, upon entering the school, to take a vow of silence for five years.

There was a school of philosophers in ancient Greece, known as Hylozoists, in distinction from the Atomists, whose speculations have a decidedly pantheistic flavor. Strato Lampsacenus was a master in this school, and is represented by Cudworth as the teacher of a certain crude pantheism. "Strato's deity," says he, "was a certain living and active, but senseless nature. He did not fetch the original of all things, as the Democritic and Epicurean atheists, from a mere fortuitous motion of atoms, by means whereof he bore some slight resemblance of a theist; but yet he was a downright atheist for all that, his god being no other than such a life of nature or matter as was both devoid of sense and consciousness, and also multiplied together with the several parts of it."[1] Coleridge was no doubt right in saying that "pantheism was taught in the mysteries of Greece." Yet it is hardly fair to study those ancient systems, as too many critics seem to have done, with the foregone conclusion, that so far as they were not polytheistic they were pantheistic. The presupposition of pure monotheism would explain certain portions of them just as well. Men who think, and who find their data in consciousness, are exposed to pantheism when

Hylozoists and others.

[1] Intellectual System, Vol. I., pp. 149, 150.

they forsake the true God; and this is enough to establish the fact that many of the Greek philosophers, though we dare not say precisely which ones, were forerunners of Spinoza.

<small>The Orientals.</small> Of the contemplative Orientals it is far more true than of the Greeks, that, in their ignorance of the true God, they inclined to pantheism. We find in the East a philosophy of the senses, quite as earnest as that of Democritus or Epicurus, and resulting in a vast system of Positivism; but the main current of thought there seems always to have set more naturally towards Spinozism. The ancient Hindoos, if we may trust Sir William Jones, " believed that the whole creation is an energy rather than a work, by which the infinite mind is present at all times and in all places, and exhibits to his creatures a set of perceptions, like a wonderful picture or piece of music always varied but always uniform." Here we have laid open the secret of the Brahmanical emanations, the source of the pleroma and eons of the Gnostics, the origin of nearly all that is most profound in Oriental religion and philosophy. There are many things also, in <small>Egyptian speculation.</small> the writings of the ancient Egyptians, which seem to anticipate the teachings of modern pantheism. · The inscription on the veiled image at Sais, " I am all that was, is, and shall be, and my veil no mortal could ever uplift," may have been the utterance of a pantheistic creed; as also the following words, taken by Cudworth from the Trismegistic or Hermaic books: " He (God) is both incorporeal and omnicorporeal; for there is nothing of any body which he is not; he is all things that are, and therefore he hath all names; because all things are from one father; and therefore he hath no name, be-

cause he is the father of all things."[1] Such passages abound in the sacred books of the Egyptians; but to search them out, and discriminate between those which teach pantheism and those which teach a primitive monotheism, would be a wearisome, if it were a possible, task.

Recent researches have shown, however, that not all of those old speculations were mere foreshadowings of Spinozism; that some of them, at least, are worthy to be put in a nobler category; that they may have been, and probably were, instances of a more or less pure monotheism. The study of language and mythology, pursued with such eagerness by certain German and French scholars, has nearly demonstrated that there was, far away beyond the ages of polytheism, a general belief in the God of Balaam and Melchisedek. Thus the testimony of science is confirming the scriptural record. And who knows but it may yet be found that many dwelling in the shadow of paganism, and now called pantheists, were worshippers of the true God? "We see in the history of the religions of China," says Professor Martin, of the Imperial College at Pekin, "a process directly the reverse of that which certain atheistic writers of modern Europe assert to be the natural progress of the human mind. According to them, men set out with the belief of many gods, which they at length reduce to unity, and finally supersede by recognizing the laws of nature as independent of a personal Administrator. The history of China is fatal to this theory. The worship of one God is the oldest form of Chinese religion, and idolatry is an innovation."[2]

Primitive monotheism.

The Chinese.

[1] Cudworth, Vol. I., p. 589. [2] New Englander, April, 1869.

There is evidence also in the Orphic poetry of Greece, that the most ancient thinkers of that land believed in one God,—"one supreme, unmade Deity, the original of all things." Was there nothing of this nature in the mind of the Greek poet when he wrote, "Nothing is accomplished on the earth without thee, O God, save the deeds which the wicked perpetrate in their folly"? And what shall we say to the words of Sophocles in the Œdipus? "May destiny aid me to preserve unsullied the purity of my words and of all my actions, according to those sublime laws which, brought forth in the celestial heights, have Heaven alone for their father, to which the race of mortal men did not give birth, and which oblivion shall never entomb. In them is a supreme God, and one who waxes not old." Or listen to this, found on a roll of papyrus in the coffin of an Egyptian mummy: "I am the Most Holy, the Creator of all that replenishes the earth, and of the earth itself, habitation of mortals. I am the Prince of the infinite ages. I am the great and mighty God, the Most High, shining in the midst of the careering stars, and of the armies which praise me over thy head. It is I who chastise and who judge the evil doers and the persecutors of godly men. I discover and confound the liars. I am the all-seeing Judge and Avenger; the guardian of my laws is the land of righteousness." Here, now, is a voice, coming to us out of the ancient wonder-land, from a time far beyond its degrading idolatries, which seems to catch up and sound forward the words spoken to Adam and Noah.

Ernest Naville, late Professor of Philosophy in the

University of Geneva, has taken pains to gather up these vestiges of ancient monotheism, in his able work entitled "The Heavenly Father;"[1] and he asks, in view of the mass of evidence they afford, "Did humanity begin with a coarse fetichism, and thence rise by slow degrees to higher conceptions? Do the traces of comparatively pure monotheism first show themselves in the most recent periods of idolatry? Contemporary science," he adds, "inclines more and more to answer in the negative. It is in the most ancient ·historical ground, that the laborious investigators of the past meet with the most elevated ideas of religion. Cut to the ground a young and vigorous beech tree, and come back a few years afterwards: in place of the tree cut down you will find coppice wood; the sap which nourished a single trunk has been divided among a multitude of shoots. This comparison expresses well enough the opinion which tends to prevail among our learned men on the subject of the historical development of religions. The idea of the only God is at the root; it is primitive, polytheism is derivative. A forgotten, and as it were slumbering, monotheism exists before the worship of idols; it is the concealed trunk which supports them, but the idols have absorbed all the sap." Nor does Professor Naville reach this conclusion by any path in which his own faith in Christianity might sway him. Distrusting himself, he appeals to those who may claim to speak with authority on the subject; and the response which he gets from one of the most learned of archæologists is, "The general impression of the most distinguished mythologists of the

Conclusion of Professor Naville.

---

[1] Published by W. V. Spencer, Boston, 1867.

present day is, that monotheism is at the foundation of all pagan mythology."[1] It is now generally held by the best mythologists, that fetichism is a less ancient form of religion than the worship of ancestors. Religious honors, paid to famous progenitors, were the rites which naturally grew up first, after men had forgotten the true God. A distinguished ancestor had some symbol, — a dog, crocodile, reindeer, or other natural object, — by which he was known among his contemporaries, and which gradually became the fetich of his descendants. The synonyme for "fetich," in the dialect of the North American Indians, seems to have been "totem;" and the religious worship which grew up among them has been called *totemism*. Hence Longfellow says, in one of his poems, —

Origin of fetichism.

The totem of the Indians.

> "And they painted on the grave-posts
> Of the graves, yet unforgotten,
> Each his own ancestral totem,
> Each the symbol of his household;
> Figures of the bear and reindeer,
> Of the turtle, crane, and beaver."

But whether or not we have here a true account of the origin of fetichism, "it is enough for my purpose," again using the words of Naville, "to have shown that it is not merely the grand tradition guaranteed by the Christian faith, but the most distinctly marked current of contemporary science, which tells us that God shone upon the cradle of the species. The August Form was veiled, and idolatry, with its train of shameful rites, shows itself in history as the result of a fall which calls for a restoration,

[1] Pictet.

rather than as the point of departure of a continued progress."

Therefore, without going farther into the history of ancient systems, and admitting that the leaven of pantheism was in many of them, to a greater or less extent, I come back to the lonely exile of Amsterdam as our proper starting-point in the survey undertaken. It is cheering to find that the latest researches of scholars and critics are falling in so well with our inspired traditions. This look into the remote past, through the glass of science, also strengthens our position as to the first origin and the genesis of all unbelief. Separated from God, the human mind becomes lost in its own speculations. As it turns back to him, it partakes again of the spirit of a pure monotheism, which the students of history may have sometimes unjustly condemned as pantheism. Presuming it to be such, they have found it to be such, as there are not wanting those who have found the same thing in the New Testament. Where, however, the human mind has not thus turned back, but has kept on with its face away from God, it has taken one or the other of two opposite paths of infidelity. Which of these two paths it has in any case taken, has depended on its inherent tendency, whether to make the outward or the inward its starting-point of inquiry. There did unquestionably exist in ancient times, and in various countries, men occupied with philosophy and religion who sought their data in the inner world of consciousness. So, far as those thinkers were without knowledge of the true God, they undoubtedly inclined to pantheism,—losing the

margin: Spinoza our starting-point.

human in the divine, substituting emanation for creation, and confounding the Maker of all things with the work of his hands.

But this ancient pantheism was unshapen, Vagueness before him. changeable, crude, indeterminate, vague. It was forever repeating itself in one form or another; slightly varied, to suit the genius of different countries and ages, yet on the whole confirming the truth of Dugald Stewart's remark, who says, in view of the frequent recurrences of the same essential error, "One is almost tempted to believe that human invention is limited, like a barrel organ, to a specific number of tunes." Gleams of the vast conception, now eagerly grasped and now cast aside, flash out upon us all along in the pathways of ancient thought; but that conception seems never to come forth, and plant itself in solid proportions before us; it never unfolds into a well-adjusted and comprehensive system. We catch only elusive glimpses of the vision; vague hints and impressions, with no fixed centre about which to crystallize; faint foreshadowings of the doctrine whose elaborator and expounder was yet to come.

Course of religious thought sketched. The weary ages of paganism circled on. Humanity, cut off from God, groped after its ancient blessedness, but went sounding on a dim and perilous way. The great lights of philosophy burned out, one after another, or withdrew into the heavens. Then "the Desire of all nations" appeared. Wise men followed his star, and, paying their homage at his feet, found again the glory which had been lost. But not all were wise. "He came unto his own, and his own received him not." And that nation of despisers and rejecters, dashed in pieces for its unbelief, was scattered over the world. The Great Light, seen of them that sat in the region and shadow of death, rose towards the meridian; and to it the moon and stars did obeisance. After displaying for a time its glory, so full of grace and truth, the mists of human selfishness began to obscure it. It was hidden from the world on which it had briefly shone in triumph, and the night of the dark ages descended. And not until those ages had passed away, in the full morning of modern literature, when the Bible was in the hands of the people, and humanity everywhere was awaking as to some new destiny, did the high priest of pantheism appear. Born of the proud but rejected stock, spurning Judaism, and seeing no beauty in Christ, he braves the religious faith of his own time, and claims to interpret the dream of benighted philosophy.

Yes, to Spinoza belongs the honor, whatever that may be, of grasping the principle of former impressions and tendencies, and fixing forever the laws and limits of pantheistic speculation. He seized the essence of the world-old dream. And not only that, but he made it stand forth so completely in his exposition, that he may be said to have necessitated the formulas of his most famous successors; as Newton, when he enunciated the principle of gravitation, became virtually the author of all subsequent astronomy. The influence of Spinoza in the history of pantheistic thinking, reminds us of the great river which flows through the central valley of the United States. His mind was the point, far up in untrodden wilds, where previous tendencies were first gathered into a single fountain head. He scooped the

Spinoza's system the receptacle.

channel into which the brooklets emptied themselves, and which drained the neighboring swales and marshes. It was the rush of his tireless genius that gave unity, direction, and momentum·to the stream. He has had many successors; but, drawn irresistibly towards the main current, they at length lose their independent life, and become, as it were, the tributaries of his greatness.

I must not omit here, in claiming this precedence for Spinoza, to mention one other name which is nearly related to the rise of pantheism in modern times. Giordano Bruno is thought by some to deserve the place assigned to the great Hebrew thinker. Even Willis, the biographer of Spinoza, and editor of his Correspondence and Ethics, inclines to this opinion. He thinks it impossible that Spinoza should not have been familiar with the works of Bruno, and wonders that he nowhere alludes to them, while they so thoroughly anticipate the main doctrines of his system. "In the present day," says he, "we should hold the man who borrowed so freely as our philosopher has certainly done from his predecessor, to be guilty of unmitigated plagiarism, did he fail to acknowledge the obligation."[1] But it is by no means certain that Spinoza deserves this wound in the house of his friends. He must be acquitted of anything approaching dishonesty. He had too much intellectual pride, to say nothing of his general character, ever to deck himself with the plumes of another. Bruno certainly had as many advantages as the outcast Jew for becoming the leader of his school, if he deserved to be. He was not of the rejected race, but a Christian Catholic. He had

Claims of Bruno.

---

[1] Life, Correspondence, and Ethics, General Introduction, p. 11.

the favor of public position in his native Italy, resided in England for a time, where he was the friend of Sir Philip Sidney and received many attentions from the queen, was an expounder of the views of Copernicus, and finally acquired the renown of martyrdom at the stake for his scientific heresies. His writings had been before the world three quarters of a century, when the Ethics of Spinoza appeared. It is certainly strange, considering the whole case, that Spinoza, if a mere copyist of his views, should have so thoroughly displaced him, and usurped all his honors. The natural conclusion is, that Bruno, though a pantheist in many of his utterances, was not always consistent with his theory, and that he lacked the systematizing power which was so remarkable in Spinoza. But whatever the verdict of justice should be, as between these two masters, it is idle to quarrel now with the judgment of history. The scholarship of two centuries has spoken, nor is it probable that any good cause can be discovered for reversing its decision.[1]

Spinoza did his work with every help towards doing it well. The gracious God, who makes his sun to rise on the evil and the good, withheld from the daring thinker no advantage. It was the seventeenth century; that century unsurpassed for triumphs of the human intellect in the higher and more difficult fields of inquiry. Luther died eighty-six years before Spinoza was born. It was the age of the Dutch Republic; of the

Intellectual activity of the age favorable to Spinoza.

The Reformation.

---

[1] Mr. Lewes, the warm eulogist of Bruno, and who has given us a graphic sketch of his eventful life, says of his philosophy, "Its condemnation is written in the fact of its neglect." — Biog. Hist. Phil., p. 388.

English Commonwealth; of Richelieu, and the French Academy, and the Sorbonne. Bacon's great work, though completed, was yet a buried seed, not destined to rise and overshadow the schools of thought till after Spinoza had passed away. The founder of the pantheistic school of free-thinkers lived, and died, amidst the full blaze of the philosophy whose most recent master had been Descartes. He must have known the story of the Pilgrim Fathers, who, not long before his own family, had, like them, sought refuge from persecution in Holland. His life synchronized with the palmy period of the Puritan theocracy in New England. Prodigies of human energy, not merely in individuals, but on a national scale, were enacting all around him. Richelieu's administration was the wonder of Europe. Spinoza watched the career of Cromwell, and saw him at the height of his power. In the near past was the story of Dutch heroism, struggling to rescue a country from Spanish tyranny, and from the invading sea. The many examples of endurance and devotion thus afforded could not fail to inspire the ardent Hebrew. It was a time for mediocrity to keep out of sight. To venture forth, and claim a place among the leaders of the age, became only such as were conscious of their ability to measure swords with giants. John Locke was born in the same year as Spinoza; but his influence, especially in the sphere of religious thinking, belongs to a later age. Sir Isaac Newton was ten years younger than Spinoza; but his imperial genius, though following in the track of Bacon and Locke, gave a lustre to the times of which it was born. It was the age of the Bodleian Library, the age of faith in the moderns. Men had grown less servile towards the old masters, and the Baconian maxim that "we are the ancients" was in every student's mouth. We have seen that Spinoza corresponded with Leibnitz, and that he was courted by Louis XIV. of France. Surely, if there were any possibilities of greatness in him, the attentions he received, and the examples all about him, must have aroused them to do their utmost.

Scientific research was everywhere active, and crowned with remarkable success, in the time of Spinoza. It was in his century that Harvey made his famous discovery of the circulation of the blood; that Galileo became known as the expounder of the law of the equilibrium of bodies, the laws of accelerated and retarded motion, and the parabolic nature of the curve described by projectiles; in his age that Torricelli and Pascal solved the problem of the pressure of the atmosphere; that Napier invented the logarithmic tables; that the binomial theorem was discovered, letters used for notation, algebra applied to the investigation of the properties of curves. Pascal and Descartes expounded the cycloid; Kepler showed that the circle is composed of an infinite number of triangles, the sphere of an infinite number of pyramids, the cylinder of an infinity of prisms. Spinoza beheld, in astronomy, the most wonderful discoveries of modern times. Kepler, a believer in the old philosophy rather than the new, had discovered that the planetary orbits are ellipses; that the sun is fixed in

[margin: Triumphs of science.]
[margin: Mathematics.]
[margin: Astronomy.]

one of the foci of all those orbits; that the radius vector of each planet passes over equal spaces in equal times; that the square of the time of revolution is, in every instance, as the cube of the mean distance from the sun. In the midst of these sublime achievements, optics came forward to lend its helping hand. The telescope, invented by Galileo, vastly widened the field of "the science of space." The moons of Jupiter were observed; and the phases of Venus, and the occultations of the planets, were used as data in determining longitude.

Optics.

But it was not alone in the study of nature that this age excelled. Spinoza was the contemporary of the greatest lights in modern literature, — the greatest lights in all literature. The first half of the seventeenth century was the golden age of the drama. Corneille, Calderon, Shakespeare, Jonson, Beaumont and Fletcher lived and wrote during that period. Cervantes gave to the world Don Quixote in this age. John Milton was the contemporary of Spinoza. To show the activity of the theological and religious mind in this era, it is needful only to name the Westminster Assembly, the Synod of Dort, the controversy between Augustinians and Arminians, Port Royal, Jansenism. What splendor of intellect, what keenness of logic, what patience of labor, and how great wealth of piety and burning devotion are called up to our minds by the mention of such names as John Howe, Richard Baxter, Jeremy Taylor, Isaac Barrow, John Owen, Stillingfleet, Tillotson, Fénelon, Bossuet, Fléchier, Bourdaloue; all of which belong to the age of Spinoza.

Literature of the seventeenth century.

Theological activity.

It was in the very focus of all this unparalleled brilliancy of thought, with a mighty hunger for truth, driven to his task by the persecution of friends, and every energy aroused to its utmost by the great examples about him, that the champion of pantheism took up his problem. God seemed, in his providence, to have specially arranged for the solution under the most favorable circumstances possible. The man, the age, and the immediate influences under which he acted, were all that the most earnest friends of the cause could desire. If it failed despite these signal advantages, it would fail utterly and irrecoverably; and therefore God did not withhold them. Wishing to show to his children that the speculation they had chased so many ages was a baseless dream, he allowed it every opportunity for proving itself true. When all things were ready, and victory seemed most likely to crown the adventure, the word was given, Come forth into the arena; produce your cause, and set in order your arguments.

<small>Divine purpose.</small>

LECTURE II.

THE NATURE AND GROUNDS OF PANTHEISM.

Definition of pantheism. A GENERAL definition of pantheism may be given in few words. It is the doctrine that God includes all reality, and is identical with it, nothing besides him really existing. To use the Greek phrase, he is τὸ ἓν καὶ τὸ πᾶν — the One and the All. Spinoza's way of stating it is, "Besides God, no substance can exist, or be conceived to exist."[1]

How it differs from theism and atheism. The doctrine thus enunciated will be made clearer, perhaps, by comparing it with theism and atheism. The theist separates nature from God, in his system, and recognizes the existence of both; the atheist starts from nature, and denies the existence of God; the pantheist starts from God, and denies the existence of nature. Atheists and pantheists agree in opposing the theist, alleging that his doctrine involves a species of dualism, — not the dualism of Zoroaster and the Manichæans, which asserts the eternity of matter and of moral evil, but that distinction between the Creator and the creation which admits of secondary causes in nature, and of free-will in the rational creature. The dualism is only that which is necessary in order to moral govern-

[1] Ethics, Part 1, Prop. xiv.

ment and responsible action. Yet objection is made to it, as not evolving all reality out of a single principle; as implying an ethical universe, whereas all existence is embraced under the natural, and must be so regarded, or there can be no simple and perfect philosophy. The atheist and pantheist are alike in starting with a single postulate, which, they claim, is all-inclusive; and they throw out the matter of freedom and responsibility for the assumed philosophical advantage of entire unity of system. But though alike in standing upon a basis of monism, they seem nevertheless to be in direct and necessary antagonism to each other. One of them does not believe in any God, the other believes in nothing but God. This hostility is apparent rather than real, however, at least in its religious aspect; is not so much in ideas as in language. When the atheist has explained what he means by the word "nature," and the pantheist defines that which he chooses to call "God," it is often clear that they both mean the same thing; that they occupy common ground in their attitude towards Christianity, although their methods of philosophizing may be opposite. One denying nature, and the other everything but nature, it is clear that they must alike reject the *super*-natural. The uninitiated reader gets a profound impression of the piety of Spinoza while reading the pages in which Novalis extols him as "the God-intoxicated man;" but when he learns that the "God" which produced this intoxication was only an impersonal substance constituting the universe, he knows that he has been misled by a verbal juggle. Piety quite as good as this might be legitimately felt, and no doubt was, by Auguste Comte, if not also by Baron d'Holbach.

Wherein atheism and pantheism agree.

Language of pantheists often ambiguous.

And here we discover, at the very threshold of its temple, one of the vices of pantheism. It is less honest than atheism. Has it at first sight a somewhat noble and captivating look? This is because it puts on disguises. It uses the language of theism, and even of Christianity, to inculcate a doctrine which no Christian or theist can for a moment think of entertaining. Herder and Schleiermacher, pointing to the verbal dress in which Spinoza's thoughts were at times put, might seem to have a warrant for insisting that he was a Christian; and Schleiermacher might say that he was not as impious as his critics declared him to be, when once in the midst of a sermon he exclaimed, "Offer up with me a lock of hair to the manes of the rejected but holy Spinoza." It would seem, however, from the manner in which it is here proposed to honor Spinoza, that the enthusiastic preacher, to say nothing of the philosopher himself, was in a state of mind bordering on paganism. Justly does Mr. Morell say, speaking of the theistic language of Spinoza, "A being to whom understanding, will, and even personality is denied; a being who does not create, but simply *is;* who does not act, but simply unfolds; who does not purpose, but brings all things to pass by the necessary law of his own existence, — such a being cannot be a father, a friend, a benefactor; in a word, cannot be *a God* to man, for man is but a part of himself. It may be more correct to term the philosophy of Spinoza a pantheism than an atheism; but if we take the common idea or definition of Deity as valid, then assuredly we must conclude that the God of Spinoza is no God, and that his pantheism is only a more imposing form of atheism." There is a tradition that Spinoza, when about to publish one of his pantheistic writings, showed it to a friend, and that the word "God" was not to be found in it, but only the term "nature," where the other word stood in the printed volume. His friend, it is said, induced him to make this change wherever he could, substituting the theistic for the atheistic term, fearing that if he did not; the treatise would make no disciples, but only arouse dangerous hostility. It is easy enough to see that Spinoza uses these terms interchangeably. He says, in the Introduction to the Fourth Part of the Ethics, "The eternal and infinite being whom we call *God* or *Nature*, as he exists of necessity, so does he act of necessity." He therefore might have altered his manuscript to mislead or conciliate a class of readers. But the story may well be doubted; for Spinoza, whatever must be said of his system, was a thoroughly fearless man, despising hypocrisy, and scorning to turn his hand over in the hope of disarming opposition. The tradition may have arisen from the fact that some of his works were published under fictitious names in various parts of Europe, though without consultation with him, and with such changes as his admiring disciples thought would help to give them currency in the philosophical world.

This extraordinary use of language, even if not intentionally dishonest, has, as a matter of fact, deceived many. It also enables the pantheist to make a show of denying, and indignantly repelling, any charges of irreverence or impiety that may be brought against him. He can subscribe to the whole Christian vocabulary, without making it apparent, except

Many names for one thing.

to those who understand his system and his definitions, that he resolves all religions, together with everything else, of whatever claims or appearance, back into an eternal nature-process. Any terminology, from that of apostolic fervor down to the hardest scholastic barbarisms, can be made to serve his turn. John Sterling, replying to a remark made to him one day by his friend Thomas Carlyle, said, "That is flat pantheism." "And what if it were pot-theism, if it were true?" was Carlyle's rejoinder.[1] The audacious hero-worshipper was utterly indifferent to terms. They were but the "clothes" of philosophy to his view, and might be changed never so often, he cared not how often or in what way, so long as the substance within them remained intact. In the biography of Sterling which Carlyle wrote, and in which he labors so hard to make Sterling out a religious doubter essentially at one with himself, he shows that he was not above playing the juggler, and that, too, with so sacred a matter as his friend's religious convictions. His complaint of Archdeacon Hare for emphasizing the Christian faith of Sterling, might, so far as it implies a one-sided treatment of the subject, be more properly made against him. Among the terms frequently used by pantheists, and which they regard as synonymous, or nearly so, are Father, All-Father, Heavenly Father, Nature, Substance, God, Subject-Object, World-Ego, Indifference of the Subjective and Objective, the Identity-Point of Existence and Non-existence. The language hardly seems a caricature, in which an English Satirist represents the later disciples of Spinoza as saying, —

[1] Carlyle's Life of Sterling (Boston, 1852), p. 107.

"We worship the Absolute-Infinite,
The Universe-Ego, the Plenary-Void,
The Subject-Object Identified,
The great Nothing-something, the Being-Thought,
That mouldeth the mass of chaotic Nought,
Whose beginning unended, and end unbegun,
Is the One that is All, and the All that is One."

Thus it appears, from this very slight examination of the pantheistic use, or rather misuse, of terms, that we must know the system if we would not be deceived by popular expositions of it.

I pass, therefore, to the premise from which Spinoza set out, and the method by which he finally reached his pantheism. And here I must bespeak the forbearance of all, knowing how difficult it is to represent his system adequately. Fortunately my purpose does not require me to undertake an exhaustive statement of Spinozism. I am not assuming the office of an historian of philosophy, but simply sketching the general course of speculative thought, so far as may be needful to show the origin of a class of popular infidelities. By keeping to the plain starting-point and clear drift of Spinozism, and not attempting what would be superfluous, I shall hope to be sure of my ground, and at the same time to accomplish all I have purposed. *Knowledge of Spinozism which the purpose of this work requires.*

I have already intimated that Spinoza was a student of Descartes. It will be proper, therefore, to say a few words of that philosopher, and of his peculiar doctrines. The question has been argued at some length whether Spinoza found the germs of pan- *Descartes was Spinoza's guide.*

theism in Cartesianism, or in another and earlier system. One theory is, that he was a follower of Averroes, and that he took the elements of his thinking from the Arabian philosophy. Others have maintained stoutly that he was a Cabalist, and found the principles of his pantheism in the comments of Maimonides and Aben-Ezra on the Hebrew Scriptures. But Spinoza's French translator, Saisset, after discussing each of these views carefully, rejects them both as untenable, and affirms that the true filiation is with the Cartesian philosophy. This conclusion I have adopted, for reasons yet to be given.

This doubted.

Opinion of Saisset.

René Descartes was born near the end of the sixteenth century, of one of the noble families of France. He is said to have been a sickly child, of diminutive size, noted for thoughtfulness in his earliest years. In this he reminds us of Spinoza, as also in the fact that he was carefully nurtured in the faith of his fathers. His education was intrusted to the Jesuits. But like the Hebrew youth, yet to follow in his steps, he soon began to distrust the lessons of his teachers. He set almost no value on all they taught him, with the single exception of mathematics. "As soon as I was old enough to be set free from the government of my teachers," says he, "I entirely forsook the study of letters; and, determining to seek no other knowledge than that which I could discover within myself, or in the great book of the world, I spent the remainder of my youth in travelling."[1] He therefore had before him a double work to perform: first he must divest himself of all notions thus

Parentage of Descartes.

Early purpose.

[1] Huxley, Lay Sermons, Addresses, and Reviews, p. 321.

far acquired; and then he must find some criterion by which to distinguish the false from the genuine, in his search for truth. The rule he at length adopted was certainly rigid enough, if adhered to, to guard him against any impositions of error: it was — to accept no doctrines but those the truth of which was too clear to be questioned. *Criterion of truth.* We are to see in what direction this principle led him, and whether he or Spinoza was more faithful to it in the pursuit of wisdom. But even in regard to this criterion of truth, the originality of Descartes has been doubted. May Spinoza not have taken this, too, from the Arabian philosophy? Mr. Lewes, in his charming sketch of Algazzali, quotes that remarkable thinker as saying, "It was evident *Not original with Descartes.* to me that certain knowledge must be that which explains the object to be known, in such a manner that no doubt can remain, so that in future all error and conjecture concerning it must be impossible."[1] By this rule, strictly applied, the Oriental student found himself shut up to his own consciousness in the search for truth. He found in the sect of the Soufis, the mystics of the East, the best examples of his principle in action; though he says that some of them went too far, "imagining themselves to be amalgamated with God, or identified with him." Avoiding this extreme, which would have made him a Spinozist before Spinoza, Algazzali says, "I declare that the conviction was forced upon me that the Soufis indubitably walked in the true paths of salvation. Their way of life is the most beautiful, and their morals the purest that can be conceived."

[1] Biographical Hist. Phil., p. 363.

Testimony as to Descartes' position. But though the Cartesian maxim for discovering truth had been held by others, this does not detract from Descartes' real merits. He was not a plagiarist in the discreditable sense of the word, any more than Spinoza was while pursuing paths already trodden by Giordano Bruno. Descartes should, no doubt, have the somewhat questionable honor of being the real master of the founder of pantheism. And inasmuch as Spinoza claimed, and might with a degree of justice claim, that his conclusions were a logical development of Cartesianism, it will be necessary to look at some of Descartes' fundamental doctrines. Besides the coincidence already noticed, it will appear, I think, that Fontenelle was right in saying that Spinozism is "Cartesianism pushed to extravagance." So far as conclusions go, the remark of Dugald Stewart is, no doubt, correct, that "no two philosophers ever differed more widely in their metaphysical and theological tenets;" but if we consider only premises and methods of reasoning, it seems to me far from true that Spinoza, as Stewart says, "agreed with Descartes in little else than his physical principles." That it was from Descartes especially that Spinoza took the principles of his system, will appear, I think, as we go forward. The maxim, that that only is to be accepted as true which cannot be rationally doubted, was, as no one has attempted to deny, a cardinal rule with Spinoza. This appears in his whole statement of the doctrine of knowledge; where he rejects as "hearsay," or as "inadequate," all those notions which do not come through the immediate grapple of the mind with the very substance of truth. We shall see how strictly he adhered to this rule, at least in purpose, and how quick he was to see and expose any violation of it in the reasonings of Descartes.

The points in the Cartesian philosophy, which may be regarded as paving the way to Spinozism, if not indeed its very germs, are four in number: 1. The renowned formula *Cogito, ergo sum ;* 2. The argument for proving the divine existence; 3. The doctrine that there are no second causes; 4. The theory that all truth is susceptible of proof by the method of mathematics. In all cases of disagreement with Descartes, Spinoza, as can be successfully shown, I think, disagreed with him simply as a logical and thorough-going adherent to these postulates. *(Four main points in Cartesianism.)*

The formula *Cogito, ergo sum* (I think, therefore I am), was laid down by Descartes as expressive of the spirit of his whole system. In this sentence a broad meaning is given to the word "think." Descartes understands by *thought* any fact in consciousness, whether intellectual, emotional, or voluntary. "I designate by the word 'thought,'" says he, "all those facts of which we are internally conscious; and of these our consciousness itself is one. And so not only to know, to will, and to imagine, but even to feel also, is here the same thing as to think."[1] But it has been stoutly denied that the Cartesian formula proves even personal existence. Gassendi thought it a flagrant breach of the philosopher's own rule that nothing should be held true which admits of rational doubt, to infer the fact of a person from the bare existence of thinking. *(Criticism of Gassendi and Huxley.)* The thinking alone is in consciousness; and to say that *I*

[1] Principia Philosophiæ.

think, is a begging of the question. "Prove that *you* think," says Descartes' critic, "and the assertion that *you* exist will follow of necessity. The criticism is valid, no doubt; and it has been presented quite recently by Huxley, under a modified form. The formula is analyzed by Huxley, and shown to contain three distinct propositions, one of which asserts the action of a person, another conscious thought, and the other personal existence. But only the second of these propositions, that affirming conscious thought, can endure the Cartesian test of certainty. "Descartes," says Huxley, " determined as he was to strip off all the garments which the intellect weaves for itself, forgot this gossamer shirt of the *self*, to the great detriment, and indeed ruin, of his toilet when he began to clothe himself again."[1] The inference from this criticism is, that Descartes, when pushed back into his main position, turns out to be the true predecessor of James Mill and his school, teaching us that we have nothing to do with substances, whether spiritual or material, but only with sensations, aside from which there is no ground of certain knowledge.

The justice of these criticisms I do not deny. But in showing the relation of Descartes to Spinoza, he must be taken as he understood himself, and as the pupil took him. Strictly speaking, we cannot be conscious of personality; though we may be said to be, in a larger sense of the term. The "self" is something which rests upon the primary beliefs of the soul. Those beliefs, as defined in more modern times, do not seem to have occurred to Descartes as a basis of certitude.

<small>Descartes to be taken as he understood himself.</small>

[1] Lay Sermons, Addresses, and Reviews, p. 328.

He must perhaps be regarded as holding to consciousness only in the more restricted sense; and therefore we must grant that his reasoning is illogical, although the work before us requires that his conclusions be allowed to stand in their historical connections. He clearly means to assert that our personal existence is not an inference, but a datum of consciousness. What if a man doubts his own existence, runs the argument. Yet he cannot doubt that he doubts; therefore in any case the existence is a foregone conclusion. It is so true a truth that the most obstinate scepticism cannot at all invalidate it. Of one thing, then, Descartes was absolutely certain; and on this immovable rock he planted himself, resolved to make it a basis for the reconstruction of human knowledge.

But having found this standing-place, his next desideratum was the Archimedean lever. This second requisite he claimed to have secured in his method. The basis of certitude was consciousness; and the method of certitude was deduction,—called mathematical because always followed in the processes of mathematics. The mistake which Descartes here made, and which Spinoza did not correct, was in making mathematics a universal science; in assuming that all truth lay within its domain, and could be reached by its methods. Spinoza says, in the Introduction to the Third Part of the Ethics, "I shall discuss human actions, appetites, and emotions, precisely as if the question were of lines, planes, and solids." But our minds are shut up to a very small sphere of knowledge, if we can know only what may be demonstrated like so many theorems in geometry. The method is inadequate, and we cannot explain Descartes'

The Cartesian method.

adoption of it, unless, perhaps, he was biassed by his great fondness for mathematics. He achieved astonishing results in the prosecution of this science, and might properly claim to be its especial champion in his times. This fact, together with his declared distrust of any doctrine which rose only to the level of probability, may account for his error. He entered a path from which, as we shall soon see, Spinoza found him tripping. The refugee from Judaism, no less than the revolted pupil of the Jesuits, held the maxim that only what cannot be rationally doubted is worthy of belief. "All original truths," he contended, " are of such a kind that they cannot, without absurdity, even be conceived to be false; the opposites of them are contradictions in terms."[1]

Regarding the formula *Cogito, ego sum*, as an instance of mathematical reasoning, in strict conformity with the Cartesian test of certainty, we are able to see how Descartes' conclusion in the case follows. *I think* is a datum of consciousness; and the conclusion *I am* is involved in that datum, so as to be a necessary deduction from it. The two propositions are, in mathematical phrase, identical. That is, the thinking may stand as the first term of an equation, and the existence as the second term. One is just as true as the other, the truth being in each case assumed; and therefore, since things which are equal to the same thing are equal to each other, they may be put side by side, with the sign of equality between them. Thought is an indisputable fact, and thought equals being; therefore being is mathematically demonstrated.

Descartes' first step.

[1] Froude's Short Studies on Great Subjects (New York, 1868), p. 280.

Yet even here is a joint in the Cartesian harness, into which the ready critic may thrust his weapon. Descartes did not seem to see the dangerous admission which his statement involved — the welcome to Spinozism, broad and manifest. In strict fidelity to his own method, he had not proved being in itself, or as an objective fact, but only the subjective being of which he was conscious. His universe is shut within the limits of his own thinking. Has he proved existence? That we grant him; but this assured existence amounts, after all, to nothing but the contents of his own consciousness. All mathematical proof is a series of identical propositions. $2 + 2 = 4$; that is, two added to two, and four, are simply different ways of saying the same thing. Only the being of the subject involved in the thought is deducible from the fact of thinking, on mathematical principles. Therefore we must not go out of ourselves, but must draw the whole universe of reality into ourselves, and make it in some way an integral part of our own consciousness, if we would know the universe as the mathematician knows his conclusions. We must cease groping abroad, and unravel the tangled skein of our own conscious exercises; for in these alone are all demonstrable truths contained. Thus does the doctrine of Spinoza find a foothold in that of Descartes. If the master attempts to prove, by the professed method, any objective world, whether spiritual or material, the pupil may turn upon him, and assail him with his own weapon. It can be shown, beyond the possibility of refutation, that Cartesianism must come at last to nothing but a species of subjective pantheism. It gives the seeker for truth no outlet,

A foothold for Spinozism.

but keeps him hopelessly shut up, "cribbed, cofflned, and confined," within the narrow sphere of his own consciousness. God, nature, and humanity, considered as objective realities, are swept out of existence at a single stroke. The only reality left to every man is the conscious being which he finds in his own thinking; and this conclusion follows from the Cartesian formula, according to the mathematical method, as used by Descartes himself in the search for truth.

The recognition of Reid's doctrine of necessary truths would have saved Descartes.
It is easy for thinkers of the present day, who are familiar with the Scotch or intuitional philosophy, to point out the fatal error in Descartes' system, and to show what the a-priori philosophy needed, in order to guard it against the approaches of pantheism. Those necessary truths, first earnestly insisted on by Reid, and afterwards more clearly defined by Hamilton, are our only escape from the bondage to which Cartesianism dooms us. They alone can break open the door of the prison in which our consciousness holds us fast bound, and cast up a sure highway outward, from the subjective into the objective. They bridge the chasm, not only between thought and that which thinks, but between the *me* and *not-me;* between the one and the many, the conscious and the unconscious, the spiritual and the material. They carry us abroad, out of the narrow circle of individual consciousness, to the limits of the universe of truth. Under their ministration, the contents do not drop out of our ideas, so as to leave us but the residuum of blank idealism; nor, on the other hand, do they allow our identity to become lost in the matter of our thoughts; but saving us

equally, both from pantheism and from pure rationalism or sensationalism, they reveal to us substance in phenomena, and body under the dominion of spirit. Descartes did not discover, and the purpose of Spinoza forbade him to notice, this outlet of the a-priori philosophy from the terrible grasp and confinement of pantheism.

But as we have kept faithfully to the path indicated by Descartes' famous formula, in reaching the point to which we are now come, so it will be in strict accordance with his principles that we shall reach yet other consequences. His demonstration of the being of God completes the basis which we have already noticed, in part, for the argument in proof of pantheism. "I think, therefore I am," is impregnable when judged by the Cartesian test of truth, as Descartes and Spinoza both thought. And the next question is, how to rise from our own thought to as solid a ground on which to rest the divine existence. Is it possible for us to prove, by the exact mathematical method, in a way which shall preclude all doubt, the being of a God who is external to our thinking, and wholly independent of it? Descartes answers in the affirmative, and speaks substantially as follows, in the effort to make good his assertion: I have a necessary idea of an absolutely perfect being; but no idea of a being can be absolutely perfect unless that being exists, for his existence must be one of the elements of his perfection; therefore the absolutely perfect being, God, exists. It does not fall within my present plan to notice the usual criticisms of this argument. Whatever may be said about the assumption that actual existence is involved in the idea of a perfect

The Cartesian argument for the divine existence favors Spinozism.

being, — real objective existence, I mean, — no one who comprehends the case will deny that Descartes' conclusion follows legitimately on pantheistic ground. But to say that it follows on the ground of pure theism, we must assume that Descartes anticipates, here, the philosophy of Reid; that he means, by "necessary idea," one of those primary truths which are the foundation of all thinking. Thus only can it be shown that his conclusive logic does not necessitate pantheism. The theological world seems, more and more, to be coming to the position that our belief in God is fundamental; that it is one of those postulates of the human reason on which we plant ourselves in advance of every inquiry after a God; that all our a-posteriori arguments, so far from begetting, only serve to clear up and deepen this necessary conviction. It is one of the truths which lie about us in our infancy, as Wordsworth puts it in his Ode on Immortality; which we bring with us when we come from God, who is our home; truths that wake to perish never;

"Which neither listlessness nor mad endeavor,
Nor man nor boy,
Nor all that is at enmity with joy,
Can utterly abolish or destroy."

Descartes seems, at times, to have come very near this ground. Mr. Lewes quotes him as saying, "By the word *idea*, I understand all that can be in our thoughts; and I distinguish three sorts of ideas: *adventitious*, like the common idea of the sun; *framed* by the mind, such as that which astronomical reasoning gives of the sun; and *innate*, as the idea of God, mind, body, a triangle, and, generally, all those which represent true, immutable, and eternal essences." But his precise meaning in these words is uncertain, for we again find him explaining, "When I said that the idea of God is innate in us, I never meant more than this — that nature has endowed us with a faculty by which we may know God; but I have never either said or thought that such ideas had an actual existence, or even that they were a species distinct from the faculty of thinking." This language, therefore, shows us on what ground the famous demonstration of a God must be regarded as standing. The God whose existence is demonstrated must not be held to be anything distinct from that which thinks, and conceives, and reasons. The Cartesian idea of a most perfect being is only a form of the thinking faculty revealed in consciousness. It is not a truth independent of all experience, but simply a shadow of the "self." And therefore the thinker, who is conscious of it, is still within the circle of his own subjectivity. The being he has found is not outward, and personally separate from himself; he is inward, and constitutes in very deed the thinker's own essence and modes of consciousness.

How his argument legitimates pantheism.

If it should be denied that this pantheistic conclusion follows from Descartes' position, and his theistic friends should say that he has proved the being of an objective deity, independent of the human consciousness, then they are confronted by his *method* of proof, which confirms the argument against them. To deduce the outward from the inward, as the Car-

The Cartesian method helps the tendency to pantheism. tesian formula did, was doing violence to the law of mathematics which requires that the conclusion should be found *in* the premise. I think, and therefore I exist. Now show in consciousness that God thinks, and it will be mathematically true that God exists. Just here, as already intimated, comes the inevitable leap into pantheism. In order to know absolutely that God thinks, as I know that I think, God and I must have one and the same consciousness. I exist, for I am conscious of thinking; and in order to prove mathematically that God exists, I must be likewise conscious of his thinking. This is the position to which an inexorable logic brings us. Man is absorbed into God. Our consciousness of thinking is not ours, but God's; and because God thinks, God exists. Thus the existence of a certain something, God, Nature, Substance, whatever we choose to call it, is demonstrated on mathematical principles; and beyond this self-conscious and absolute Substance, there cannot be proved to be any reality.

Is further evidence needed to show that we have followed Cartesianism out to its logical ultimate? That evidence is at hand, in the doctrine of Descartes respecting second causes. He denied that any such causes exist. This tendency further strengthened by his denial of second causes. Mr. Morell states his views on this point as follows: "Creation itself Descartes attributed to *the will* of the Almighty, making even necessary truth dependent upon that will, rather than upon the nature of things." Therefore two and two are equal to four, and the sum of the angles in any triangle is equal to two right angles only because God wills that it should be so. "More important still, however," says Morell, "was his doctrine respecting the act of creation itself. To Descartes the whole dependent world, both of mind and matter, is a vast mechanism, carried on by external laws, — a mechanism which requires the act of creation to be ever reproduced, in order to keep it in perpetual and harmonious operation. According to this view, there can be no direct action of matter upon matter, because it is the perpetual efflux of the 'vis creatrix' by which all such action is maintained; and, consequently, secondary causes can be nothing more than modifications of the first cause. In like manner, also, there can be no direct influence mutually exerted upon each other by mind and matter, for the action of both is dependent on the continuity of the creative power, as seen in the laws or mechanism of body and soul. In this affirmation, *that the universe depends upon the productive power of God, not only for its first existence, but equally so for its continued being and operation*, there are involved the germs of the several doctrines of pre-established harmony, of occasional causes, and, finally, of pantheism itself, the ultimate point to which they all tend."[1]

So near had Descartes himself come to the edge of the abyss into which Spinoza "pushed" him. What was there worth contending for, between this scheme of emanation, making God the author of all human actions even, and pantheism? The disciple was severely true to the principles of his master. If he reduced the universe to a single self-conscious substance, it was done in the alembic of Cartesianism. The followers of Descartes had no just cause to shout forth

<small>Spinoza's logic faultless.</small>

[1] History of Modern Philosophy (New York, 1854), p. 120.

their indignation from all parts of Europe, thus putting the life of the Spinozists in peril. The feeble-bodied, but giant-minded, outcast from Judaism had been more faithful than any other to the fundamental theses of the great idealist. Those Cartesians who still claimed to be on Christian ground foamed at the charge of pantheism thus laid at their own door. Nor did it make them any the less, but only the more wrathful, to find that the charge could by no means be refuted. We may grant, what is undoubtedly true, that Descartes did not mean to teach such a doctrine. But neither did the good Bishop Berkeley mean to teach the scepticism which Hume deduced from his premises. As a matter of fact, the germs of pantheism were in the Cartesian philosophy, and needed only the acute and logical mind of Spinoza to develop them. Given the premise of Descartes, that all truth begins in consciousness; then allow his method, which is that of mathematical demonstration; and with these join his limiting of causation to the Deity, and you have all that is essential to Spinozism. The premises of the pantheistic system were given to it by Descartes; and from these, as Coleridge has well said, "the deduction is a chain of adamant." Spinoza can be refuted, and his appalling system be shown to be a baseless fabric, in very few words. All truth does not begin in consciousness; the necessities of thought give us a sure standing-place outside of our own conscious thinking. Furthermore, many things which cannot be mathematically demonstrated are nevertheless true. And there are efficient causes in men, if not in nature, which can never be merged into the one great First Cause. We

The premises of pantheism untenable.

need not fear the might of this self-reliant Hebrew. He is vulnerable, like the hero of the Iliad. However well protected at all other points, there is one point at which he may be successfully assailed. But spare his premise, the exposed heel of this logical Achilles, and, like the victim in the fable, you must follow where he leads. Bidding a last farewell to all your convictions of freedom, of independent personality, and of real existence; confessing yourself to be a mere phenomenon, an unsubstantial shadow of the one absolute Substance, you must go with him through that gate upon whose portal the dread line of Dante should be written, "All hope abandon, ye who enter here."

I do not claim, in tracing pantheism, as I now have, to the philosophy of Descartes, to have followed the exact track of Spinoza; but I am fully persuaded, whatever may have been the precise nature of his earlier inquiries, that he needed but to keep hold of the Cartesian clew while striding forward to his pantheistic conclusions. It is necessary only that we enter in through the doorway of our own consciousness, if we would reach the persuasion that we stand face to face *The central position of Spinoza.* with the one reality; if we would hold, on logical grounds, that our personality, yea, all personality, is merged in that absolute whole, is indeed an integrant part of it, while it, in so far as it is real, is thereby impersonal. This great One, which is the essence of all things, Spinoza calls *Substance*, applying this name to it because it *stands under* and constitutes the whole reality of all those phenomena of mind and matter which engage our attention.

It is upon this basis of the one absolute Substance, that Spinoza proceeds to build up his dogmatic system. To follow him through, and see how he accomplishes this undertaking, would be a laborious and tedious task. The form of his exposition is such that it cannot be condensed. Every step in it is a vital part of the whole. I must therefore be content, as my purpose permits me to be, with a simple account of the main drift and features of his work. Having seen what his fundamental doctrine is, it is natural that we should desire some such brief sketch of its plan of development. I shall confine myself, in what follows, to the chief work of Spinoza, which he called "Ethics;" though he has set forth his doctrine in other treatises, especially in the Tractatus Theologico-Politicus. This work is a plea for the broadest toleration of private religious opinion, while at the same time it argues that the civil power should insist on prescribed forms of religious observance. Religious worship seems to be regarded somewhat in the light of military drill. It is a kind of Papal system, with the soul left out; an external order, conducive to social uniformity, and necessary to the perpetuity of the state. Forms of worship should have nothing to do with actual religious beliefs, and should be enforced by the civil authority as a discipline which its own safety requires. A full account of the views advocated in this treatise may be found in Willis's Life of Spinoza, pp. 337-352.

The dogmatic result.

Taking up, now, the exposition of pantheism in the Ethics, the first thing to be noticed is, that Spinoza distinguishes three kinds of knowledge, or more strictly, perhaps, three methods of inquiring

Three kinds of knowledge.

after truth. The First kind of knowledge is that which we gain by the method of hearsay. And under this are included not only history and tradition, but all those impressions which we get through the medium of the senses. Knowledge of this sort is vain and unreal. However much it may have to do with the outward life of men, it is merely phenomenal, and therefore unworthy of the true philosopher. The Second kind of knowledge, Spinoza observes, is that which we attain by applying the logical understanding to outward appearances, so as to trace in them certain resemblances, or classify them under the laws by which they are regulated. This is knowledge in the Baconian sense, and is to be rejected as having no place in a system of demonstrated truths. The Third kind of knowledge, which alone Spinoza regarded as deserving the name, is that which "arises when by an effort of the reason we grasp the very substance of things when we gaze upon Being itself."[1] A more precise view of Spinoza's doctrine of cognition may perhaps be obtained from Props. XXIX. to XLIII., inclusive, Part. II. Under Prop. XL., Scholium 2, he says, "We perceive many things and form many notions: 1st, from *singulars* altered to us by our senses, and represented confusedly and without order to the understanding (vide Coroll. to Prop. XXIX.). Such perceptions I am therefore accustomed to characterize as cognition *from vague experience*. 2d, from signs; for example, because from certain words which we hear or read we remember things, and form certain ideas of these like to those by which we imagine the things themselves (vide Schol. to Prop. XVIII.). Both of these modes of contemplating

[1] Morell, p. 125. Froude's Short Studies on Great Subjects, p. 279.

things I shall for the future designate as cognition of the first kind — as *opinion* or *imagination*. 3d, and lastly, inasmuch as we have common notions and adequate ideas of the properties of things (vide Coroll. to Props. XXXVIII. and XXXIX. and Prop. XL.), I shall speak of these under the titles of *reason and cognition of the second kind*. Besides these two kinds of cognition there is a third, as I shall presently show, which I shall entitle *intuitive*, and which proceeds from the adequate idea of the real essence of some of the attributes of God to the adequate cognition of the essence of things." Under Prop. XLIII., Demonst., he says, "The true idea in us is that which is in God, in so far as God is expressed by the soul of man, and it is adequate."[1] Here we see, in the definition of knowledge which he gives, how Spinoza seeks at the very outset to draw us within his charmed circle. It is true that many have accepted this definition, or its equivalent, without becoming involved in pantheism; but they were held back, and saved, by a power which philosophy can never bring to bear.

Some account of the Ethics.

That immediate cognition of the essence of things, that is, of God, or the one substance in consciousness, is the only true and adequate knowledge Spinoza everywhere assumes. This appears in the First of the five parts into which the Ethics is divided, though more especially in some of the subsequent portions. Reversing the order of parts, so far as to make the First come in last for notice, I will now endeavor to state, as briefly as I can, the topic of each part and the manner of treatment. In the Second Part of the Ethics, the origin

[1] Willis's translation.

and nature of Mind are considered. The human soul is there held to be, not an independent thing, but purely a mode of the divine attribute of thought. **Subject of the Second Part.** There are prefixed to the forty-nine demonstrated propositions, with their corollaries and scholia, seven definitions and five axioms. Reality (Def. 6) is defined to be the same thing as perfection. To be is to be perfect. The first proposition declares that thought is an attribute of God, and the second that extension is an attribute of God. Individual thoughts express the nature of God. The soul itself is not substance or being, but simply a mode of one of the attributes of substance.[1] Nor can we know the soul save through this underlying substance. It is a thing which must be comprehended in the infinite idea of God.[2] If considered by itself, it appears only as a succession of fleeting phenomena. Following this changeful process, and not penetrating through it so as to gaze on being itself, Spinoza regards as the road to self-ignorance. The observer mistakes appearances for the reality.

The Third Part of the Ethics treats of the source and nature of the Affections. **Subject of Part Third.** "It will doubtless appear strange," he says in the Introduction, "that I should set about treating the vices and follies of mankind in a geometrical way. Yet such is my purpose." He begins here with three definitions, the second of which is important. We *act*, he says, when we are the soul or adequate cause of what takes place within us or without us; and we *suffer* when anything thus occurs of which we are only partly the cause. He also lays down three postulates, the first of which says that the human body may be variously affected, so that its power of action shall be

[1] Part II., Prop. X., Scholium 2.   [2] Part II., Prop. VIII.

increased or diminished. Then, in the fifty-nine propositions following, it is attempted to show that all the pleasurable emotions, such as hope, joy, love, occur through the increase of that power of action, and that all the disagreeable emotions, such as despair, grief, hatred, result from the diminution of that power.[1] It is, in each instance, the flowing or ebbing of the one substance. There are times when all the emotions of which the soul is capable are in such a state of activity as just to balance each other. It is the peace of God, of which we are conscious, whenever this equilibrium ensues. Then any greater influx of the divine essence causes an overflow, which is some one of the specific forms of pleasure;[2] and any withdrawal of that essence causes a diminution, which we may include under the generic name of sorrow.[3]

Subject of Part Fourth. Spinoza goes on next, in the Fourth Part, to treat of Human Slavery, or the Strength of the Affections. We are enslaved just in proportion to the strength of the emotional element in us. It is the tendency of the affections to take from a man his power of self-control, and to compel him to pursue evil paths even while he sees and approves the better course. To labor for a given end is a species of slavery; for "a final cause, as it is called, is nothing but a human appetite or desire considered as the origin or cause of anything." God is not under this bondage of the affections, since he has no final cause in what he does. "The cause why God acts and why he exists is one and the same, and as he does not exist for any end or purpose, so does he not act for any end or purpose."[4] Everything, that is, is slavish which is

---

[1] Prop. XI.
[2] Part III., Prop. LIII.
[3] Part III., Prop. LV.
[4] Part IV., Introduction.

not purely spontaneous. This doctrine is made to rest on a basis of eight definitions and one axiom, and is built up into seventy-three propositions, with their demonstrations, corollaries, and scholia. "It is impossible," we are told, "that man should not be a part of nature."[1] And the equilibrium of nature, or the balance of all the passions in God, is lost in their coming forth into our consciousness. The rays of the colorless beam are dispersed and but partially comprehended. This is the subordination of the absolute substance to the particular manifestation; and it is the slavery of the human mind.

In the Fifth Part the reverse of this case is considered — the power of the understanding, or human freedom, when the mode of the attribute embodies its essence. There is most freedom in us when we are least conscious of the self, and lost in beholding the one substance which constitutes all that is real in us. The whole of God is revealed in our contemplation, no ray refracted, and all so blended as to make one passionless experience. Perfect liberty is the perfect spontaneity of the infinite God or Nature, and its absolute necessity is that which renders it perfect. Spinoza declares, in this portion of the Ethics, that "God is without passions, and is not affected by any emotion of joy or sorrow."[2] He also undertakes to demonstrate that "no one can hate God."[3] Beatitude is that perfect balance of the passions in their manifestation, which amounts to the absence of passion. True love is purely intellectual, not emotional; and "the intellectual love of the mind towards God is part of the infinite love wherewith God loves himself."[4] "I say that

Subject of Part Fifth.

[1] Part IV., Prop. IV.
[2] Part V., Prop. XVII.
[3] Part V., Prop XVIII.
[4] Part V., Prop. XXXVI.

a thing is free," says he, "which exists and acts by the sole necessity of its nature; and I call that constrained which is determined to exist and to act in a certain definite way by something external to itself. Thus God, though existing necessarily, exists freely, because he exists by the necessity of his nature alone. So also God understands himself and all things freely, because it follows from the necessity of his nature alone that he understands himself and all things else. You see, therefore, that I place freedom not in any free decree of the will, but in free necessity."[1] The explanatory words show that Spinoza did not recognize such a thing as freedom either in God or man, save in a way that would apply to all the outgrowths of nature equally well; for these, quite as much as he claims in any case, exist and act from an inherent necessity.

Subject of the First Part.

I will return now, after this look forward through Spinoza's system, to what he says more directly concerning God, which occupies the First Part of the Ethics. I do this, not with the hope of adding to the imperfect outline just given, for my sketch must, at the best, be far from adequate. But it may not be out of place to introduce here a specimen or two of the manner in which this system of pantheism is constructed. He begins with laying down eight definitions. The first

Definitions.

of these says, "By a thing which is its own cause, I understand a thing the essence of which involves existence, or the nature of which can be considered only as existent." The third in the series says, "By substance I understand that which exists in itself, and the conception of which does not require the conception of anything antecedent to it." The fourth of

[1] Letter to Dr. Schaller, Willis, p. 383.

them is, "By attribute I understand that which the mind perceives as constituting the very essence of substance."[1] The sixth of these definitions says, "By God I understand the being absolutely infinite, i. e., the substance consisting of infinite attributes, each of which expresses an infinite and eternal essence."[2]

If we are not yet persuaded that there may be such a thing as the geometry of metaphysics, let us follow Spinoza a step farther. From Definitions he proceeds to Axioms. There are seven of these prefixed to this First Part of his work, such as, "Everything which is, is in itself or in some other thing;" "That which cannot be conceived through another must be conceived through itself;" "The knowledge of an effect depends on the knowledge of its cause."[2] But let us not stop here. Let us follow this geometrical pantheist a little into his propositions, demonstrations, corollaries, scholia, and the letters q. e. d., appended here and there; thus we may be able to see how it is that everything in the treatise, from beginning to end, seems nearly as rigid and concise as the procedure in Euclid. The fifth proposition, which is decidedly pantheistic, declares, "It is impossible that there should be two or more substances of the same nature or attribute." The eighth proposition I will give, together with the demonstration, it being one of the simplest, and

---

[1] It will be noticed that the distinction which Spinoza makes between Attribute and Substance, is perhaps what may be called subjective rather than objective. In a letter to his friend Simon de Vries he refers to these third and fourth definitions, and explains: "By Attribute I understand the same thing [as substance], save that Attribute, in respect of our understanding, is regarded as attaching a certain specific nature to Substance." Willis, p. 279.

[2] Lewes, p. 473.   [3] Lewes, p. 474.

a good example of Spinoza's method: "Prop. VIII. All substance is necessarily infinite. *Demonst.* Substance of one attribute exists not save as one (by Prop. V.); and to exist belongs to its nature (Prop. VI.). It will therefore be in its nature to exist finitely or infinitely. Not finitely, however, for then it would have to be conceived as limited by another substance of the same nature (by Def. 2), which would also have to exist necessarily (by Prop. VII.); in which case there would be two substances of the same attribute, which is absurd (by Prop. V.). Substance, therefore, exists infinitely: q. e. d."[1]

A demonstration.

Perfection of Superstructure.

I shall be readily excused, no doubt, for not attempting to report Spinoza's argument any farther. It seems a little discouraging to one at first, when he thinks of going through a metaphysical treatise constructed after this fashion. But I can assure any one who proposes to make the attempt, that the progress is so steady, and the demonstrations are so clear, that when once fairly started he will find himself drawn irresistibly forward. Let him forget how utterly insecure the foundations are, and he will feel an ever-growing wonder as he sees this temple of pantheism rising up, throwing out its battlements, lifting arch above arch, and rearing aloft its towers, — every joint perfect, each stone and each timber going to its destined place, the sharpest scrutiny unable to detect anywhere the least break, or flaw, or weakness. The doctrine of One Substance is the material of which the whole edifice is made. That substance has two infinite attributes, Thought and Extension.[2] Each of these attributes, fur-

Two attributes of substance.

[1] Willis, p. 418. [2] Ethics, Part II., Props. I. and II.

thermore, has, while expressing the essence of the One Substance, an infinite number of modes, which modes make the whole varying phenomena of what we call finite mind and matter.[1] All those phenomena which are viewed in their subjective relation to consciousness, are modes of the infinite attribute of thought, and all those which are seen in objective relations, ordinarily regarded as the affections of matter, are modes of the infinite attribute of extension. Spinoza seems to regard these attributes as mutually dependent, so that neither can be conceived to be, apart from the other — an opinion which is important, as implying that there can be no thought, and therefore no conscious immortality, where everything which answers to our idea of bodily organization is wanting.[2] This dualistic manifestation of God must go forward in our consciousness in order that he may know himself as still existent. And he is all. Matter and finite mind, viewed by themselves, have not a real, but simply a phenomenal existence. Soul and body are the same thing; and neither of them is anything but a transient evolution out of the universal substance. The earth, the heavens, the waters, the continents, man, beast, fishes, the birds, the flowers, have no proper being; they are the same great all-in-all, — the absolute substance manifesting itself.

Bearing on question of Immortality.

"All nature, he holds, is a respiration
Of the Spirit of God, who, in breathing, hereafter
Will inhale it into his bosom again,
So that nothing but God alone shall remain." [3]

[1] Ethics, Part II., Props. VIII. and XIII.
[2] See Froude's Short Studies, &c., p. 315.
[3] Longfellow's Golden Legend.

According to Spinoza there is no such thing as a created universe. He denies the possibility of creation.[1] Cause and effect are but different aspects of the same energy, *natura naturans* and *nātura naturata ;* God, nature, the absolute, the cosmos, or whatever one may choose to call it, continually going out of itself and returning into itself. This process, corresponding to what Herbert Spencer calls evolution and dissolution, is what we name growth and decay, birth and death, in our inadequate language. This terrible God, this insatiate Chronos, devouring his children as fast as he begets them, has perfect freedom, according to Spinoza. Yet here, as already noticed, words are not used in their prevailing sense; for the freedom spoken of has no reference to liberty of choice, but is only the ceaseless power of activity. This all-ingulfing divinity cannot act otherwise than it does,[2] nor can it ever pause in its action. Its spontaneity is necessary and eternal. We have then at last, as Spinoza does not shrink from admitting, a scheme of universal and invincible fatalism. "Free will," he says, "is a chimera, flattering to our pride, and in reality founded on our ignorance. All that I can say to those who believe that they can, by virtue of any free decision of the soul, speak or be silent, or, to use a single word, act, is, that they dream with their eyes open. Nothing is bad in itself. Good and evil indicate nothing positive in things considered in themselves, and are nothing but modes of thinking. Not only has every man the right to seek his good, his pleasure, but he cannot do otherwise. The measure of each man's right

Fatalism.

---

[1] See Appendix to Part I. of the Ethics.
[2] Ethics, Part I., Prop. XXXIII.

is his power. He who does not yet know reason, or who, having not as yet contracted the habit of virtue, lives according only to the laws of his appetites, is as much in his right as he who regulates his life according to the laws of reason. In other words, just as the sage has an absolute right to do all that his reason dictates to him, or to live according to the laws of reason, in the same manner has the ignorant man or the madman a right to everything that his appetite impels him to take; in other words, the right to live according to the laws of appetite. And he is no more obliged to live according to the laws of good sense than a cat is obliged to live under the laws that govern the nature of a lion. Hence we conclude that a compact has only a value proportioned to its utility. Where the utility disappears, the compact too disappears with it, and loses all its authority. There is, then, folly in pretending to bind a man forever to his word, unless, at least, a man so contrive that the breach of the compact shall entail for him that violates it more danger than profit." No comment is needed on these plain words. It follows from them inevitably, nay, is earnestly maintained in them, that there can be no such thing as responsibility for moral action, and that right and wrong, as commonly understood, are a pure delusion. Ethical or natural evil is a notion which ignorance frames to itself, with no shadow of actual foundation; and man, in order to enjoy the largest happiness, and attain the fullest development, should seek, first of all, to lose his consciousness of such airy phenomena, and be identified in thought with the Absolute Substance which fills and upholds all things.

108 HALF TRUTHS AND THE TRUTH.

The question here arises, What shall be said of Cartesianism in view of the conclusions of Spinoza? Is it fallacious? Ought it to be altogether eschewed in the search for truth?

The a-priori philosophy not to be judged by Spinozism.

While not taken rigidly, but as commonly understood, it certainly is not to be avoided, even if that were indeed possible. Many of the first thinkers of the time are essentially Cartesians, as many have been in every past age, and as will continue to be the fact hereafter. The inherent peculiarities of such minds make them what they are. If they think. at all, it must be on the basis, and by the method, of Descartes. This was true of the celebrated writers of the school of Port Royal; more or less true of that wonderful genius and Christian writer Blaise Pascal; it was true also of the pious Fénelon, and of Bishop Berkeley — so devout a worshipper of the true God, though in his theory of the world so deluded. Descartes himself was a sincere believer in Christianity. If his works were condemned as heretical by the Papal church, this was not because he had denied the Lord that bought him, but on account of certain physical discoveries, owing to the criterion of truth which he set up, and because he had subverted the philosophy of Aristotle as interwoven with her scholastic theology. The great master of a-priori thinking, whom many leading minds even at the present day follow, was a firm believer in the living God of the Scriptures; so firm, that he seems to have mistaken his faith for logical demonstration.. While Spinoza took from him the principles of pantheism, Malebranche, on the other hand, beginning from the same source, deduced a body of Christian mysticism. No doubt Spinoza was

Malebranche.

the more acute and logical pupil. It was the ardent piety of Malebranche, his strong hold upon the personal Jehovah, that saved him. "The union of the soul to God," says he, "is the only means by which we acquire a knowledge of truth. Let my readers judge of my opinions according to the clear and distinct answers they shall receive from the Lord of all men. Let us repose in this tenet, that God is the intelligible world, or the place of spirits, like as the material world is the place of bodies; that it is from his power they receive all their modifications; that it is in his wisdom they find all their ideas; and that it is by his love they feel all their well-regulated emotions. And since his power, and his wisdom, and his love are but himself, let us believe, with St. Paul, that he is not far from each one of us, and that in him we live, and move, and have our being."[1] No doubt the keen-eyed Spinoza would have found his own doctrine here, as easily as in Descartes. But Malebranche was not a logical machine, and therefore not a pantheist. His language expresses his deep sense of the need of divine illumination in the search for truth; the conviction that we see falsely through the senses, the imagination, the understanding, the inclinations, and the passions; but always truly, when we see all things through reason restored to its right relations with God.

The world-renowned Leibnitz was a Cartesian; and he bent all the energies of his great mind to refute the conclusions of Spinoza. He did refute them, in the judgment of his friends, but not till he had added to the philosophy of Descartes certain very important principles. He restored to the idea of a Supreme

Leibnitz.

[1] Hallam's Literature of Europe.

Being that creative power for which Descartes had too nearly substituted simple emanation; and in his theory of *Monads*, or independent forces, not only is the doctrine of second causes restored, but the later doctrine of intuitions or necessary truths is foreshadowed. Herein it was that he hinted at the basis on which alone the a-priori philoso-

The safe-guard. phy can be saved from pantheism. With him, as with Malebranche, faith in a personal God, and in his own independent personality, predominated over any logical faith in Cartesianism. Like many others, both in earlier and later times, they walked safely along the "high priori road" cast up before them. But it was not in themselves, while they thus went forward, nor in the system they adopted, to direct their steps. That Great Light, which is the only true light of philosophy, illumined their pathway; and the Hand on which the universe depends upheld their goings.

LECTURE III.

THE GERMAN SUCCESSION.

THE startling conclusion which Spinoza had reached, and from which he could not be driven by Cartesianism, was followed by a general revolt from that philosophy. Thinkers gave up their faith in consciousness as the basis of a system of truth, and began to build more and more on experience. The a-priori method yielded to the a-posteriori. Deduction was exchanged for induction. Sensuous observation took the place of spiritual conviction. *A reaction.*

Thus a fresh impulse was given to the philosophy expounded by Bacon, and which had been carried forward into the realm of mind by Gassendi and Locke. Bacon wrote a century earlier than Spinoza, Gassendi just before him, and Locke was his contemporary. This school had therefore gained a foothold, and could boast of powerful adherents, when the real nature of Spinozism began to be known. Hence the ripened seed of Descartes' philosophy, which the astute Hebrew had gathered, was not immediately sown broadcast. It lay buried in the congenial soil of Germany; destined, however, to spring forth into a prodigious growth, when empiricism should have run its course and proved itself, too, a failure. *Empiricism.*

It does not belong to the present part of my plan to trace this empirical movement in the world of thought; a movement which became so powerful towards the close of the seventeenth century, and which was subverted in the eighteenth. The Positivism of our times may, I think, find in this its lineal predecessor. Condillac, Bonnet, Helvetius, Saint Lambert, Condorcet, Baron d'Holbach, were its high priests in France. One of its strongest early advocates in England was Thomas Hobbes. David Hume held the same relation to it as a critic which Spinoza held to Cartesianism. Taking it upon its own premises, that is, he showed its logical ultimate to be universal scepticism; just as Spinoza had shown that Descartes' principles led to pantheism. This keen sighted Scotchman was to arise, and cut up by the roots the empirical metaphysics of Locke; then Kant was to introduce, instead thereof, the germs of a-priori thinking again; and then the doctrine of Spinoza was to experience a resurrection, and to have a development which is one of the marvels of speculative philosophy. "The God of Spinoza, which the seventeenth century had broken as an Idol," is the remark of Saisset, "becomes the God of Lessing, of Goethe, of Novalis." It is with this German pantheism,— only so far, however, as it appears in the philosophy of the period,— that I am now concerned. Lessing the sceptic, who deemed it less blessed to possess truth than to search for truth, was among the earliest of the Germans to awaken an interest in the study of Spinoza; but he belongs to the department of criticism and literature, rather than that of philosophy. His Nathan the

Wise is perhaps as good a reproduction as we have of the spirit of Spinozism, and I shall repeatedly have occasion to refer to him; but the present starting-point is more properly Kant's Critique of the Pure Reason, from which the stream of pantheistic thought flows steadily on, through the writings of Fichte and Schelling more especially, till it comes to an end in the Absolute Idea of Hegel. It is with very great diffidence that I enter this path, along which so many able critics have been found stumbling. There is a tradition that Hegel, near the close of his life, said, "Only one of my followers has understood me; and he has misunderstood me." Even with the best of qualifications, therefore, I might well shrink from the attempt to represent German pantheism with thoroughness. But fortunately my plan does not require this; nor is it probable that the numerous class which I hope to reach would be greatly aided by such an effort, however successful in itself. I shall undertake only so much as is requisite in order that certain forms of unbelief, more or less popular at the present day, may be seen in their historical connections. I do not claim to be a master of the German tongue, nor to have read the works of the famous authors just referred to, in the original text; but I have taken pains to verify any statements which seemed to me to require it by recourse to that text, and have used only those translations which have the sanction of high authority. Though preferring to walk over the bridge rather than swim the river, as Mr. Emerson puts the case, I have not hesitated to plunge in and make examination, where anything seemed insecure. The writer whom I

What is here attempted.

shall quote chiefly, in sketching the course of thinking from Kant to Hegel, is Heinrich Moritz Chalybæus, of whose book, rendered into English by Alfred Tulk,[1] so competent a judge as Sir William Hamilton says, that it is "a perspicuous and impartial survey of the various modern systems of German philosophy, at once comprehensive and compendious." It will be seen I am confident, even in the imperfect and fragmentary sketch which alone I can hope to give, that there is, in all a-priori thinking, a danger on the side towards pantheistic forms of unbelief; and my object will be fully accomplished if it is made clear that the philosophy of consciousness is not a sufficient guide in the search for truth, save where it is supplemented and upheld by a divine energy, but carries one fatally on to emanation, and the confounding of effects with their causes, with no promise of a logical resting-place short of the One Substance with infinite attributes in which Spinoza at last rested.

Relation of Leibnitz to the new movement.

Leibnitz, who was mainly a Cartesian, may be said to have nourished the life of Descartes' philosophy in the German mind, during the period of its feebleness. He was, notwithstanding his seeming arrogance and impatience of contradiction, in many respects a remarkable thinker. Nothing short of the limitless universe of truth seemed an adequate field for his powers, over which his intellect swept on imperial wing. But besides this largeness of range, he had, what is more to the present point, the rare faculty of kindling

[1] Historical Survey of Speculative Philosophy from Kant to Hegel (Andover, 1854).

enthusiasm in other minds. This last trait has no doubt done much towards perpetuating his influence; for the works which he finished with his own hand have been less valued than some of those which he stimulated others to undertake. It was his mission to open new doors of knowledge, to point out with eagle eye the errors of previous and contemporaneous thought; to make suggestions and start hypotheses which, in the minds of the rising class of thinkers, unfolded gradually into systems of philosophy.

This influence was especially manifest in the case of John Christian Wolf, who was perhaps the leading thinker of Germany at the beginning of the eighteenth century. So closely did he adhere to the teachings of his master, in the numerous works which he published, and which were scattered over Europe, that it has been said of him, "He dried, cut up, and sold the philosophy of Leibnitz." This criticism seems unduly severe, however, for there is evidence that Wolf anticipated some of the views of later and more famous thinkers; it is in his writings that the term *Rational Psychology*, used in the sense of the Kantian school, first occurs. But even granting that he added no new material to the subject, he was a master of method, and gave the discoveries of Leibnitz a systematic shape, whereby he taught them many years, and with no small success, to his countrymen. It was not an age of great intellects. Frederick the Great had drawn around him a class of French writers, who were spreading the worst results of Sensationalism, and thus a kind of shallow eclecticism had grown up in the very home of Leibnitz.

[sidenote: The Leibnitz-Wolfian philosophy.]

But Wolf, breasting this popular current, marshalled to his aid what little was left of the indigenous Teutonic spirit, and kept it ready for the dawning that was to come. He was, besides all else, the instructor of Immanuel Kant. He thus stands as in some sort a connecting link between the philosophical source of pantheism in the seventeenth century and of pantheism in the eighteenth and nineteenth centuries. As there could have been no Spinozism but for the philosophy of Descartes, so without Immanuel Kant there could have been no Fichte, Schelling, or Hegel. It is very true that Kant did not abide by the Leibnitz-Wolfian doctrines; but the whole influence of Wolf strengthened his natural bias, and saved from pre-occupation the field in which he was to sow afresh the seeds of a-priori speculation. " Wolf," according to Tenneman, whom Mr. Morell quotes as a thoroughly competent witness, "assumed bare thinking as his starting-point, overlooked the difference between the formal and the material conditions of thought, considered philosophy as the science of the possible in so far as it is possible, made the principle of contradiction the highest principle of human knowledge, placed mere ideas and verbal definitions at the very head of all research, made no difference between rational and experimental knowledge, and, though following the geometrical method, neglected to distinguish that which is peculiar to mathematics on the one hand, and philosophy on the other, both in their form and in their matter."[1] Here, now, as may be readily seen, especially in the primacy assigned to " bare thinking," was something which could not fail to awaken the national

[1] History of Modern Philosophy, p. 152.

hunger in young Kant's mind. Yet no sure basis of hope was given that the hunger thus awakened would be appeased, so large was the intermixture of empiricism all along in the development.

Kant was of Scotch descent on the father's side, though so unmistakably German in his habits of thought. The subjective tendency in him, however, did not prevent him from holding for a time the dogmatic position of Locke. He was early in life a student of the Sensational philosophy, and seems never to have rescued himself altogether from its power. Not substances, but phenomena, the sensations of the mind itself, he held to be the proper material of our knowledge. It was to this school of English and Scotch thinkers, rather than to that represented by Thomas Reid, that Kant partly belonged. Though he seems at times to come so near the position of Reid, in his treatment of the ideas of the reason, he never clearly reaches it. He condemns, in the founder of the intuitional philosophy, that affirmation of objective truths which he himself afterwards tries to make on less solid ground. It was with the speculations of the school of Locke chiefly that Kant contented himself, before undertaking his critical philosophy; and the impulse to this great work, which removed him so entirely from Locke's position, came also from the famous Scotch critic Hume. "I freely confess," he says, "that it was David Hume who first roused me from my dogmatic slumber, and gave a different direction to my investigations in the field of speculative philosophy."[1] By his "dog-

Kant's earlier views.

The need of a critic suggested by Hume.

[1] Chalybæus.

matic slumber" we are to understand the mental security with which he had gone forward in the search for objective truth, while bestowing no attention on the powers and limitations of the cognitive faculty itself. He agreed with Locke that the material of our knowledge is given to us in experience; the question still remaining was, whether our notions of efficiency, essences, cause, and especially of a First Cause, are purely imaginary, as Hume had shown that they must be on the ground of Locke. Knowledge can never transcend experience, was the premise which had been laid down. But our experience is limited to the mental processes of which we are conscious. Therefore, is the inevitable conclusion, we can have no knowledge either of cause or substance, or of any phenomenon save as it is a part of our own thinking. This surely followed, as Kant saw by the aid of Hume, from the position taken in the Essay on the Understanding. But had that Essay given a full account of man's cognitive powers? If it had not, and there was a way of knowing besides experience, the universal scepticism which Hume had deduced from it might perhaps be escaped. Hume afforded him no light on this new question. Still, the violent blow which had been given to the received philosophy "struck a spark." Kant could not accept the dreary conclusion, that subjective truth alone is possible to human knowledge. Fully persuaded as he was, that we may know objects external to our own thoughts, he saw at once the only way in which Hume's scepticism could be effectually met. Thus far he had neglected what it became him first of all to do. The work needing to be done was of the same nature as that undertaken by Locke, though with the hope of a very different result. The faculties of the human mind must be examined, with a view to showing, if possible, that man has a power of cognition by which he may know truths transcending his own experience. And since this was the important doctrine which Kant from the first proposed to establish, but which he failed to establish in the Critique of the Pure Reason, we treat him unfairly, I think, in supposing that the Critique of the Practical Reason was in any sense an afterthought. This second Critique alone claims to reach the end which he had in view from the start; and therefore, whatever must be said of its comparative merits, or even if it must be regarded as wholly a failure, justice requires that it be looked upon as an essential part of the design with which Kant set out.

He begins his inquiry by questioning the position of Locke, that we can know only what is given us in experience; and the first great point to which that inquiry brings him is, that we have a faculty, styled by him the *Pure Reason*, by which we may know truths transcending experience. This faculty he proceeds to analyze, calling his analysis a *Critique*. The pure reason dwells in a sphere which experience cannot reach; and it gives, out of that transcendent sphere, certain ideas, forms, or regulative principles, which the understanding is forced to recognize in construing the matter of our knowledge. Our experience does not indeed amount to knowledge without them. They are "synthetic judgments a-priori;" that is, logical forms joined to the facts of experience, coming from a region above experience, under which forms those facts

Critique of the Pure Reason.

Relation of the reason to the understanding.

must be known in order to be true science. The dealing of the understanding with the mere matter of knowledge is nothing, without those regulative principles which the Pure Reason gives to the understanding. Kant's proof of these transcendental elements in all true knowledge is the same as Reid's proof of the principles of common sense,—namely, their *necessity* and their *universality*.

These logical forms of the reason are, in the world of sense, Space and Time. All men are compelled to know every object of sense under both these two forms. The understanding does not merely apprehend the material given it in sensation, and make up secondary notions therefrom by its own unaided action; but evermore joins with the material of its knowledge these two a-priori data of the Pure Reason. It is as true in the province of reflection as in that of sensation; as true when our minds analyze their experience as of the primary experience itself, that these transcendental forms are present. The reason is continually furnishing them, wherever the understanding finds any new notion. They are synthetic judgments a-priori, without which the notion would be impossible; and because they are in every case thus indispensable to knowledge, even in the world of experience with which the understanding deals, Kant calls them the "categories of the understanding." There are twelve of these logical forms of the reason, three severally having to do with each of four different judgments of the understanding. Thus: where the understanding finds quantity in the matter of our experience, the pure reason supplies the logical form of unity, plurality, or totality; where the understanding finds quality, the rational form of reality, negation, or limitation will be present; where the understanding finds relation, reason compels that lower faculty to see what it finds under the form of substance, cause, or reciprocity; and where the understanding discovers modality, there is present the a-priori form of possibility, existence, or necessity. These are the categories of empirical knowledge, all coming from that mental realm which is above experience, and all proved by the infallible test of necessity and universality.

But not only are these regulative principles thus furnished in all our empirical knowledge. Besides the categories of the understanding, there are what Kant calls the *Ideas* of the reason. The existence of those ideas is proved just as that of the logical forms was: all men have them, and no one can help having them. Though coming from the same transcendental source as the judgments of the understanding, they yet differ from them, in that they are not susceptible of a synthesis with any matter of actual knowledge. There is no possibility of applying them to anything else. They stand alone, pure and simple, cognizable only as ideas in their own peculiar sphere, and defying all attempts to actualize them elsewhere. These ideas of the reason are three in number: (1.) that of the Soul, which is the basis of rational psychology; (2.) that of the World, which is the basis of rational cosmology; (3.) that of God, which is the basis of rational theology. Neither one of these ideas has anything to do with objective reality, but they are all framed by the reason, with the consciousness that no object anywhere an-

Ideas of the reason.

What they are.

swers to them. They are purely transcendental. They remain the peculiar possession of the reason which gave birth to them. Their presence within us is inevitable, whatever our experience, of which they are independent. They go with us, and are pre-supposed in all our investigations; yet they can never be brought down, and made a part of the subject-matter of our inquiries. They stand by themselves, isolated, purely subjective; they involve nothing corresponding to them in the actual world. It Their subjective nature. is an ideal world, an ideal soul, an ideal and subjective God in which they force us to believe. Neither one of these ideas is anything but a regulative principle within the province of the reason itself, and we are cheated with the emptiest possible of illusions if we believe them to involve any reality beyond themselves. We are compelled to entertain the idea of a God, yet this idea furnishes no ground for the belief that God actually exists. While on the one hand it pursues us, and will not let us escape, on the other hand, it equally refuses to go beyond us, or let us pass behind it. It forevermore follows us as an ideal, but we are forbidden to hope that we may ever behold it as actual and real.

Where this Critique leaves us. Now, it may well be asked, at least so far as the most precious beliefs of the human race are concerned, whether the Critique of Kant is a whit more valuable than the Essay of Locke. Had it revealed a new region of truth? Yes, but that truth had no objective validity; it was purely subjective and ideal. Did the sage of Königsberg close the door against Hume's scepticism? Yes, but in doing so he had opened a door of blank idealism, from which, as we shall see, the step was easy into pantheism. The thinking world was rescued from one source of infidelity only to be exposed to another. Once more philosophers turned from sensuous impressions, and began to build on the intuitions of the reason; but they only exchanged Hume for Spinoza; they recoiled from the rock to be drawn back into the whirlpool. "We see distinctly," says Chalybæus, "how near Kant was to expressing himself in the manner to which Hegel, at a far later period, found himself constrained, when on the same path of inquiry: the absolute God is the mere essence which is thinking and thought of, because it is that in us which thinks; thinking is identical with what is thought; the absolute is the thinking process itself. Thus the ontological proof can succeed only upon the basis of an absolute idealism, or idealistic pantheism."

But it would be wrong to infer that Kant intended any such result as that now indicated. At least we must presume, in simple justice to him, that he saw beyond it another result of a positive nature, to be reached by a different path of inquiry. He certainly leaves the ground of a solid theism, even if he does not tread on the edge of pantheism, when he says that, "for aught we can tell, the unknown base of mind and matter, despite their divergent phenomena, may be the same." But he was no pantheist. It was contrary to his plan, as conceived from the first, to allow his subjective idealism to absorb the whole material of philosophy. As Chalybæus justly says, and as we shall soon see, he could not consent to that line of argument in reference to the infinite God, when he came to lay the basis of our ethical action, and of a practical theology. If, on

Kant's plan broader than this sphere of the reason.

the one hand, he had shown the inadequateness of the empiricism of Locke, and on the other hand had struck a blow at the ontology of Anselm and Descartes, it did not therefore follow that he meant to subvert the great truths of the soul, a world-system, and a supreme God. They were indeed subverted, and could by no means be proved true, on the ground of the speculative reason; but Kant had in view another faculty of the human mind, held back thus far in his reasoning, which he now brings forward as a means of proving the objective validity of those truths. He had not imperilled them at all, as the case stood to his view, for the *Practical Reason* was that on which he had relied from the beginning to establish their absolute verity. His *Critique* of the Practical Reason was, as has been charged, the life-boat in which he escaped from the wreck made by his Critique of the Pure Reason. Yet it should be remembered that he had the wreck in view from the outset, and planned the boat with reference to that emergency, regarding it himself, whatever others may think, as an abler and far more important work than the one published before it. Having shown that the realm of ontology cannot be reached by way of pure intelligence, he undertakes to open a way into that sublime region upon an ethical basis. The moral nature of man, in distinction from the purely rational, is the ladder on which he may feel himself ascending and descending. The law of our moral nature, its *Thou shalt* and *Thou shalt not*, Kant calls "the categorical imperative." This voice of command in conscience is just as universal, and just as necessary, as any idea of the speculative reason; and it is

Another faculty.

Function of the Practical Reason.

something which, in order to its own integrity, must be realized in experience; and therefore it carries us back of itself to a self-determining soul, and up to a divine executioner, thus planting our foot "upon the unconditioned, absolute, or intelligible world." This categorical imperative, which issues forth from the practical reason, looks only to its own actualization, regardless of such ends as happiness, beneficence, and reward; and it establishes the otherwise unproved being of a supreme God, since it is upon no less a basis than this that its autocracy can be upheld. Now, if Kant had simply meant, in this reasoning, to give us the usual moral argument of theologians, all would have been well enough. Then he would have come clearly out upon the ground of the intuitional philosophy, and might have affirmed, *Result not satisfactory.* as the truest of all truths, that conviction of man which he says is "not to be called a true knowledge and cognition, but only a belief." Yet such a step, evidently, would have placed him in open antagonism with the doctrines of the speculative reason; and even as the matter stood, such a conflict was apparent to others, though not to himself. If his first Critique was to stand, as its immense popularity had already insured, then must the intelligible world be reached, not by the outward pathway of our moral nature, but by bringing it into the ideas of reason, and in some way identifying it with the processes of rational thought. At least this was the method which the leading minds of Germany, in their efforts to know the absolute, were determined to adopt. However conclusive Kant's argument may have seemed to himself, for them it had an air of constraint, and was so much weaker than what had gone before it as to retain no steady hold upon them. It gave the thinking principle no outlet, which pure science could recognize as adequate. The circle of knowledge which it had begun could be completed only by merging the objective and subjective in one pantheistic result.

<small>Critique of the judgment.</small> Kant was evidently troubled by the charge of schism which was brought against his philosophy, and he firmly believed that he could show the essential harmony of his system without accepting the alternative of Spinozism. He was himself the first to attempt a reconciliation of his ethics with his metaphysics — an attempt which we need not discredit as a mere afterthought, but may regard as part of his original plan. He claimed that the real and ideal elements of his philosophy could be united on a common basis, thus making one complete whole. That this union of the two principles might take place he sought to show in a third work, — his *Critique of the Judgment*, containing his *Æsthetics* and *Doctrine of Final Causes*. The object of this work was to fix the central principle of a Kantian school of philosophy. I can give no account of it here, except to say that it was a kind of bridge whereby his realistic or empirical doctrines were brought over to his idealism, — not to retain their independent life, but to be overmastered and devoured. A few of his disciples tried, for a short time, to stand upon this middle ground, holding in equilibrium the two antagonistic Critiques.

<small>Its object not attained.</small> But no one was able to keep the position long. The dualism of the Kantian philosophy was what struck men as its most obvious trait. They failed to see the new foundation, and felt that only another crisis had been reached in the

history of thinking. Idealism and empiricism, they contended, could not be brought together into an harmonious system, and each at the same time preserve its own integrity. The question with them therefore was, which should fall before the other. And the question was not a very hard one to decide. When a meteor is revolving midway between the sun and the nearest planet, we know to which body it must ultimately come. The distance being the same on either hand, the attraction must be as the mass of matter. The little finger of Kant's idealism, whatever he thought of it, was, in its impression on other minds, thicker than the loins of his empiricism. As often as they met in fair encounter, the latter was sure to go to the wall. "The two principles," says Chalybæus, "were still held dualistically together. We could, while arriving through the reason at absolute unity, either acknowledge the one idealistic principle to be the genuine root of all knowledge, and abide subjectively by this alone, or we could in turn make empiricism, and consequently a multitude of objective beginnings and principles, the point of our departure."[1]

Whether I have now succeeded in giving any correct impressions of Kant's system or not, it is at least clear that three distinct schools of thought might proceed from him. Directly before him was the path indicated by his Critique of the Judgment, in which Reinhold and Fries tried to go forward; on the one hand was his realism, which Jacobi and Herbart pursued, though from opposite sides, and on the other hand was his idealism, which Fichte, Schelling, and Hegel carried out to

Three distinct tendencies in Kant.

[1] History of Speculative Philosophy, p. 57.

its extreme results. The last of these three paths will chiefly claim our notice, though something should be said of the other two.

Reinhold. Of those who tried to hold the middle course, seeking a principle which should mediate between the real and the ideal, Carl Leonhard Reinhold deserves to be first named. Chalybæus intimates that Fries was the more earnest in advocating Kant's centre-theory; but of the few sentences devoted to them both, almost all have reference to Reinhold. Under his treatment the Æsthetics of Kant becomes a representation, oscillating between the subject and the object, in which their essential unity is to be found. This representation being one of the data of consciousness, he is led by it to speak of the importance of an examination of that faculty. This work he never undertook himself, but it became a fruitful subject under the treatment of other thinkers, especially in the hands of Fichte, to whose views Reinhold gradually inclined." [1]

Jacobi. I shall attempt no statement here of the views of Herbart, who developed strongly the empirical side of the Kantian realism, and shall speak only of Friedrich Heinrich Jacobi, who, while starting from the same point as Herbart, leaned towards idealism in his thinking. He was one of the noblest men of his time. We are charmed by his character, as it comes out both in his writings and his daily life. Yet the tendency of his mind was

His mystical tendency. towards a certain mystical quietism. He pursued the image of truth, not outward by way of the understanding and senses, but inward

[1] Morell, p. 178.

till caught in the subjective idealism of Kant, where he gave up the chase, and asserted that our conviction of reality is a thing to be reverently accepted, but which no one should dare attempt to account for. "All our knowledge," he says, "must rest ultimately on faith, and not on reasoning." His system has been aptly termed a Faith-Philosophy. Starting with the demands of our moral nature, and holding, with Kant, that they involve in each instance an actual world, human freedom, and a supreme God, he argued that an objective result might be similarly reached in the sphere of pure knowledge. "Has not Kant," he asked, "adopted the matter-of-fact existence of the ideas in his practical philosophy, and regarded them as being the ultimate and most certain point? Does he not here content himself, and rightly, with letting the matter-of-fact existence of the moral law (the so-called categorical imperative) hold good as the most irrefragable of all? If he did this in the theory of the practice, how could he presume to do directly the reverse in the theory of knowledge? Why should that which in the former case was irrefragable count for nothing in the latter?"[1] These questions are certainly well put, and, as addressed to Kant himself, they cannot be answered. But they made almost no impression on German thinkers, for they assumed the correctness of that side of Kant's system which was regarded as a mistake and an excrescence. The speculative tendency of the times, taking the Critique of the Pure Reason for its gospel, was not satisfied with a theory which made faith, or mere feeling, the ultimate basis of all knowledge. It demanded that

Argues against Kant's first critique.

[1] Chalybæus.

the ideas of freedom, a world, and a God, be brought forth from their concealment in the misty depths of feeling, to undergo scientific study. There was no sanctuary into which the torch of knowledge might not be thus carried; no veil on the image of truth which the hand of inquiry might not dare to lift. Jacobi stood almost alone in asserting that the three great ideas of the reason are an awful treasure in the depths of the human consciousness; in refusing to sound those depths by the scientific method; in his dread of Spinozism, to which he foresaw that such an investigation must lead. An extract from the famous conversation of Jacobi and Lessing, at their first meeting in 1784, will help to make this point clear. Lessing had no dread of the results of idealism, and made haste to say, as soon as he found occasion, "The orthodox ideas concerning God are no longer mine. I have no pleasure in them now. 'Εν και παν, One and All, I know nothing but this." Jacobi's reply is, "Then are you greatly at one with Spinoza." To this Lessing rejoins, "Did I rank myself with any one, it were with none but him." Whereupon Jacobi says, "Spinoza is well enough; yet is it but a sorry kind of healing that we find in his name."[1]

This partial agreement with Spinoza, which Jacobi gave at different times, led his opponents to charge him with timidity. They said that he lacked the scientific spirit, in refusing to push on to the logical goal of his admissions, holding himself back through fear of offending the orthodox party. However this may have been, no one questioned the goodness of his

[1] Willis's Life, &c., of Spinoza, p. 152.

character, or failed to be charmed by the beauty with which he expressed his deep and suggestive thoughts. His style was said to be like Plato's; and many, who could not rest in his intellectual quietism, yet studied his works with confessed profit and delight. Hegel, whom no dread of pantheism kept from working out scientifically the contents of his consciousness, says of Jacobi, "He is like a solitary thinker, who, in the morning of his day, found some ancient riddle hewn upon an eternal rock. He believes in this riddle, but he strives in vain to guess it. He carries it about with him the whole day, allures weighty sentiments from it, spreads it out into doctrines and images, which delight the hearer, and inspire him with noble wishes and hopes: but the interpretation fails; and in the evening he lays him down, with the hope that some divine dream, or the next waking, will pronounce to him '*the word*' for which he longs, and on which he has so firmly believed."[1] This beautiful system of faith-philosophy did not start from that side of Kantism which was most complete, and which most powerfully affected the speculative mind of Germany. The realism of Jacobi, like the seven goodly ears of corn in Pharaoh's dream, sprang forth only to be devoured up by the hungry idealism of Fichte, Schelling, and Hegel.

<small>Hegel's criticism.</small>

Fichte, wholly discrediting that side of Kantism to which Jacobi clung, seized with a powerful grasp the doctrine that the ideas of the reason have respect only to themselves. Laying this down as the grand premise, from which all true philosophy must

<small>Fichte.</small>

[1] Hegel's Miscellanies, quoted by Morell, p. 602.

132 HALF TRUTHS AND THE TRUTH.

be deduced, he did not fear to push on to the logical result. The human consciousness — that is, his own self-conscious thought-activity — is his starting-point. This thinking process is, in the first instance, the veritable Ego; nor does it presuppose any essence or substance, such as is commonly understood by the word *soul;* and to it, whether considered as infinite or finite, all knowl-

Thought-activity the only knowable thing.

edge is strictly limited. Beyond the simple thought-activity, there is nothing real. The images and sensations which constitute its material, and which are imprisoned within the consciousness, cannot be traced to any external origin. The whole process is purely subjective; in no sense from without, but altogether a creation of the Ego itself. Fichte could not believe that Kant was, in any honest sense, a realist; nor was he willing to give up this opinion till Kant publicly protested against it. But Fichte went on. Of all the advocates of subjective idealism, he was perhaps the most thorough-going. He did not, in so many words,

The non-Ego.

deny the existence of the world, as his opponents charged him with doing, but recognized it under the designation of the non-Ego. Yet he defines it not as any real thing, after all, but as only that consciousness of limitation which the Ego experiences; and he probably would have never conceded even this much, had not the criticisms of Schelling led him to qualify some of his earlier statements. But that he is strictly an idealist still, is clear from his saying, " I can absolutely *know* nothing beyond what is present within me." Our consciousness is not due to impressions made by things outside of it, but the thinking process itself creates the objects with which it is concerned. Having himself posited the object of this thought, a man cannot say that he holds a passive relation to it, or that the Ego of which he is conscious is its effect; for the object itself is rather the effect of the thinking process.[1] There are certain images and sensations, going to make the consciousness in any case, but to seek an external origin for them is to quit the track of true science; just so far as they reach the standard of scientific knowledge, they are a part of the thinking process itself. "The being, the objective reality, can be for us merely a being that is thought; a thought reality, thought by us, and consequently in this sense self-produced." Thus it is, in strict fidelity to Kant's first position, that the theoretical is made to lay hold of the practical and wholly absorb it. Consciousness is the source of all knowledge, and this is limited to its own processes; hence beyond consciousness there can be no knowledge, but pure guess-work only. If we say that the soul may know itself, yet that soul cannot be a substance, but only a thinking process; and beyond the play of this self-conscious thought-activity there is no demonstrable truth.

A product of the Ego.

It is not necessary to go any farther into Fichte's doctrine of science, to see that it places him on the edge of a precipice. He can no longer be said to occupy the ground of the ordinary theist; the only alternative before him is atheism or pantheism. The outward world being to him simply an image projected from himself, he could not rise from it to a Creator, as do those who hold it to be an objective real-

The alternative of atheism or pantheism.

[1] Chalybæus, p. 155.

ity. The thinking process is the creator, "being that operation which mirrors itself in each of its acts;" and if this be not absolute, there is no absolute. For a time Fichte's utterances were thought to incline towards the atheistic side of the alternative; so much so that he was forced to resign his chair of philosophy at Jena. To meet the odious charges thus raised against him, he gave a new direction to his thoughts, though by no means changing his theory of knowledge. He affirms that the Ego itself, viewed under its transcendental aspect, is the Absolute One. "This, then, is the sum and substance of our belief," he says. "The living and active moral order is God; we need no other God, and can comprehend no other." If we suppose a personal God in the usual way, we are guilty of anthropomorphism; mere imitators of the ancient Greeks, who enthroned their own imperfections on Olympus. "God is not a being or existence," says he, "any more than man is; "but a pure action, i. e., the life and soul of a transcendent world-order." It is at this point, being hard pressed by the speculations of Schelling, that he turns back from the atheistic path, and makes choice of pantheism. Every human consciousness being an Ego, there is, consequently, as viewed from the empirical side, an infinite number of these. Yet viewed from the transcendental side, they are all but the make-up of one absolute Ego — a universal self-consciousness, which is the single divine reality amid all that appears. "We, as intelligent essences, are, in respect to what we are in ourselves, by no means that absolute Being," says Fichte; "but we are connected with it by the innermost

Accused of atheism.

Becomes a pantheist.

root of our existence, since apart from it we could not be
or exist." This language is not meant to assert, as it
seems to do, that Fichte held the absolute to
be an essence or substance in the sense of Spi- <small>Unlike Spinoza.</small>
noza. The universal activity, the absolute think-
ing process, is all that he affirms. Spinoza's God was a
substance in the proper sense, and thought one of its infinite attributes; Fichte's God is that attribute, and he
denies that there is any reality besides it. Spinoza was
intoxicated with his absolute substance; Fichte loses himself in his absolute process.

It is our highest wisdom, he teaches us, to <small>The true wisdom.</small>
know this only God; to forget the Ego in so far as
it is empirical, and behold it as the transcendental reality
filling all things. "So long as ever man yearns to be anything, God does not come to him, for no man can become
God. So soon, however, as he purely and radically annihilates himself, God alone remains, and is all in all. Man
cannot engender God, but he can annihilate himself as the
true negation, and then he sinks or relapses into God.
He has no fear for the future, for the absolutely Blessed
guides him towards it; he has no repentance over the past,
for in so far as he was not in God he was nothing, and the
past is now past, and for the first time since his reception
into the Deity is he born unto life; in so far, however,
as he was in God, is that right and good which he has
done." [1]

We may say, then, that the a-priori philosophy, reinstated
and more strictly defined by Kant, had, in the hands of
Fichte, vitalized the pantheism of Spinoza. If the distinc-

[1] Quoted by Chalybæus, pp. 182, 183.

tive feature of Spinozism was rest, that of Fichte's system is activity. Yet while insisting on this dynamical life of the absolute, he banished from it all containing substance. This it was the aim of Schelling to bring back. And it is a striking comment on the history of human speculation, that these two men, after all who had preceded them in their school of thought, could only leave the great problem so nearly where Spinoza had left it a century and a half before.

Fichte's pantheism considered defective.

Schelling.

Schelling begins by objecting to Fichte, and that with great force, that the bare *process* of thinking is in no proper sense of the word *knowledge*. There must be some real matter or essence involved in the process, which our thoughts can separate from it; something around it, beneath it, or within it, which is to our minds as really objective as the thought-process is subjective. Knowledge can begin only when our thinking has found something which it did not originate. Thus far Schelling is on the sure grounds of our primary beliefs. But he is possessed by the German madness for the absolute one, the monistic all-in-all. The real content of our thinking becomes, with him, only an integrant portion of the one *noumenon*, which mirrors itself forth not only in our thinking but in all phenomena. Not the human ego, therefore, even when considered as a substance, but the absolute Ego which underlies and constitutes it, is the true a-priori conception. At this point all true philosophy must begin. This essence may be contemplated in itself, and as apart from the thought-process,

Grand objection to Fichte.

Schellingian doctrine of knowledge.

How Schelling reaches the position of the pantheist.

when it is the object; or it may be contemplated as entering and filling that process, when it is the subject. It may therefore be properly named the subject-object. Call it by what name you please, — nature, God, noumenon, absolute reality, infinite one, — it is that in which our thinking and the content of our thought are one and the same thing to consciousness; and therefore the scientific treatment of it is truly styled the Identity-Philosophy. Pantheists are fond of repeating Schelling's celebrated remark, that "all difference is quantitative." This assertion of the one, and of the identity of all things in it, is a complete rendering of the doctrine of Spinoza. It is pantheism crowded into a single sentence. The following quotation will perhaps place before us the Schellingian doctrine, so far as demanded by the present inquiry: "The multiplicity of determinations is not evoked in us by the influence of manifold external objects or things in themselves, but it is the birth or product of the potential fulness of our nature. It is, really and truly, the universal world-nature which here acts in me, as in one of her innumerable points, as well as everywhere else; and on *His system described.* that account we have an immediate knowledge of this nature; or, more correctly speaking, it is the universal nature, that here within us knows something of or perceives itself, — the nature which has organized itself into human souls, into humanity, and by means of these its organs cognizes itself. We human beings are, as it were, but the innumerable individual eyes through which the infinite world-spirit regards itself. We are real or actual as regards our internal essence; that which is imaginary and unsubstantial in us is the absolute personality with which the individual flatters himself." [1]

Agreement with Spinoza. It is therefore plain, if language can make anything plain, that Schelling's Identity is the Substance, and his subject and object the thought and extension, of Spinoza. If he has improved at all upon his master, it is by giving heed to the words of Fichte; that is, by emphasizing the inherent activity of his world-nature. He even speaks of the freedom of the subject-object. But Spinoza insisted that the one substance is free. Yet here is no real liberty of will asserted, in the former case more than in the latter. The freedom of God, as understood by both these thinkers, is simply that automatic power of action which pertains to the universal consciousness. This essential activity has three distinct manifestations; three *potences* Schelling calls them. The first of these is the potence of "reflection;" that is, the movement by which the infinite and absolute seeks to mirror itself forth in finite phenomena. The second is the potence of "subsumption;" that is, the effort which the absolute makes to return from a mere phenomenal, back into its essential mode of being. The third is the potence of "reason;" that is, the act by which the absolute recognizes itself as indifferently present, and forever one and the same, in the other two movements.

Three potences.

How they work in the evolution of spirit. But this is not all. The first double movement of the absolute, in trying to realize itself, indicates two distinct lines of evolution, which it forever follows. Nature and spirit are these

[1] Chalybæus, p. 204.

lines; these directions of the absolute, in its self-evolution through the three potences. And in each branch of this twofold evolution there are three successive stages, called *sphéres*, in which the threefold movement forever goes forward. I will not attempt to give the whole scheme of development, as thus foreshadowed, but only some faint glimpse of it as it occurs in the department of spirit.[1] Here the three potences give, in the first sphere, which is that of knowing, feeling, reflection, and freedom. In the second sphere, which is that of action, they give individuality, the state, history. The third sphere in the domain of spirit is genius, and in this the three potences blend, constituting the noblest evolution of which the one essence of all things is capable. Within the sphere of genius the threefold movement of the absolute, thus blended into a single state of consciousness, becomes the inspiration of finite intelligence. To its presence and action, being indeed but another name for itself, all fresh inventions and achievements which excite our wonder are due. In religion, philosophy, and poetry, also, those discoveries which carry the horizon of the soul abroad, or fill it anew with pure and sublime thoughts, are but the three potences of the absolute, blending in the one movement which constitutes genius, and thereby carrying itself up nearer to that point of perfect realization which it never attains.

The difference between nature and man, according to Schelling, is one of degree rather than kind, so that the two spheres in which the world-essence is evolved are less unlike than we might at first think. The same absolute, as the following

<small>Distinction between nature and spirit.</small>

---
[1] The whole subject is treated by Morell, pp. 433–456.

extract will show, fills them both. "With the stars is inborn the most exalted number and geometry, which they execute in their movements without any notion of such plan. More distinctly, though still incomprehensibly to themselves, appears the living perception in animals, whom we see, though wandering here and there without deliberation, to perform countless works far nobler than themselves; the bird, intoxicated with music, excelling itself in tones that are full of soul; the small, art-gifted creature, without practice or instruction, producing light works of architecture; but guided by a superior spirit, which already shines in single flashes of intelligence, but nowhere comes forth as a full sun except in man."[1] Man, as we thus see, is the true wonder-worker. In him alone is genius; in him alone, that is, the immanent absolute so realizes itself, in the blending of the three potences, as to be an inspiration. Thus it is, as Schelling does not hesitate to say, that we have the Homers and Isaiahs, the Platos and the Pauls, of history. Even the recognized God-man himself, who came forth in heavenly beauty among the hills of Galilee, was but the one world-essence, rising into the form of genius, and moving amid bright visions which its own magic had cast. It was the identity of the living finite with the living infinite, in his consciousness, that made him the founder of the sublimest of all religions. That same identity may be traced wherever there is genius, though showing itself in less noble displays. There is no supra-mundane Creator; no God who sitteth upon the circle of the earth. According to Schelling, says Mr. Morell, "all difference between

How Schelling would account for Christianity.

[1] Relation of the Plastic Arts to Nature, quoted by Chalybæus, p. 251.

God and the universe was entirely lost; his pantheism becomes as complete as that of Spinoza; and as the absolute was evolved from its lowest forms to the highest, in accordance with the necessary law or rhythm of its being, the whole world, material and mental, became one enormous chain of necessity, to which no idea of free creation could by any possibility be attached."[1] The doctrine of a supernatural Creator, as Schelling viewed the case, leaves the creation a piece of dead mechanism. God is in his works; is himself their essence, their life, their soul; his immanence is their mystery, his emanence their glory. Thus is the mighty problem of the universe solved, thought Schelling. All is but the eternal ebb and flow of the one absolute substance; and without this no man, no nature, no God is possible or conceivable.

The spirit of Schelling's system.

It is remarkable how soon this school of pantheism came to an end. Fichte died only ten years after Kant; and Hegel, who stands last and highest in the succession, was but eight years younger than Fichte. Schelling outlived them all, and in his old age sought to reinstate his system, which had already fallen into decay. The rise, growth, and downfall of this whole vaunted system of philosophy covered a period of only about fifty years. Kant, as we saw, was assailed with charges of dualism, and failed to rest his speculations on any satisfactory middle-ground. Fichte also, feeling the inadequacy of his earlier views, sought to modify them later in life. And so of Schelling. He did not seem to see the revolutionary tendency of his thinking

Short continuance of this school of pantheism.

---

[1] Modern Philosophy, p. 448.

till the mischief had been done. As a logician, he was faulty. He did not possess the philosophical temperament in large measure. He clothed his speculations in the language of poetry, rather than in that of metaphysics. There are passages in his works to which the language of Edgar A. Poe, in his Essay on the Material and Spiritual Universe, bears a striking likeness. Poe called his essay a Prose Poem; and it is a notable instance of the power of a pantheistic imagination. The Eureka of Poe is the subject-object of Schelling.

Nor did Schelling seem to be aware of the destructive tendency of his doctrine, till Hegel's logic compelled him to see it.

Schelling and Edgar A. Poe.

Culminated in Hegel.

The labors of Hegel are a lesson forever to all the friends of truth, that the surest way of overcoming error is to let it clearly state itself. Tolerance of opinion is an effective method of opposing wrong opinions. The human mind was made for truth; and it instinctively recoils from error, when that error is clearly defined to it. The complete overthrow of pantheism by its especial champion is a signal instance of this. He showed clearly, and in all its practical bearings, what the system was. This was enough. It needed no other refutation. Bellerophon carried on himself the letter which condemned him. There was a general recoil of the better-class of minds. Hegelians sought to show that their master had been misunderstood. Schelling was drawn from his retirement, to prove, if possible, that his doctrine, at least in its moral and political bearings, differed from the extreme views imputed to Hegel. But he attempted an impossible thing. The darkness had come to the light, and been reproved. Men saw what it was, in its practical tendencies. Dreading the social chaos it legitimated, they cast from them its glittering bands; and the reign once broken, there was no power by which it could be restored.

Is it not a little discreditable to our Anglo-Saxon intellect, that a theory which the best minds of Germany had repudiated should, more than a generation after, have been the boasted faith of so many English and American writers? Is it worthy of men claiming to be thinkers, to make so much of that which has been overthrown in the country of its birth? to be like that class of paupers who come around to the back doors of our houses, to gather into their baskets the stale pieces of bread and meat which the family cook has been ordered to throw away? But the friends of truth, surely, need have no fear of an enemy which is dead at the heart. The claws of the tiger may continue to feel after his prey, although the fatal shot of the hunter has brought him to the ground. This movement of the extremities is but spasmodic, however. That which has ceased to be alive at the core must soon give up the ghost altogether.

An anachronism.

Hegel was a trained logician. He possessed the philosophical temperament to an eminent degree. He had that cool fearlessness, so remarkable in Spinoza, which shrinks from no logical result of the premises laid down. It is said that he studied the works of Spinoza with the utmost enthusiasm, caring but little, in comparison, for what had been achieved by other modern thinkers. He saw in the subject-object of Schelling the substance of Spinoza. From this he dropped out the

Hegel.

objective element, as that whose existence was the same as its non-existence, and the subjective process which remained he called the Absolute Idea. The nature of this idea he undertook to expound, or to show how it unfolds itself, from a primary being which is non-being, to an ultimate being which is also non-being. This part of his system is the Hegelian logic. Kant had discovered, in connection with his categories, certain contradictions which he named *antinomies;* that is, it was possible, from different data, to prove direct opposites in regard to the same thing. But he applied this law of contradictories only in the sphere of natural philosophy. Hegel, seizing hold of this Kantian principle, claimed that it was universally applicable, and made it the comprehensive law of his logic. These antagonisms were only for the understanding, however; the reason beholds steadily that higher unity into which they are constantly rising. His whole system of logic is therefore a triplicate process. As described by Professor H. B. Smith, "There is first a statement expressed in the positive form; then there follows the negation of the position; and then the two contradictory statements are resolved into a higher unity. And so the system proceeds, from stage to stage, — positive, negative, and the union between the positive and negative. This union becomes in turn a positive, a negative is set over against it, and this new contradiction is resolved into another and higher unity."[1]

But the Hegelian dialectics are not simply logic, in the usual abstract sense of the word. A vital movement is

[1] Bibliotheca Sacra, Vol. II. p. 274.

everywhere intended. The recognition of the absolute idea, under its threefold aspect, constitutes in nature Natural philosophy. Here we are conscious of a "becoming," answering to Spinoza's infinite at- *Natural philosophy.* tribute of extension. This nature-movement, throughout all its stages, conforms to the fixed logical arrangement. It illustrates, like everything else, the presence of the Hegelian trinity. Not only natural philosophy as a whole, but its divisions,—mechanics, physics, and organized bodies; and not only these, but their subdivisions and sub-subdivisions, down to the minutest representatives of the action of nature, conform to a single law. They exist only by a constant struggle of affirmations and negations, through which the reason beholds them rising all the while into a fuller development and perfect unity.

Not only in nature, but in mind or spirit also, the Hegelian trinity is everywhere present. Mind, considered absolutely, was to Hegel an infinite process, not differing from nature in the final analysis, and corresponding to Spinoza's infinite attribute of thought, so far as an empty process may be said to correspond to *Philosophy of spirit.* a substance. The true philosophy of mind or spirit is the exposition of the threefold movement in consciousness, by which it is unfolded. Our thought-activity affirms itself by a positive movement answering to Schelling's potence of reflection, and also denies that positive by the potence of sub-sumption; while the reason has, in the mean time, held the two contradictories together in perfect union, under the higher idea of the absolute spirit. The propriety of the distinction between nature and mind is a little hard to see, looking from the point of Hegel's subjective idealism; though it enables the logician to reach certain facts of history which otherwise might seem to escape him. The absolute spirit, Hegel says, "is the absolute idea known and understood. The three stages of its development are art, religion, philosophy. Philosophy, in the system of Hegel, is the highest state to which the consciousness of man can be brought. It is not merely the union of art and religion, but it is this union elevated into the state of self-conscious thought."[1]

Religion, therefore, is simply one of the factors *Its theological result.* of a true philosophy; one of the potences of an absolute thought-process, which started from nothing and proceeds to nothing. All the knowledge of existence to which we can ever attain is this triplicate movement of the Hegelian dialectic. Being, which is the same thing as non-being, lies behind us and before us. From it we came, and to it we hasten, by a process of constant " becoming," the law of which is the universal logic, and which constitutes all that we distinguish as God, man, and nature. God, for instance, is first thought into being; but this thought is completed only in the contradictory thought of non-being, the two opposites so uniting as to give rise to the pure idea of a "becoming." This is the only existence in the case, and it is the product of the dialectic movement; therefore, exclaims the audacious logician, "I have created God."

The following is related as occurring between Kant and Hegel. In an argument one day, Hegel had been contending that what we call the outward reality is never

[1] Bibliotheca Sacra, Vol. II. p. 285.

anything but the idea which we have of it. The thinking process posites the object. Kant could not accept this, for he believed in a real external world; and he replied to Hegel, with great shrewdness, "There is considerable difference between *having* a hundred dollars and *thinking* you have them." But the absolute idealist was not at all confused. Drawing himself up with proud disdain, he met his opponent on common ground, and effectually silenced him, saying, "Your poor *empirical* dollars are things with which philosophy does not concern itself."[1] No argument, or ridicule, could move him from his conclusion, that the only real existence is a self-moved process out of nothing into nothing. *[margin: Hegel and Kant.]*

Plainly, then, no written revelation, or positive system of worship; no political, social, or domestic institution, can hold its own a moment in the sweep of this all-consuming philosophy. Polytheism, monotheism, Christianity, the instant they touch it, melt like wax in the furnace. Strauss brings the story of Jesus of Nazareth within its reach, and straightway that beautiful life and sacrifice are licked up by its tongue of fire. Schleiermacher exposes to it the doctrines of theology built up by mighty minds through the slow ages, and instantly, like the servants of Nebuchadnezzar, they are slain. It would be pleasant to feel sure that the trans- *[margin: Consequences of the system. Strauss. Schleiermacher.]*

---

[1] The following passage (Logic, Chap. I., C.) would go far to sustain this anecdote: "Being and non-being are the same thing; also it is the same thing whether I am or am not, whether this house is or is not, whether these hundred dollars are in my possession or are not."

lator of Plato, and the great Berlin preacher who had such power to lift the minds of men up into heavenly realms of truth, escaped from the abyss of pantheism into which he early fell. But Julius Müller concedes as much, probably, as the strict truth will bear, when he says, "The truly Christian view of sin and redemption, which Schleiermacher adopts in his superstructure, is in direct contrast with the foundation of his theory. Firmly agreeing with Schleiermacher as to the superstructure, we are obliged to reject the theoretic foundation of his doctrine."[1]

Net result. While thinking of the system of Spinoza as perfected by Hegel, and of the way in which all divine and human institutions, and the realities of the external world, vanish in its embrace, it seems to us like a mighty ocean, heated by the rays of a vertical sun; into which the Bible, the Church, the State, history, nature, society, as if they were but so many tall and resplendent frost-vessels, are forever moving down to melt out of sight, and to blend with its weary, aimless, ever rolling, and unfathomable waters.

Lesson of the survey now taken. The lesson of this brief and fragmentary survey of Neo-Spinozism is plain. In the midst of the garden in which the Lord God has placed

---

[1] The following is Schleiermacher's eulogy of Spinoza, the first sentence of which I have already quoted: "Offer up reverently with me a lock of hair to the manes of the rejected but holy Spinoza. The great Spirit of the universe filled his soul; the infinite to him was beginning and end; the universal his sole and only love. Dwelling in holy innocence and deep humility among men, he saw himself mirrored in the eternal world, and the eternal world not all unworthily reflected back in him. Full of religion was he, full of the Holy Ghost; and therefore it is that he meets us standing alone in his age, raised above the profane multitude, master in his art, but without disciples and the citizen's rights."

us, is the tree of knowledge. And the latest voice of history only re-echoes his own earliest word, that in the day we depart from him and eat of that tree, aspiring to know as he knoweth, we do surely die. Well does Julius Müller say, " There is but One perfectly free from error and free from sin — CHRIST. He alone could lay claim to the faith of men in himself as one who spoke the truth, on the ground of his moral purity; and he therefore can pronounce judgment upon whatever does not receive and harmonize with him, as a wandering into the paths of darkness; he alone can analyze its connection with a depraved bias of will. That which Protagoras the sophist said of man subjectively, that he is 'the measure of things,' is objectively true of the MAN who is our Lord and our God. But as for us, seeing we are never free from sin, and are therefore continually liable to error, it is our highest wisdom not to trust ourselves, still less to make ourselves the 'measure of things,' but to rise above ourselves to Him who alone is holy, and who, as he is the life, so is also the truth." [1]

Testimony of Müller.

[1] Christian Doctrine of Sin, B. I., Pt. I., Chap. III.

LECTURE IV.

THE PANTHEISTIC CHRISTOLOGY.

<small>Philosophy cannot be separated from religion.</small> THE questions of philosophy are always closely related to those of religion. This is no more true when the relation is óne of sympathy than when it is one of antagonism; no more true of pantheism than of positivism. Even a sensuous philosophy opens anew the whole field of religious thought by denying its reality. The human mind, while gratifying its natural thirst for the discovery of truth, either concerns itself directly with the primary facts of religion, or with theories which involve the question of their existence. Naturalism does not, any more than transcendentalism, remove us from the realms of theism. The inevitable recoil of our antipathy, as surely as any direct impulse of sympathy, is constantly bringing us to those realms. This necessary connection is more apparent, however, in the case of the a-priori philosophy. The material on which Fichte, Schelling, and Hegel wrought, is the same as that of <small>This connection more manifest in transcendentalism.</small> Christian theology. The nature of God and all existence, and the origin and tendency of things, were the themes on which they speculated, in common with Augustine, Anselm, and Descartes, though in a different spirit. Pantheism itself is no less a

religion than a philosophy; a religion to reverent and poetical natures, which love to look at truth through the haze of the affections or prism of fancy; a philosophy to purely inquisitive minds, which study all subjects in the dry light of the intellect.

In one view of the case, therefore, it might seem superfluous to consider the attitude of pantheism *towards* the doctrines of religion. Why go on beyond it to speak of that which lies within itself? But we use the word "religion" in two senses. There is a natural religion and a revealed religion; a subjective religion of the human consciousness, and an objective religion of authoritative precept; an idealistic religion, and an historical religion. It is the former of these that constitutes the essence of the pantheistic system : what becomes of historical religion, under the handling of pantheism, is a question still to be considered. The nature of its investigations is such as to make this, almost of necessity, our first inquiry from its point of view. If it is to have any development at all, if it is not to be forever a fountain without an outlet, it must begin to flow forth by this channel. Pantheism takes us through the whole realm of religious ideas, and claims to bring us, at last, to a universal solvent. If that solvent is not to lie in our minds unused, but to be applied to the phenomena of human life and society, the particular historical religion which we may happen to hold, will naturally be the first thing to come under its power. If Hegel had lived in China, and made disciples there as he did in Germany, his philosophy would have been applied to the writings of Confucius; if he had lived in Turkey, his followers would have straightway applied that philosophy to the religion of the Koran; but living, as he did, where Christianity is the historical religion, those who accepted his views began, at once, to use them in accounting for the New Testament records. Hence the rise of the Pantheistic Christology, more generally known under the designation of the Tübingen School, which has filled so large a space in the biblical criticism of the last half century, and to which I propose to devote the present lecture.

Religions to which pantheism may be applied.

Let us recall here, so far as the nature of our undertaking requires, the central doctrine of Hegel's philosophy. It is that of the progressive development of the Absolute Idea, through a triplicate and never-ending process. By the Absolute Idea I understand him to mean the one sole reality, besides which nothing either is or can be conceived to be. In its logical results, though not in its essence, it is the same thing as Spinoza's Substance. In like manner it agrees with the Subject-Object of Schelling, while it seems hardly to differ, in any respect, from Fichte's World-Ego. This idea is not a substance or entity, at least in our conception of it, but a process. The absolute, considered in itself, is either something or nothing. As apprehended in consciousness it is a "becoming," an endless evolution which had no beginning. In the evolution, or "becoming," there is all the time affirmation, negation, and higher affirmation. This triplicate movement, forever carrying the absolute idea out into more and more perfect manifestations, con-

Re-statement of Hegelianism.

The absolute idea.

A triplicate process.

stitutes the whole material of our knowledge. The movement goes on, not only in the phenomena of the universe considered as one, but in each division and subdivision, down to the least province of discovered facts. It is the method of progress in all civilizations, in all histories, in all arts, in all religions. Taken in the broadest sense it constitutes philosophy, which is that manifestation of the absolute idea in which its self-consciousness culminates. The doctrine may be clearer to us, perhaps, if we compare it, or rather contrast it, with Comte's threefold law of progress. According to Comte the facts of observation are accounted for: first by hypothesis, either theological or metaphysical; then there is a negation of the hypothesis, through a destructive criticism; and then there is an advance from hypothesis to the positive laws of phenomena. It is only in this threefoldness of movement, however, that the two schemes even suggest each other. With Comte the process is but intellectual; with Hegel it is real and universal. Comte recognizes only a limited movement in time, while Hegel makes it absolutely eternal. In Comte the three steps of the movement succeed each other chronologically, till at last only the third remains, which is permanent; in Hegel these steps are simultaneous, and every one valid, and will continue to be forever. The absolute idea, even when asserted most rudimentally, is not an hypothesis, but all the reality there is for the time being. The negation and criticism of its forms do not destroy it, as Comte makes theology and metaphysics fall before positivism, but are ever resulting in its higher affirmation.

Compared with Comte's "three states."

In civilization, for instance, this triplicate movement is always repeating itself. Men find themselves living together in one of the primitive stages of society. This rudimentary life is the absolute idea affirming itself; the positive form of the "becoming," or evolution in consciousness. But in the mean time humanity is outgrowing this form of civilization, and recoiling upon it, contradicting and destroying it. The effect of this conflict is another positive manifestation of the absolute idea, in some better form of civilization. And the higher ground thus reached, instead of being a resting-place, is always a point of departure to something still higher. In this way primitive barbarism rose to hero-worship, hero-worship to monarchy, and monarchy to the government of society by laws and constitutions. This unfolding of the absolute idea is history, and the recognition of it, and interpreting of human progress by its action, constitute the philosophy of history.

Illustrated in the history of civilization.

The absolute idea in art.

Within the province of art, also, the Hegelian scheme reveals its essential nature. At first men made for themselves a few rude implements and ornaments. Jubal was the father of such as handle the harp and organ; Tubal-cain, an instructor of every artificer in brass and iron. This was an actualization of the absolute idea in art. But that idea, being an eternal process, does not stop at this point. It goes beyond, and reacts upon what *is* with destructive effect. And it brings back with it, into the place of the forms it destroys, other forms which more perfectly embody its own possibilities. In all departments of life, as in art and civilization, there is forever a conservative party in conflict with a destructive party, and the result of their struggling against each other is constant progress; the further unfolding, that is, of the absolute idea. Whatever be the thesis on any subject for the time being, antithesis is steadily lifting the general consciousness to some higher thesis.

Progress and conservatism.

Such being the universal necessity, it follows that religion, like everything else, is subject to its action. The absolute idea was here first actualized, let us assume, in the form of fetich-worship. But immediately it began to recoil upon this affirmation of itself. And the result of the conflict was its higher affirmation as polytheism. Polytheism is now the thesis, and upon this, too, the absolute idea straightway reacts by antithesis, thus lifting the religious consciousness of the world into the form of monotheism. In this way monotheism, as at first imperfectly held, became that which the absolute idea affirmed. But by the necessity of its development, the idea still reacted destructively on what it had affirmed, and thus rose to the positive conception of Christianity. Christianity, as a temporary embodiment of the absolute idea, is now the thesis in religion. The antithesis, which assails this, and destroys its formal expression in the New Testament records, is the Tübingen school of criticism; which criticism, however, so far from doing any harm to religion itself, as conceived under the absolute idea, only clears the way for some manifestation of it more noble than the Christianity of the Bible. Thus it is that pantheism, under the handling of Hegel and his school, finds within itself a place for the Christian religion. That

The absolute idea in religion.

Christianity one of the temporary forms of the absolute idea.

Christianity is, however, only a transitory embodiment of the absolute idea, which idea alone is permanent, in religion as everywhere else. This winds its all-crushing folds about the historical Christ, destroying him as it gave him, for the sake of its own higher manifestation. The so-called historical Christ is a myth, and the absolute idea, which wrought in the religious imagination of men to create that myth, and which even now is seeking a nobler incarnation, is the only and the whole, the all-one reality.

The followers of Hegel soon separated into a "right" and "left;" and these two parties straightway went to war with each other, and are still at strife, evolving *him* through their disputes, about as interminably as his contradictories evolve the absolute. His influence, even upon Christian theists, may be easily accounted for.

Different views of Hegelianism. He died suddenly, at the age of sixty, while the praises of his philosophy were resounding far and near. No young thinker, much less any German thinker, wished to set himself against so great a name. Those who held to orthodoxy, and to conservative views generally, yet professed Hegelianism, lest this glory should all pass over to the revolutionary party.

The "right." They sought to show that Hegel's philosophy did not subvert historical Christianity, nor the positive institutions of the church and the state. But the absurdity of their effort was too manifest to make much headway. Though revived from time to time, even to the present day, the attempt to prove that Hegelianism agrees with orthodox Christianity has been generally regarded as a failure. Julius Müller, a thoroughly competent witness, says, "No place is to be found in this system for a finite life unfolding itself progressively, in pure and undisturbed harmony with God and with itself, and the attempt to force such an idea into it is vain. Hegel, therefore, in his logic, is fond of using 'infinitude' and 'holiness' as correlatives, and in his lectures upon the Philosophy of Religion, he uses 'the finite' as the correlative of 'evil,' with the additional limitation that 'evil is the extreme of finitude.'"[1] Those who take the "left," construing Hegel's system to the overthrow of positive institutions, may well charge their opponents with a lack of the scientific spirit; with looking to practical results, that is, rather than to the real nature of what Hegel taught. Take the self-contradictory thought-process, which is the absolute idea eternally evolving itself, and go on fearlessly with it, say they, never turning back to guard your prejudices, and warning final causes, historical Christianity, and all other obstacles to save themselves as they best can. But this party, even if true to the logical tendencies of the system, were yet false to the spirit of their master. They, too, like their extreme opponents, sought to make use of the new philosophy in furthering their practical views of social and individual life. But was it possible that so great a man as Hegel should wish to be only a destroyer? that he should seek to cast off all bands of order from men, and bring in a social chaos everywhere? This was the question now raised by some of his disciples, to which they could return only a negative answer. And hence arose a third party, called the "centre," though left-centre would have been the more accurate term, perhaps. These claimed to stand

The "left."

The "centre."

[1] Christian Doctrine of Sin, Book II., Chap. IV.

midway between the other two parties, and laid special claim to that scientific spirit which they alike had forsaken. And here again we are reminded of the Hegelian dialectics, the same idea evolving itself anew through the conflict of its opposites in manifestation.

Strauss. One of the first and most earnest of this "centre" party was David Friederich Strauss. He, while still a youth under twenty, had sat in the vast audience of learned men who listened with delight and wonder to the ripest utterances of Hegel. None were more receptive than he, none more enthusiastic in their advocacy of the new system. It was under this impulse that he went to Tübingen, where Hegel had been educated, to lecture at the university, and also to be connected with the theological faculty. As we might expect, *At Tübingen.* he looked at all subjects through the system of philosophy which he brought with him. He was a pen in Hegel's hand, a tongue to the Hegelian philosophy. But he wrote and spoke, for the most part, on subjects connected with the biblical teachings. We are at present concerned, therefore, to see what the method was by which he found a place for Christianity in this pantheistic temple.

His Life of Jesus, which has given him so wide a notoriety, was published within five years after the death of Hegel, and when Strauss himself was but *The " Life of Jesus."* twenty-seven years old. It was a work of youthful enthusiasm, and not free from the faults wont to mar such efforts. Other critics, agreeing with him in the main, especially Ferdinand Christian Baur, have written more ably and accurately. It is not *what* Strauss did, so much as the state of religious thought at the *time* of his doing it, which has made him, throughout the world, the popular representative of the school to which he belongs. The style of biblical criticism which he boldly adopted had for a long time been cautiously growing up. And the destruction of the Evangelical record, in which his criticism issued, was no shock, but an omen of hope, to those who would resolve everything back into an eternal thought-process by which all things are evolved.

Strauss took the ground that all positive religions, Christianity among them, are but transient forms in which the absolute idea, under its religious designation, manifests itself. These forms are constantly changing, even while their names are retained; and they can never have any but a secondary value. Our so-called historical Christianity is only the flowing dress in which the imaginations of Christians have clothed the religious idea. That idea itself, being the absolute in one of its phases, is the only important thing. And not only this, but since it is part of the eternal thought-process, as such it is the only real thing in Christianity. The temporary embodiment of the process, whether in the form of narrative, discourses, conversations, dogmatic treatises, natural or so-called supernatural events, is of but little account. It may be altogether fictitious, or a nebulous mass of fiction clustered about some small nucleus of fact; or it may be a string of fabulous inventions and parables, antedated afterwards by some

The idea in religion alone important.

The question of historical truth but trivial.

unscrupulous editor, who would thus make it seem to fall within certain historical limits. No matter what that embodiment for the time being is, provided it is a suitable form in which the imagination of man may express his religious ideal. So long as it admits of this, in the case of those who accept it, its office is fulfilled. The question of fact or fiction need not be raised; for it serves its turn all the same, be it history, fable, poetry, legend, myth, or a mixture impossible to define.

When Strauss was dismissed from the faculty of theology at Tübingen on account of his heresies, he took the attitude of surprised and injured innocency. He thought it very hard that he should be driven forth for affirming that Christianity was of so little account as Essential Christianity. history, and as such might be either true or false, while he held with all his might to the idea which evolved it. The story of the Nazarene symbolizes to us the working of the moral ideal in man, at a certain stage of the general progress. That ideal, wearing such dress as representative writers saw fit to give it, passes before us. It is God manifest in the flesh, it dies, it rises, it ascends into heaven. The whole beautiful picture, so far as it has any value or significancy, is but a movement in the human consciousness. The scene is not objective, but purely subjective; not the won- How the idea produced the so-called record. der-working of one who brings help down to us from above, but the many-hued robes of an ideal Christ which humanity thinks into being. If we would know how the Evangelical record grew up, Strauss would say, let us consider how the Iliad, Paradise Lost, and Hamlet were produced. The only difference is that these are the works of individuals, thinking partly in secular channels, while that may be regarded as the work of a whole people, under the lead of the religious imagination. Humanity is always in a state of progressive thinking, on religious as on other subjects. This is the grand truth, and all the truth. Man's religious thinking is not to be put under restraint. It may array itself in such garments as it likes; may appropriate history, or put its own inventions into the form of history; may seize upon any marvellous tales floating about in tradition; may make use of the actual, the possible, and the impossible, in giving "a local habitation and a name" to its "airy nothings" which are everything.

From this theory Strauss passes, by a natural inference, to his Life of Jesus. All the temporary forms of religion are legitimate game for the critic, — who loves to discern between the historical and the poetical in literature, and who seems to think it but fair that he, provided he holds firmly to the absolute idea in religion, should be allowed to amuse himself with trying to destroy the Christian religion. It is not at all surprising that such a target should have been chosen by the Hegelian, on which to prove his marksmanship. The paths of religion and philosophy, where not co-incident, are near each other. Neither of them can be pursued very far by itself. This is shown in the case of Strauss. There was but a step between his lighted torch and the Christian records. And having been bred up in a philosophy which assigned a lower seat than its own to every form of religion, it did not occur to him that he was at all sacrilegious or irreverent, though somewhat re-

Criticism deals with the non-essential.

gardless of prevailing prejudices, in brushing aside the whole drapery of an historical Gospel. So much of the Evangelical record as had ceased to express the scientific thinking of the age on religious subjects, had become an obstacle to the further progress of religion. Its reign was broken. It was a discrowned and lifeless body. And the still more glorious manifestation of the absolute idea, required that it should be hidden away as soon as possible.

<small>Evidence that Strauss was a pantheist.</small> But what is the evidence, some may ask, that I have stated the real spirit of the Tübingen criticism? Such evidence abounds. A little of it I will now proceed to give. Strauss quotes the remark of Schelling, that "the incarnation of God is an incarnation from eternity;" and he says that Schelling "understood, under the incarnate Son of God, the finite itself in the form of the human consciousness."[1] This is his own doctrine. The God-man is the absolute idea coming to self-consciousness in man's religious thinking. This thought-process in humanity is the eternal Son, the Word, that by which all things are made, and in which God loves the world. "The recognition of God as a spirit implies, that God does not remain as a fixed and immutable infinite, encompassing the finite; but enters into it, produces the finite, nature, and the human mind, merely as a limited manifestation of himself, from which he eternally returns into unity."[2] It is

<small>His view of the incarnation.</small> in the race of men, therefore, that the incarnation of God takes place. The Gospels are a picture of what is forever going forward in our religious consciousness. Jesus is a symbolical, ideal char-

---

[1] Life of Jesus, Evans' translation (N. Y., 1856), Vol. II., § 150.   [2] Ibid.

acter, imaging to us the workings of the humam mind; all springs from its depths and divine impulses. "That history is a beautiful poem of the human race,— a poem in which are embodied all the wants of our religious instinct. The history in the Gospels is in fact the history of human nature conceived ideally, and exhibits to us in the life of an individual, what man ought to be, and can become." What was fact and certain history to the four Evangelists, is to us "a sacred mythus and poetry." "The points of view only are different: human nature, and the religious impulse in it, remain ever the same."[1] "To know the ideal Christ," says Strauss, quoting Spinoza, "namely, the eternal wisdom of God, which is manifested in all things, in the human mind particularly, and especially in Jesus Christ, alone is necessary."[2] "The key to the whole of Christology is this," he again says: "That an idea, instead of an individual, is set forth as the subject of the attributes which are attributed to Christ in the Church doctrine. Humanity is the union of both natures. Humanity is the miracle-worker. Humanity, not the individual, but the race, is the sinless one. Humanity is that which dies, and rises again, and ascends towards heaven. This alone is the absolute subject-matter of Christology: the circumstance that it appears in the person and history of Jesus of Nazareth, is but the poetical dress of the doctrine."[3]

The origin of the Gospels.

Accepts Spinoza's view of Christ.

Strauss even makes the Evangelists themselves profess pantheism, where they say of

Thinks the conscious-

---

[1] Life of Jesus, Vol. II., § 149. [2] Ibid.
[3] Dr. W. H. Mill's "Observations on the Attempted Application of Pantheistic Principles to the Theory and Historic Criticism of the Gospels" (Cambridge, England, 1861).

ness of Jesus would have responded to his criticism. Christ "that he recognized God as his Father, God's cause as his own, was conscious of knowing the Father, and resigned his own will to the divine, where he speaks expressly of his oneness with the Father, and sets himself forth as the visible manifestation of the same. Such utterances were without pretension, arising from no transient elevation of mind, but from the conviction of his whole life. All his acts and discourses were penetrated with this consciousness as with a soul."[1] The Gospels portray to us such a personage; and his existence is not historically but ideally true, which alone is scientifically possible. He is the absolute idea, shining forth in the human consciousness for a season, and then sinking back into the infinite depths, to be succeeded by another and more glorious theophany, in the progressive thought of the race. We may compare the doctrine of Strauss, or rather of Hegel, to the phenomena of evaporation in nature. The waters above the firmament are one with the waters under the firmament. The mists, which pile themselves in fleecy masses of silver and gold along the calm heights of the sky, are still the ocean which sent them up, and they are constantly falling back into it, as it is all the time rising into their beautiful forms. In the Christology of Strauss, the absolute idea is the ocean,— a sea unfathomed and without shore. This, coming forth into the human consciousness, paints that piece of gorgeous cloud-scenery, the story of the Nazarene. But the abysmal depths are forever reclaiming the iridescent vapor which they send up. The sweet Evangel cannot retain that which fills it with its rainbow hues. Even while we

The Gospel record a piece of cloud painting.

[1] Dr. Mill, p. 56.

look it is not the same, but changing every moment. The one changeless and eternal thing in all this, is the absolute idea; which these moving splendors serve but to reveal, and besides which there is no value or reality in the whole display.

Now this pantheism of Strauss, from which he undertook the criticism of the Gospels, gave him a certain vantage-ground. It enabled him to deal a death-blow to the naturalistic school of critics, of which Paulus was the leader. This school was already in its decadence when he wrote. It had tried to apply to the Christian Scriptures such rules of interpretation as Evemerus, an ancient Greek critic, applied to the classical mythology. Evemerus held that the Greek gods and heroes were extraordinary men, who to increase their power had surrounded themselves with a nimbus of divinity, or whom tradition had invested with superhuman attributes.[1] The Wolfenbüttel Fragmentist was among the first of modern interpreters to apply this theory to the biblical record. He would not even admit the honesty of the great leaders and teachers whom the Bible names. They were designing men, who feigned inspiration and intercourse with the God of heaven, to gain influence over the masses of the people. To this extent Paulus did not go. He still claimed that men of such benevolence as Abraham, Moses, David, Paul, and who really accomplished so

Advantage of this pantheistic position.

The Paulists.

Evemerus.

His method revived by Lessing, editor of the Wolfenbüttel Fragments.

How used by Paulus.

---

[1] For some account of Evemerus see Grote (Harper's edition), Vol. I., pp. 411, 412.

much good, could not be wilful deceivers. But they might be self-deceived. They might mistake their natural enthusiasm for a supernatural afflatus. Their conviction of the vast importance of what they were doing, might give rise to a belief of divine authority to do it. No miracle is to be admitted anywhere; yet the honesty of the writers and actors, and the historical character of the record, are to be maintained.

Results of the theory. Wild as the attempt may seem, yet it is a fact that Paulus sought to explain the Bible on this theory. Our first parents ate some poisonous fruit, which planted in them the seeds of hereditary disease: this, on naturalistic principles, may be regarded as the historic fact of the Fall and its consequences. Moses built a large fire on Mount Sinai, and just then a thunderstorm arose. When he came down to the people, his face shone as the natural effect of so much excitement. So, too, in the New Testament. Early one morning Christ is with three of his disciples in a mountain. He is above them, towards the east, on the highest peak; when the sun, suddenly rising behind him, makes his whole person shine, so that the disciples are blinded by looking at him. Peter did not find the tribute-money in the mouth of the fish; this is only a nice way of telling what did occur, namely, that he caught the fish and sold it for the money. Christ and his disciples took wine with them to the wedding at Cana; and it was their putting this into the six water-jars, through a quiet understanding with the servants, which constitutes the historical matter in the narrative. Thus would a Paulist go along through the record, enucleating so much of it as is not supernatural, and holding that this, or some equivalent, is literal history; while the rest is but embellishment, — the result of a rich Oriental fancy, or of that tendency to exaggerate which is in all great story-tellers. Paulus has some followers even at the present day, as the work of Schenkel on the Character of Jesus may serve to attest. No one, excepting always a German with a theory to maintain, can fail to see that the naturalism of Paulus was an ignoble failure. His attempt made it plain, if it was not clear before, that we must admit the supernatural in Revelation, or we cannot regard it as in any proper sense historical.

Regarded as a failure.

Eichhorn, who was contemporary with Paulus, applied the method of Evemerus to biblical interpretation. The same is true also of De Wette to some extent. But these scholars either lacked the intrepidity of Paulus, or they had a keener sense than he of the puerile tendencies of his criticism. They did not wish to divest the Scriptures of all dignity. Therefore, while pursuing a course which in many things sustained the orthodox faith, in some things they leaned towards the view of Paulus, and in other things they were inclined to grant the Tübingen theory of a poetizing fancy. The inspired writers are communicating truth everywhere, but in some cases their enthusiasm makes the dress in which they clothe it. It is this concession of an unhistorical element, by De Wette, but more especially by Eichhorn, which Strauss does not fail to seize upon as a partial and cautious approach towards his own theory of the mythus. Indeed, he goes back of them, even to Origen and Philo, for the germs of his theory. I am not careful here to

Eichhorn.
De Wette.

Strauss sees in them the germs of the myth-theory.

defend either of those early interpreters. Philo was an acknowledged Neo-Platonist; and Origen felt the influence of the Alexandrine pantheism. Therefore they may have both applied a pantheistic exegesis to the sacred records. But it is certain that Origen, to say the least, did not deny the historical validity of the Scriptures. His allegorical sense was not a creative energy, but a meaning which he found in the narrative. No doubt there is some ground for what Strauss says of himself, that he only matured a theory of interpretation which had been growing up for a long time. The enthusiastic reception his work met with, in various quarters, proves that the minds of many biblical critics had come to be in sympathy with him. The appetite which his mythical theory gorged, had been, to say the least, awakened. Even the orthodox party read him, not sorry to see their old foes, the naturalistic rationalists, falling under his sturdy assaults. Yet they themselves were in no better plight. Strauss saved them from the Paulists, only as the hawks saved the doves from the kites. They were, like Samson, crushed themselves by what they pulled down upon their enemies. Paulus admitted that the Bible is historical, but not supernatural; Strauss denied that it is either. To his view the Bible, and especially its Christology, is the product of the absolute idea, working in the religious imagination of the Hebrew race for the most part. This idea, coming to self-consciousness in the religious thinking of men, is the whole reality in sacred Scripture, as Hegel had taught him to say; and in just this fact, that Strauss was a Hegelian

Thinks Origen and Philo held his theory.

Relation to other schools of criticism.

Secret of his popularity.

speaking to a generation of Hegelians, is the secret of the prodigious popularity of his work.

The orthodox principle of interpretation is, that the biblical record is historical, and much of it supernatural, — as it ought to be, since it describes a coming down of the omnipotent God into nature to save sinful men. The naturalistic rationalist admits its historical validity, but tries to get rid of the supernatural. The mythologist denies that it is either history or miracle, making it a product of the religious imagination. The mythical theory differs from the legendary, — the latter granting some weight to historical facts, while the former affirms that it is indifferent whether the narrative be true or false. These two theories differ rather in degree than in kind, however, while the more extreme, namely, the mythical, is that held by Strauss. So much of the record as is supernatural, is of course unhistoric, since it all is but the fruit of human thinking. And so much of it as might have happened, is given not because it happened, but because it is a convenient form in which the thought, working itself out, may be embodied. Æsop makes the dumb animals, the fishes, and the reptiles talk together with man, in his efforts to convey truth: the writers of the Bible have used a similar liberty. They tell of what did not take place, and of what could not take place, more or less mingled, perhaps, with actual occurrences, with the sole purpose of giving forth that religious idea which is struggling for expression within them.

In order to make room for the growth of the Evangelical

Three principles of interpretation.

The position of Strauss.

The myth.

mythus, such as his pantheistic philosophy requires, Strauss puts the origin of the Gospels forward into the second century of our era. Jerusalem had been destroyed at least fifty years, and the Christians were scattered abroad throughout the Roman empire. None of the immediate friends of Jesus of Nazareth, not even any who had conversed with those friends, were now living. There was, among those thus scattered abroad, a tradition that Jesus had been a Rabbi of a singularly pure and noble character, who had suffered a most cruel death some time before their dispersion. This story, handed on from the elder to the younger, and carried from place to place in an unwritten form, naturally grew on the lips of the exiles, and shaped itself to their ideas and feelings. It became a type of their calamity, and of their hope; that is, a mythus, — like the legend of William Tell, mistaken by some for actual history, which is but a symbol of the Swiss struggle for liberty. The Jewish nation has been violently overthrown; and the story ran that the good Rabbi from Nazareth was cruelly killed. But the Jewish nation is to be restored; therefore Jesus, its mythical type, is imagined to have risen from the dead, and ascended into heaven. The Messianic spirit, having thus seized upon the tradition, connects it with Old Testament prophecies. Therefore a birth and childhood of Jesus are imagined, and a public ministry and sufferings, answering to the early predictions of a Messiah. "Such and such things must have happened to the Messiah; Jesus was the Messiah; therefore such and such things happened to him."[1] The

How Strauss makes room for his theory.

The story the product of the idea.

[1] Life of Jesus, Vol. I., p. 67.

mythus is "the product of the idea." Jesus is greater than any that went before him, therefore greater marvels must have attended him. Because the face of Moses shone, he must be transfigured. There were twelve Jewish tribes, hence he must have twelve disciples. Whatever the Messiah was expected to do, he is fancied as doing; and the name Son of God, given to him, grows out of the feeling that the Hebrew nation, which he ideally typified, is the chosen favorite of heaven.

Thus did the Gospel narratives grow up. They belong to the post-apostolic age. They are not history, but national religious poems; not the work of particular individuals, but of a whole people, which certain persons after a while took the liberty of reducing to writing. If we ask Strauss why these writers did not put their own names to their works; why they have practised a fraud upon us in representing those works as written by the companions of Christ and the apostles, his reply is, "The most reputable authors, amongst the Jews and early Christians, published their works with the substitution of venerated names, without an idea that they were guilty of any falsehood or deceit in so doing."[1] Such is one of the exigencies into which the theory of Strauss brings him. In order to give the Evangelical mythus time to grow up, the Gospel narratives are declared to be post-apostolic. Thus he is obliged to admit that the writers practised literary forgery. Yet he sees no immorality in their conduct, but thinks they were under the influence of the most exalted motives! The absolute idea of religion, revealing itself in the national mind, is what

What follows if the Gospels are post-apostolic.

[1] Life of Jesus, Vol. I., p. 68.

we are to see and admire, — revering it not the less, but the more, for working itself out through so much storytelling and innocent trickery! This may meet the highest demands of a Straussian conscience, perhaps; but there are still a few persons in the world of so singular a turn of mind as to refuse the nostrum, preferring a little less absolute, and a little more honesty. We think it not so likely that the authors of the four Gospels should occupy themselves with inventing lies, as that this Whittington-and-his-cat theory of the life of Christ should be false. We claim strong internal evidence for our conclusion; since it is the charm of the Gospels that they have none of the air of poetic fiction, but everywhere give us what profess to be actual events, in the simplest and plainest style. There is nowhere any impression or hint of a myth. If a fraud, it is the wickedest of all frauds, for every word of it has the historic stamp. That which not only so stirs us, but is so real to us in all its alleged facts, cannot be mere literary invention. Its roots must go down into the world of objective truth, which man beholds but does not create, and which will be the same when his place knows him no more.

Internal evidence against Strauss.

But we do not rely on this internal evidence alone — evidence which the impotent charge of forgery does not brush aside. There is strong external evidence, going to confirm our conclusion, that the Gospels were written by the men whose names they bear. Before the time to which Strauss assigns the origin of the Evangelical writings, they were quoted as works well known among the Christians. Already, even in regard to the Fourth Gospel, the last

External evidence agrees with internal.

written, Justin Martyr, Papias, and others had testified to its existence, by quoting from it and repeatedly referring to it. In order to escape this historic testimony, Strauss invents the fiction of a Gospel afterwards lost, to which the apostolic fathers and the early critics refer, and on which those we now have were founded. But however grand or fruitful the Hegelian philosophy may be, we must be excused for thinking it a little grandiose in fruitfulness, when it not only sets aside well-attested history, but invents history of which there is no record, for the sake of an unproved assumption. Not only the testimony of the early fathers, and of infidels even, as well as the intrinsic character of the Gospels, but the geography of Palestine itself, is to-day a refutation of the theory of Strauss. The origin of the Gospels was not mythical, but historical. They are not merely ideally but objectively true. No hypothesis solves the problem of their origin, as presented in the light of contemporary events, but that which affirms them to have been written by the men whose names they bear, eyewitnesses and ear-witnesses of the supernatural facts which they record.

How Strauss would evade it.

The argument for the historical origin of the Gospels unanswerable.

The Tübingen school of criticism would have fallen into disrepute sooner than it did, but for the efforts of Ferdinand C. Baur, perhaps its most skilful representative. He does not, in the same unqualified sense as Strauss, seem committed to the philosophy of Hegel. He wrote an adverse criticism on the Life of Jesus, when that work first came out. But however the

Baur.

two men may differ as between themselves, in their attitude towards historical Christianity they agree. Strauss regards the Messianic idea in the mind of the Hebrew race as the germ of the Gospels. The view of Baur, though mythical like this, is that the writings of the New Testament must be traced to a less poetical source, namely, the conflict which had arisen between Jewish and Gentile Christianity. His statement of this theory, as well as his defence of it, is very ingenious. There were two parties in the early church, — a Petrine and a Pauline party. The latter were desirous that the Jewish faith should merge itself into a world-religion, the former wished it to be kept strictly within the old national limits. In the dispersed condition of the Jews, living in Roman and Greek communities, everything naturally favored the Gentile party. It grew steadily, especially by the incoming of Gentile converts, while its rival faction as steadily lost ground. As time passed on, and the once clear authority of the Mosaic laws had grown dim, even in the minds of the Petrine or conservative party, certain of the progressive or Pauline party stepped forward, and supplemented the Old Testament records by inventing the writings which compose the New Testament. They showed that the prophecies of the Old Testament pointed forward to something, and that something they supplied in the Gospels and Epistles. These writings were so shaped as to suit the ancient tradition, as to represent a long and varying struggle between Jewish and Gentile Christianity, and as in the end to give the latter the ascendency over the

Differs from Strauss.

What he thinks gave rise to the Gospels.

Traces of a conflict all through them.

former. Christ is portrayed as less and less Jewish, and more and more favorable to the Gentiles, as the feigned narrative goes forward. This is shown in his denunciations of the Pharisees, while he befriends outcasts; also in his formal discourses, and especially in his parables. The lost sheep, *[How Baur makes the narrative favor the Pauline party.]* the pieces of silver, the prodigal son, awakening so much concern in each instance, are the Gentile world. The unjust steward, whom his lord puts out of the stewardship, is Israel. The fact of descent from Abraham is to be disregarded; Christ proclaims a religion which is equally open to all men. Those on the right hand of the Judge in the last day are good Gentiles; true subjects of the new kingdom, though kept in ignorance of their relation to Christ by the Petrine teachings. Those on the left hand are bad Jews, rejected for lack of such obedience as the others have shown. Peter is more a name than a person, representing the narrow view. He has precedence in the apostolic college, as the Jews had in the matter of revelation. But he does many weak things, such as denying his Master, waiting for a vision before he will visit Cornelius, and refusing to eat with the Gentiles after his doing so had offended some *[Peter disappears.]* at Jerusalem. Gradually he is made to acquire broader views, yet he cannot quite put away his exclusive feelings; and finally, after some collisions with the party of progress, in which he is uniformly put to the worse, he sinks out of the so-called history altogether. Meanwhile the liberal tendency, for the sake of which the New Testament writings were drawn up, is described as making rapid headway, and as absorbing the whole energy and piety of the church. Not only does it show to advantage throughout the Evangelical mythus, but especially in the Acts of the Apostles. Paul, the representative man of this movement, is the great missionary, entirely eclipsing Peter, withstanding him to the face because he was to be blamed, and forcing him at last to yield his pretensions. Various treatises are added, which, to increase their influence, are called the Epistles of Paul, or of those who in the main accepted his views. Even Peter is made to indorse the Pauline party, in his Epistles, so called. Baur concedes that some of the treatises ascribed to Paul were written by him; but the Gentile spirit predominates in these no more than in those whose authorship is uncertain. The object of them all is, to impress it upon the minds of the early Christians, that either the liberal party in the church must triumph, or the whole Evangelical idea, as well as the Messianic idea back of it, must be given up. Baur thinks that many a Judaizing Christian, in the second century and near the beginning of the third, falling in with the New Testament writings and reading them thoughtfully, must have been persuaded to give up his Judaism, and accept the newer doctrine of a world-religion. To beget such a persuasion was the purpose of the authentic treatises, and of the feigned letters and narratives. This purpose emboldened the writers, whoever they were, to do what is sometimes done by the correspondents of newspapers. They imagined the stories they wrote out; and these, for lack of a rigid criticism, such as Baur and his school now apply to them, gained general currency among the credulous friends of the broad-church party. Histories were invented, for which those who knew Jesus personally are made to vouch, and essays were composed, at the head of which stood apostolic names; and so childish was the age, and ready to be duped, that this deception passed without successful challenge. It was not till nearly two thousand years after, that the Daniel of biblical criticism, in the form of the Tübingen school, came to judgment.

It will be seen, therefore, that the position of Baur, with reference to the historical validity of the New Testament, is substantially that of Strauss. Hence the facts which refute one are a sufficient answer to the other. Having already indicated what those facts are, I need not repeat them here. Those who wish to examine the whole question of the historical validity of the New Testament, need hardly to be referred to the many volumes of recent critics, in which this matter is ably discussed. One of the best of these, for general use, is Professor Fisher's work on the Supernatural Origin of Christianity. This work makes it clear, by a full and scientific treatment of the subject, that the ground of Baur is untenable. _{A special refutation not needed here.}

To the special view of Baur respecting parties in the apostolic church, there is no objection. Such parties undoubtedly did exist. They are plainly described to us in the New Testament history. It is Baur's fault, that instead of finding them *in* the history, he makes them create the so-called history. He finds the evangelical record in his idea, rather than the grounds of his idea in the record. In doing this, he shows the peculiar vice of German thinkers. When _{There were parties in the early church.}

they have found a theory, they are inclined to make that theory the source of whatever else they find. With Baur the idea of two parties originates the New Testament writings, as the Messianic idea does with Strauss. And in this producing power of the idea they both follow Hegel, who finds in his absolute idea the creative substance of all things. We find, in the history of the United States soon after the adoption of the Constitution, two political parties,—the federal, led by John Adams, and the republican, led by Thomas Jefferson. But what would be thought of the critic who, discovering this conflict, should declare that it, for the partisan purposes of one side or the other, has created all our so-called national history; that the record is simply an imaginary dress, in which some partial champion has embodied his view of the conflict; that the struggle did not begin till some time after the date assigned; that it is very doubtful whether Adams and Jefferson are not, after all, only the myths which some politician has imagined; while it is certain that they never penned many of the writings which now claim their authorship? Yet this is not an unfair illustration of the spirit of the Tübingen criticism. Not satisfied with running its theory into the ground, it runs the ground into its theory.

Baur's treatment unfair.

The ancients had their muse of history, whose aid they reverently invoked, while attempting to set past events in order. Did they not, in this, recognize a universal human infirmity? Even our secular historians carry back their private views, to the serious discoloring of that which they would describe. It was left for Strauss and Baur to enthrone this infirmity, and make it the originator of the sacred annals. But there is a Muse of evangelical history. Holy men wrote as they were moved by the Holy Ghost. This divine inspiration saved them from the error to which all historians are liable. It kept them back from the mythical abyss into which Baur and Strauss fell headlong. It enabled them to record God's thoughts towards us, and the great facts of redemption, with no damaging admixture of subjective theory; so that we do well to take heed to their words, as to a light that shineth in a dark place. There are many arguments for inspiration, but I know of none more powerful than the rise of the Tübingen school of criticism. If we are to have a revelation from the Father of our spirits, and not sink into naturalism or blank idealism, there is no mere man whom we can dare to trust. That revelation, our sorest need, must come through persons whom God has inspired to speak his words unto us, and whom he so saves from their own imperfections, that they shall neither add anything to the message nor take anything away.

Strauss and Baur furnish an argument for inspiration.

A word only is needed, in this place, respecting the legendary theory of Renan. His Life of Jesus, and connected works, have been extensively read. And no wonder; for they clothe in a fascinating garb theories easily made plausible to minds but partially informed. Yet the careful reader soon finds that Renan's doctrine is not original; it is a French imitation. His theory hardly seems to me to require any separate treatment. Though he gives more space to the historical element than either Baur or

Renan.

Requires no separate treatment.

Strauss, — as he could not well help doing, being familiar with the geography of Palestine, and writing in the midst of it, — yet the pantheistic flavor of his thought often rises to the surface. It is true that he rejects the mythical theory, and adopts the legendary; but he still says that the criticism of the gospel-text by Strauss "leaves little to be desired." He also speaks of Christianity itself as an "evolution by which the noblest portions of humanity passed from the ancient religions." He says, with evident reference to the pantheistic doctrine of the absolute, "No passing vision exhausts divinity; God was revealed before Jesus, God will be revealed after him. Widely unequal, and so much the more divine as they are the greater and the more spontaneous, the manifestations of the God concealed in the depths of the human conscience are all of the same order." The Christian religion, that is, though more or less historic in some of its forms, is only an evolution within humanity, — part and parcel of that thought-process which is all the time going forward in man. That such is the philosophical germ of Renan's criticism, so far as it has any, and that he should be met on the same ground as other pantheists, is further indicated where he says, "If we except the French Revolution, no historic medium was so fitting as that in which Jesus was formed, to develop those hidden powers which humanity holds as if in reserve, and which she never reveals except in her days of fever and of danger." It is doubtful if any person, of less powerful imagination than Renan, would have seen much likeness between the stormy times of Robespierre and the peaceful Galilean society in which

The spirit of his criticism pantheistic.

An irreverent comparison.

the Son of Mary grew up; and with the exceedingly liberal compliment given to Jesus, by insinuating that he was only second to the leaders of revolutionary France, we dismiss this popular critic to those who ignorantly admire him, not knowing what they worship.

I only allude here, in conclusion, to the still more recent movement which calls itself Free Religion. The peculiarity of this is, that it finds more or less of religious truth in all religions, and the whole essence of religion in the human consciousness. Brahmanism, Confucianism, Buddhism, Christianity, all the forms of religion now existing, in short, should stand together in brotherly fellowship. For they have all been developed by the same idea in man; none of them are of supernatural origin, or have any supreme authority; and that in us which gave birth to these, is steadily crowding them aside with something better. It will be seen at a glance what is the parentage of this theory. While vainly striving to cling to the ghost of a departed theism, it is but the last and puny child of a philosophy already overthrown. It is the dying echo of the voice which Hegel lifted up so long ago. It is the faint resonance, on this distant shore, of a wave whose original force is spent. Let pantheism, like the divine revelation, have its "minor prophets" if it must. Yet it touches our American pride somewhat, when we see those prophets trying to convert our popular literature into a kind of Israelitish bazaar for the display of the philosophical old-clothes of the Germans. For Christianity itself, however, we have no fear. The warlike manifesto which scepticism issued

Free religion.

Its peculiarity.

May be traced to Hegel.

Christianity triumphant.

half a century ago, has resulted in its own signal defeat. The stone cut out of the mountain has smitten the pantheistic image. Its fragments, ground to powder by the chariot-wheels of truth, are but the dust of the highway cast up for the Lord's ransomed, along which they are returning to Zion, — coming with songs, and with the joy of victory on their heads.

LECTURE V.

The Culture which Pantheism Legitimates.

THOSE revolutionary tendencies of modern thought, of which we hear so much, are nowhere more manifest than in the ethical and social discussions of the day. Theories of duty, whether public or private, have forsaken their ancient base. In many instances they have even been faced about, so that what was once the front is now the rear, and the starting-point has become the point of attack. Formerly external authority was the rule, but now spontaneity is the law which tends to prevail. The doctrine that morals are intuitive, and cannot be taught, has been broached. Humanity, in its spontaneous growth, is the true basis of the state; and written compacts are hinderances in its way, which should be destroyed. Marriage should not rest on unchanging statutes, but on the free action of nature in man. The family and society, instead of depending on legislation, should be the unhindered outgrowth of forces which are a law to themselves. The conduct of the individual, of the family, of society, of the state, all of which I here include under the general notion of *Culture*, should not be regulated from without, but from within. They should be spontaneous,

A feature of modern thought.

Spontaneity.

and not suffer themselves to be guided by external authority. That authority is fictitious. They make it by their own unfolding energy, and it but marks a point in their limitless progress, beyond which they have already passed when it rises into notice.

I do not say that there was none of this revolutionary spirit in ancient times. There was much of it. But it wrought, for the most part, in a blind and aimless way, so that the theory of human culture, which appears most conspicuous to us as we look far back, is the one which rests on external standards.

<small>The elements of authority in modern times.</small>

Nor do I mean to imply that this law of culture has at length been abandoned. It was never more loyally obeyed, or thoroughly and clearly expounded, than at the present moment. In this case, as in all others, truth has been cleared up and strengthened by conflict with error. The doctrine of spontaneity in morals no doubt did good by correcting certain exaggerations, and calling attention to certain elements which had been neglected by the friends of truth. That doctrine has been thoroughly canvassed, however, and ably refuted, under the various forms it has taken since the revival of Spinozism.

<small>New theory untenable.</small>

Whether known as Agrarianism, Communism, Chartism, or simply as "the Spirit of the Nineteenth Century," when it has clamored for the abolition of the laws of property, for free marriage and free religion, its hostility to our noblest convictions has been clearly pointed out. It assumes an inborn purity in all men, and an absence of evil tendencies, which their own honest consciousness sadly denies them. It shuts them away from those heavenly ideals which they did not originate, and from that holy God, whose authority checks the evil and helps the good in their natures. Its liberty is anarchy; its spontaneity means civil convulsions, social chaos, the axe, the knife, the torch, every man's hand against every man. These disorders are defended on the ground that the whole fabric of society has been wrongly organized, on a basis of external rules; and it is claimed that all would have gone forward smoothly, if nothing had ever been put in the way of the spontaneous tendencies of men.

We can see the fallacy of the reasoning easily enough, knowing as we do what many of the tendencies of human nature are; yet we are sometimes amazed, and half persuaded into belief of the theory, amid the dazzling and bewildering sophistries which its advocates throw around us. *Relation to pantheism.* We need, therefore, to know the source of their power. They must be forced back to a point which even they themselves, perhaps, have not yet found out. The ethical doctrines, which they would apply to man and society, have the same parentage as the theories of Strauss, Baur, and Renan. Pantheism is the universal solvent. We saw how all the facts of the Scriptures disappeared in it; we are now to see how the established regulations of society, as soon as they touch it, melt out of sight. That social lawlessness seething in certain quarters, which gets itself more or less fiercely spoken now and then, may find in Hegel its legitimate source. His philosophy is its real major premise. The spontaneous culture, which it would substitute for that of positive precept, begins there; and this its philosophical origin we must clearly see, if we would dissolve its charm and expose its intrinsic ugliness. It puts on many captivating disguises. The most pure-hearted feel the fascination of some of its partial statements. Only in its source, and its relation to moral evil, do its repulsive features come out.

There are many recent writers, whose names might represent more or less this doctrine of spontaneous culture. Of these I select, as best suited to my purpose, the name of Goethe. The nature and influence of the new movement, and its relation to Spinozism, can be traced in him as perhaps in no other popular writer. It is evident, as I shall hope to show, that he ranges himself with the pantheistic school of thinkers; and it will not be denied that in variety of topics, originality, and beauty of style, he stands pre-eminent. There is a charm in nearly all that he has written, felt even by the best minds at times, the secret of which needs to be uncovered. It is for these reasons that I now call attention to him. I do not attempt a comprehensive treatment, either of the man or his writings. Those who look for this will no doubt be disappointed, and disposed to accuse me of injustice. I am concerned with a single phase of his character and influence. This is all that my purpose contemplates. I am not about to give an estimate of Goethe, but to show how a pantheistic philosophy affected him as a man and a writer. Unfortunately for me, it will be my duty to dwell on that aspect of Goethe's character which is least honorable to him. I crave only such indulgence as is fair, while doing this ungracious work, knowing as I do the great merits of Goethe, which it would be

Goethe.

Why chosen.

Viewed only in one aspect.

out of place for me here to consider. It is as a disciple of Spinoza, carrying the principles of pantheism out logically into his theory of literature and life, — in these relations and no other, — that we have now any special concern with him. He was one of the earliest and foremost of those who hold that the laws of duty are not objective, but subjective; who reject outward authority, and fall back on spontaneous impulse as the true guide of human conduct.

Goethe was enough younger than Kant and Lessing to have been moulded somewhat by their writings. From Jacobi and Herder, also, he may have received hints which gave a pantheistic turn to his thinking. But he was the senior of Schelling, and had become a famous author before Fichte and Hegel were known to the public. From this we infer that he did not take his speculative views from the German successors of Spinoza, so much as from the more original source. He wrote for the many, and they for the few, yet they and he alike followed the same master. {Relation to thinkers of his own age.}

It may surprise some to hear Goethe's name thus joined to Spinoza's. They have never regarded him as a pantheist. He has had multitudes of readers, and still has not a few, whom his superb sentences charm, but who do not perceive his underlying theory of God and the world. What that theory was we need first of all to know; and that our fairness may be above suspicion, it shall be given chiefly in his own words. {Ignorance of his speculative views.}

He has given us an account of the early working of his

mind on religious subjects. Referring to the Lisbon earthquake, which occurred in his sixth year, he says, "The boy who was forced to put up with frequent recitals of the whole matter, was not a little staggered. God, the creator and preserver of heaven and earth, whom the explanation of the first article of the creed declared so wise and benignant, having given both the just and the unjust a prey to the same destruction, had not manifested himself, by any means, in a fatherly character. In vain the young mind strove to resist these impressions."[1] This sceptical bent, he adds, was strengthened by the ravages of a hail-storm at Frankfort the year after. He had a boy's enthusiasm for Frederick the Great, which his friends, wickedly, as he thought, did not share. "In this way," he says, "I was thrown back upon myself; and as, in my sixth year, after the earthquake at Lisbon, the goodness of God had become to me in some measure suspicious, so I began now, on account of Frederick the Second, to doubt the justice of the world."[2] It would seem that, with his faith in God, his reverence also declined. For he says, referring to a later period in his life, "I had believed, from my youth upwards, that I stood on very good terms with my God; nay, I even fancied to myself, according to various experiences, that he might even be in arrears to me; and I was daring enough to think that I had something to forgive him. The presumption was founded on my infinite good-will, to which, as it seemed to me, he should have given better assistance."[3] These admissions are certainly enough to show that

---

[1] Autobiography (Bohn's edition), Vol. I., p. 19.
[2] Ibid., Vol. I., p. 33. [3] Ibid., p. 291.

Goethe's faith in the positive teachings of Christianity had been undermined, and to bear out De Quincey's charge, that he "so corrupted and clouded his mind, as not to look up to God with the interest of reverence and awe, but merely with the interest of curiosity."

Passing, now, from the negative to the positive side of Goethe's creed, we come at once upon the essence of Spinozism. This is his dogmatic position, whatever he may have rejected as a sceptic. Mr. Lewes, one of his most ardent admirers, says, "In his conception of the universe he could not separate God from it. Such a conception revolted him. He animated the universe with God; he animated fact with divine life; he saw in reality the incarnation of the ideal; he saw in morality the high and harmonious action of all human tendencies; he saw in art the highest representation of life."[1] But we are not forced to take the testimony of another, in learning the speculative views of Goethe. He himself has borne witness. At the age of twenty-one, through the works of Bayle, he became acquainted with the theories of Giordano Bruno, the pantheist of the sixteenth century. For this author he conceived a warm sympathy, notwithstanding Bayle's criticisms. And in his note-book, containing comments on what he read, is the following: "To discuss God apart from nature is both difficult and perilous; it is as if we separated the soul from the body. We know the soul only through the medium of the body, and God only through nature. Hence the absurdity, as it seems to me, of accusing those of absurdity who philosophically have

Proofs that he was a pantheist.

---

[1] Life and Works of Goethe (Boston, 1856), Vol. I., p. 74.

united God with the world. For everything which exists necessarily pertains to the essence of God, because God is the one Being whose essence includes all things. Nor does the Holy Scripture contradict this, although we differently interpret its dogmas, each one according to his own views. All antiquity thought in the same way; an unanimity which to me has great significance. To me the judgment of so many men speaks highly for the rationality of the doctrine of emanation; though I am of no sect, and grieve much that Spinoza should have coupled this pure doctrine with his detestable errors."[1] This judgment of Spinoza Goethe afterwards reversed, upon further acquaintance, as we shall see. In saying that the Scriptures are not opposed to pantheism, he simply agrees with other readers who have made their wish father to their thought. And in the same way he mistakes the monotheism of antiquity, expressed in the mystical language of the East, for downright pantheism. But what the quotation brings clearly out is, that Goethe was essentially a pantheist at this period of his life.

The faith thus early adopted was not a mere enthusiasm to be given up with youth. It marked the manhood and old age of our author as well. His views were constantly crystallizing more and more into this form. In his twenty-sixth year he procured the works of Spinoza and studied them for himself. About the same time he also made the acquaintance of Jacobi, who, like himself, was revolving, though never more than half believing, the doctrines of the great master. Here is his record of what he then thought, given in the account

Meets with Jacobi.

---

[1] Life and Works of Goethe, Vol. I., p. 103.

of his conversations with Jacobi. "Happily, I had already prepared if not fully cultivated myself on this side, having in some degree appropriated the thoughts and mind of an extraordinary man; and though my study of him had been incomplete and hasty, I was yet already conscious of important influences derived from this source. This mind, which had worked upon me thus decisively, and which was destined to affect so deeply my whole mode of thinking, was SPINOZA. After looking through the world in vain to find a means of development for my strange nature, I at last fell upon the Ethics of this philosopher. Of what I read out of the work, and of what I read into it, I can give no account. Enough that I found in it a sedative for my passions, and that a free, wide view over the sensible and moral world, seemed to open before me."[1] He declares himself especially pleased with Spinoza's definition of love to God, and of all love, — making it a sentiment which is to be regarded as a kind of personal luxury, and to be cherished by the person exercising it for his own sake, with no reference to any effect it may produce outwardly. "If I love thee, what is that to thee?" came thus to be one of Goethe's favorite sayings. But the underlying principle, though looking very much like disinterestedness in one view of it, would excuse hatred, or any other evil passion, making it nothing to any but ourselves if we choose to entertain the most malicious feelings. It is in this same connection, still referring to Jacobi, that he says, "I could not comprehend what he communicated to me of his state of mind; so much the less indeed, because I could form no idea as to my own. Still, as he was far in

[1] Autobiography, Vol. II., p. 26.

advance of me in philosophical thought, and even in the study of Spinoza, he endeavored to guide and enlighten my obscure efforts."[1]

They are the less intelligent of the friends of Goethe who deny that there is pantheism in his writings; who accuse us of reading it into, rather than in his pages. He disdains all such apology, and is at war with those who make it for him, as shown by the words just quoted. They may affirm that his works should be read without suspicion; but he, in a calm review of his life, declares that Spinoza "affected deeply his whole mode of thinking." As surely as the same fountain cannot send forth sweet waters and bitter, so surely all that Goethe wrote could be, in its religious aspects, only pantheistic. Herder says of him, alluding to a later period in his life, "The only Latin author ever seen in his hand was Spinoza." He often confessed, while arguing with friends, that he thought it better to know God with Spinoza, than to believe in him with Jacobi. Gall's phrenology pleased him, "because it connected man with nature more intimately than was done in the old schools, showing the identity of all mental manifestation in the animal kingdom." "I believe in God, is a beautiful and praiseworthy phrase," he said; "but to recognize God in all his manifestations, that is true holiness on earth."[2] He failed to see anything exceptional or supernatural in Christ; his greatness did not stand alone, but was merely of "as divine a kind as was ever seen on earth. If I am asked whether it is in my nature to pay him devout reverence, I say — certainly. I bow before him as the

(margin note: Wished to be known as a Spinozist.)

[1] Autobiography, Vol. II., p. 27.   [2] Life and Works, Vol. II., p. 307.

divine manifestation of the highest morality. If I am asked whether it is in my nature to reverence the sun, I again say — certainly. For he is likewise a manifestation of the highest Being. I adore in him the light and the productive power of God, by which we live, and move, and have our being."[1] Mr. Lewes says, "Goethe's theosophy was that of Spinoza, modified by his own poetical tendencies; it was not a geometrical, but a poetical pantheism. In it the whole universe was conceived as divine; not as a lifeless mass, but as the living manifestation of Divine Energy ever flowing forth into activity."[2] In the eighty-first year of his life, while completing the second part of his Faust, Goethe said, "What is all intercourse with nature if we merely occupy ourselves with individual material parts, and do not feel the breath of the spirit which prescribes to every part its direction, and orders or sanctions every deviation by means of an inherent law?" Not only does he deify nature, but makes man a part of it, as in the following words: "I had come to look upon my indwelling poetic talent altogether as nature. The exercise of this poetic gift could indeed be excited and determined by circumstances, but its most joyful, its richest action was spontaneous, nay, even involuntary."[3] Here, then, we have the pantheistic spontaneity; that fatalism of Spinoza which makes necessity essential to liberty. He found in himself a creative power, acting automatically, in the free play of which he sought to escape from all tumults.[4] This is the power which he described

Divineness of nature.

Free necessity.

[1] Life and Works, Vol. II., pp. 397, 398.   [2] Ibid.,
[3] Autobiography, Vol. II., p. 66.

in his Prometheus, a poem which both Lessing and Jacobi pronounced thoroughly pantheistic. The play of Egmont assumes all along the presence of a divine force working through human action in obedience to its own fatal tendencies. "Man imagines that he directs his life, that he governs his actions, when in fact his existence is irresistibly controlled by his destiny." One of the most admired passages in the whole play is the following, in which the doctrine of a free necessity is taught: "I see before me spirits, who, still and thoughtful, weigh in ebon scales the doom of princes and of many thousands. Slowly the beam moves up and down; deeply the judges appear to ponder; at length one scale sinks, the other rises, breathed on by the caprice of destiny, and all is decided." Goethe would carry this doctrine of a fate, working unhindered in and through man, so far as to make men irresponsible for their religious beliefs. "In faith everything depends on the fact of believing; what is believed is perfectly indifferent. Faith is a profound sense of security for the present and future; and this assurance springs from confidence in an immense, all-powerful, and inscrutable being. The firmness of this confidence is the one grand point; but what we think of this being depends on our other faculties, on even our circumstances, and is wholly indifferent." [1]

We should hardly expect a writer, whose chosen sphere is poetry and fiction, to make his theoretical views very prominent. We must look for them, rather, in the general tone of his works, and in the spirit actuating his favorite characters. Goethe held that it is the business of literature not to teach or mould men, but to paint the life of

[1] Autobiography, Vol. II., p. 15.

nature and society. Claiming to be only an artist in all his writings, he was careful not to give them a dogmatic or controversial air. Nevertheless, the under-current of theory is traceable almost everywhere; nor is he able always to keep back decisive utter- *Tone of his writings.* ances of his views. We have just noticed some of these; and still others remain, for one or two of which room shall be made. In his Wilhelm Meister the following words are put into the mouth of Theresa, one of the least faulty characters in the work: "I cannot understand how any one can believe that God speaks to us through books and histories. If the universe does not immediately explain our connection with him, if our own heart does not explain our obligation to ourselves and others, we can scarcely expect to derive that knowledge from books, which seldom do more than give names to our errors."[1] Even in the noble poem of Faust, that grandest creation of Goethe's genius, he does not keep his pantheistic creed out of sight. Margaret fears that the man she so tenderly loves is not a Christian. He evades her questions, and strives to quiet her mind by uttering this rhapsody: —

> " The All-embracer
> All-sustainer,
> Doth he not embrace, sustain
> Thee, me, himself?
> Lifts not the heaven its dome above?
> Doth not the firm-set earth beneath us lie?
> And beaming tenderly with looks of love,
> Climb not the everlasting stars on high?
> Are we not gazing in each other's eyes?

[1] Wilhelm Meister (Bohn's edition), p. 430.

> Nature's impenetrable agencies,—
> Are they not thronging on thy heart and brain,
> Viewless, or visible to mortal ken,
> Around thee weaving their mysterious reign?
> Fill thence thy heart, how large soe'er it be,
> And in the feeling when thou'rt wholly blest,
> Then call it what thou wilt, — Bliss! Heart! Love! God!
> I have no name for it — 'tis feeling all.
> Name is but sound and smoke
> Shrouding the glow of heaven."

This confession of faith, put into the mouth of Faust, fails to satisfy Margaret. It strengthens the suspicion that her lover is not a Christian, though it makes ample room for the religion she professes, and for all the sad indiscretion into which she has been tempted. He, and she, and the religious faith of each, and the wild love which has drawn them together, are alike but forthputtings of the divine essence of all things, every motion of which is sacred, and to obey which is our true worship for the time being, though external standards of right should condemn the act, and only feelings of bitter remorse result from it. No critic has been bold enough to claim that he fully understands this poem. Yet the clew to it, if I mistake not, is Goethe's own experience. As in nearly all his works, so here, only more profoundly, he deals with those deep heart-troubles which his own wild doings had occasioned, and seeks repose in that pantheistic scheme which makes all human conduct both fatal and divine. In all his writings, as in those now quoted, Goethe claims that he is purely an artist. But he holds that it is the province of art to represent life. Yet life means the free play of all the forces of nature, of which every passion or instinct of man is a part, and the artist must first experience whatsoever he would represent. Nothing in our humanity is evil, but it is altogether sacred and divine. True holiness forbids us to repress any longing, and consists in acting out to their utmost all our impulses and desires. "The result of all my thoughts and endeavors was the old resolution to investigate inner and outer nature, and to allow her to rule herself in loving imitation. I sought to free myself internally from all that was foreign to me, to regard the external with love, and to allow all beings, from man downwards, as low as they were comprehensible, to act upon me, each after its own kind." [1]

Now, the impression which this pantheistic view of life and the function of the writer makes on us, must depend almost altogether upon the nature of the subjects which happen to be treated. The compass of the instrument is without limit; and the tones it gives forth will excite joy or pain, at the pleasure of the performer. Goethe's theory enables him to charm that which is highest, and gratify that which is lowest, in human nature. He stands within a pantheon where our noblest and basest passions may all be gathered. If we complain that he throws a halo of divinity about vice and crime, we must also own that he paints virtue in some of its sublimer forms. He makes no difference in kind between the good and the bad, but honors them both alike in their turn. There are two Goethes, and while listening to one we almost doubt the existence of the other.

The two Goethes.

We see nothing to offend our moral sense, for instance,

[1] Autobiography, Vol. I., pp. 469, 470.

while we look at him in his scientific studies. Here the subject is one which hardly admits of moral distinctions. The pantheist may deal with natural phenomena as justly as the Christian, though indulging a worship of nature which Christianity forbids. Goethe might have been a great naturalist, had he not chosen to be a poet. As it is, his name will never cease to be mentioned with honor by the friends of science. He was an observer, rather than an interrogator of nature; and like the idealist that he was, his conclusions were generally the starting-points in researches: yet he established facts, and threw out hints, which have led on to some of the most marvellous results in scientific thinking. The history of comparative anatomy cannot be written without reference to him. His discovery of the intermaxillary bone in man overturned a false theory in science which had prevailed for centuries; it went far to establish the truth, so fruitful in the hands of his successors, that the osseous structures of all living animals are built up after a single pattern. He it was, too, who first called attention to the fact that the skull, in man and all animals, is simply a terminal vertebra in the spinal column, more or less expanded. Scientific men hailed this discovery, as they did the other, with delight; and from it sprang the doctrine, now established, that all the bone any animal has is back-bone, — either the main column or one or more of its offshoots.

In botany, also, Goethe's work on the Metamorphoses of Plants may be said to have suggested, if it did not originate, what is now the distinctive doctrine and boasted glory of modern science. He showed, more or less successfully, that all plants conform to a single type in their structure; that in their development, from stage to stage, they only repeat the universal type, — embodying it now imperfectly, and now in forms which approach perfection. This type he declared to be the leaf; and he proved, by a valid process, that even fruits and flowers are but modified leaves. Since, however, many plants lack what may be properly termed a leaf, some more general type was sought. The result was the discovery of the cell, which is common to animals and plants, thus laying the basis of absolute unity in nature. To other men, advocates of the so-called development theory, belongs the credit of working out this discovery to its wonderful results. Yet they all name Goethe as the master who gave them the right clew to nature, and an impulse which still carries them forward. In optics Goethe was not so successful. We have seen that he did not belong to the school of inductive philosophy. The unity of nature was with him a transcendental truth. Possibly this was the secret of his opposition to the Newtonian doctrine that light is a compound substance. Look- . *In optics.* ing for unity in all things, he assumed that light must be a simple substance; and he proclaimed this theory, unfortunately, when he had happened to observe a single fact which seemed to him to confirm it. The theory was a mistake. That doctrine of nature which had led him aright in the other cases, here betrayed him into error. Yet he fought for his theory as long as he lived. Neither argument nor ridicule could move him. He experimented, and argued, and wrote, with a constantly growing zeal. He contended that his doctrine of light outweighed in value all the other achievements of his life. The fact that certain a-priori thinkers, Hegel among them, inclined to believe his theory, enabled him to bear the derision of scientific men far and near.

In one class of his purely literary works, too, Goethe's pantheism does not greatly shock our moral convictions. I allude to those which are on classic subjects, simply reviving the spirit of antiquity, or which deal chiefly with the nobler tendencies of human nature. In all his works, even those which deify wickedness, we may choose out passages admirable for their moral tone; but this lofty spirit is characteristic of some, as it is not of others. His shorter poems, if we sift out a class, give charming utterance to almost everything bright or good in human life. He has written lyrics which might serve as vehicles of the purest emotion. In their simplicity and truth to nature, they are equal to the finest models of the ancients. His Iphigenia in Tauris, also, is worthy of his great powers. He transports himself into the serene air of antiquity, lives amid its scenes, breathes its loftiest spirit. Sophocles himself could not speak more nobly of the pure but fated daughter of Agamemnon. The guile of the ancient Greek is allowed to come out, in her dealing with the Taurian king; and here Goethe shows more sympathy with her fault than we could wish. But in everything essential to womanhood, as judged by the standard of those days, — in filial devotion, patriotism, maidenly innocence, and the sacrificial spirit, — he makes her fill out the highest ideal. Nor can it be denied that there are passages in the play of Egmont which are not only worthy even of a Shakespeare's genius, but in which the sharpest morality can see little to condemn. It is true that he violently distorts history, and shows a fiercely democratic scorn for social distinctions; yet we almost forget *this, together with the doctrine of fatalism running through the play, while we read the address to sleep, put into the mouth of the imprisoned Egmont; and as Clara, who had hoped to be his bride, says to the cowering Netherlanders, "I have neither arms, nor the strength of a man; but I have that which ye all lack — courage and contempt of danger. O that my breath could kindle your souls! That, pressing you to this bosom, I could arouse and animate you! Come, I will march in your midst. As a waving banner, though weaponless, leads on a gallant army of warriors, so shall my spirit hover, like a flame, over your ranks, while love and courage shall unite the dispersed and wavering multitude into a terrible host." One other specimen of this better class of Goethe's writings I must not fail to name — the beautiful poem of Hermann and Dorothea. Nothing sweeter can be found in the whole range of idyllic or epic poetry. The description of the train of exiles, of the meeting of the lovers, of the old landlord and his wife, of the village pastor and doctor, of the garden, the vineyard, the encampment, the harnessing of the horses, the finding of Dorothea, her meeting with Hermann at the well, their walk homeward in the evening, and the betrothal, cannot be surpassed for vivid and charming naturalness. Yet the whole story covers but a single day, — too short a time, we feel, for an entirely new love thus to ripen; and the noble Dorothea

Hermann and Dorothea.

seems to forget too easily her former lover, but lately slain in battle, whose golden pledge she still wears on her finger.

From this class of works, in which the law of spontaneity yields so little to offend us, we turn to another. Here the influence of pantheism, glorifying whatever it touches, fails to satisfy our moral convictions. The spontaneity which charmed us where all the tendencies were right, begins to repel us where they are wrong. We hold that man has a lower nature, which is to be repressed, as well as a higher nature, which may act itself out freely. It is the consistency of Goethe, as a pantheist, that offends us. He dares to be true to his theory, — to show how it deifies the bad no less than the good. His Faust has been mentioned. Could anything show more clearly what bitter fruit pantheism may be made to yield, than that wonderful poem? The longing of man to gratify even his lowest passions is sacred, and cannot be resisted; yet the gratification is all the time plunging him into deeper wretchedness. The only escape from this miserable fate which Goethe can suggest, is "renunciation," — not the surrender of one's self to the holy and divine law of Christ, but to this same foredoomed and tormenting activity.

Wherein his theory works evil.

Faust.

How indiscriminate pantheism is in dealing with right and wrong, may be seen in our author's first famous production, Goetz von Berlichingen. Here the law of spontaneity is seen at work in political relations. The personality of the hero, and not public justice, is made the basis of action. He finds the state in his own impulses, and he dares to obey this inward

Goetz von Berlichingen.

authority, regardless of external standards. Goetz is the ideal of a predatory baron of mediæval times. He dwells in his own castle, surrounded by his retainers, in German wilds. To the Emperor Maximilian he swears allegiance; yet no one but himself is to say what that allegiance requires of him. He often shows it by trampling on the imperial commands. With his fellow-barons he is perpetually at war. Goethe paints him as a champion of the weak; but in defending some he wantonly wrongs others, as the following case will show: A poor tailor owes two hundred florins, which he is unable to pay. He applies to Goetz for help. The sympathies of the baron are touched, and, lacking the money himself, he waylays and robs a couple of merchants, and out of the booty the tailor's wants are supplied. Thus is an impulse of generosity made to outweigh justice. The deed goes with the flighty purpose, for the law of duty is within. Not established principles, but that subjective law is the guide, and it may modify outward standards, or trample on them, as to itself seems good. Many natural traits in Goetz are noble. He values his reputation for honor among those who are of his own class. His word once given is sacred. He hesitates to break his parole even with a treacherous foe, and at the risk of his life. Viewed in the light of his own personality, and of his generosity to those whom he befriends, his conduct is admirable; but as judged by conscience, in view of the rights of society, only the verdict of strong disapproval can be given. The theory of morals which Goethe thus favors is ably refuted by Müller, where he says, "An action which contradicts the moral law is not justified by the mere

False theory of morals.

fact that, by an anomaly within an anomaly, it happens to proceed not from selfish but from good motives in some one particular case. Man is to regard the objective connection of a mode of action contrary to the law with the principle of selfishness as an unconditional veto against that action, even though he may imagine that he has in some special case the most excellent motives prompting him thereto. Indeed, in the very self-assertion of his own subjectivity, as the determining and deciding power in the face of the plain dictates of the moral law, there is an arrogance side by side with noble-mindedness, enthusiasm, and what not, whose real source is selfishness."[1] It is with reference to Goethe's doctrine that Müller thus argues; of whom he says, in another place, "There is certainly a tendency, in Goethe's view of the world, to regard power and activity as the essence of morality." Much might be quoted, besides what appears in Goetz, to sustain this charge. The following lines are a specimen, in which complaint is made that men obey external rules to the neglect of the impulses of their own natures: —

> "Laws are a fatal heritage, —
> Like a disease, an heir-loom dread;
> Their curse they trail from age to age,
> And furtively abroad they spread.
> Reason doth nonsense, good doth evil grow;
> That thou'rt a grandson is thy woe.
> But of the law on man impressed
> By nature's hand, there's ne'er a thought."

We need not wonder that Goetz was read and admired

---

[1] Christian Doctrine of Sin, Book I., Pt. I., Chap. III.

by all Germany. Besides graphic pictures of
the wild life described, it fell in with the pre- *Its popular-*
vailing temper of the times. Goethe is sur- *ity.*
passed by no writer for skill in giving such food as
the public taste may chance to demand. He was fully
aware of this gift, and in his Autobiography tells us, at
considerable length, what pains he took to cultivate it.
He watched the currents of popular feeling; he was careful to launch each new literary venture on a favoring tide.
Goetz was written for the wild, revolutionary spirit which
he saw surging about him. It gave the masses of his
countrymen, ground under foreign oppressors, just the
voice of proud defiance which they wanted. It pleased
their national vanity, and made them feel how right it is
to disobey tyrants. Goethe held that it is the function of
literature to paint life; and in his first venture he had
succeeded so well, that a whole people read in his words
the story of its greatness, its wrongs, its too long smothered wrath, its flaming thirst for vengeance.

The evil of pantheism, in making man altogether divine,
and putting him under the dominion of fate, comes more
clearly out in the Sorrows of Werther, Goethe's
second great literary venture. Here it is not *Sorrows of Werther.*
superiority to civil law, but the right to dispose
of his own life, which the individual is made to claim.
The theory that all human impulses are sacred, and a law
to themselves, is fearlessly carried out. Even the suicidal
tendency is allowed free course. Werther was read, on
its first appearance, with unbounded enthusiasm. It paints
that experience which almost all persons undergo in passing from childhood to manhood or womanhood. It enters

fully into this sentimental period, and describes, in most sympathetic words, the vague unrest, the longings, the disgusts, from which so many youth suffer. Hence its amazing popularity. Every lovesick suitor, unrecognized genius, discarded sweetheart, and hopeless aspirant for social position or public honor, read it as the utterance of a personal sorrow. If it had been a satire, ridiculing their moodiness, it might have saved them. But they found in it no such purpose. It not only voiced forth their heart-weariness to this large class of readers, but pictured their unrest as something divine and sacred. They were driven on by a fate to which ready obedience is always noble. They could say, " The coursers of time, lashed, as it were, by invisible spirits, hurry on the light car of our destiny, and all that we can do is, in cool self-possession, to hold the reins with a firm ·hand, and to guide the wheels, now to the right, now to the left, avoiding a stone here or a precipice there. Whither it is hurrying who can tell? And who, indeed, can remember the point from which it started?"[1] Their weariness of life is not portrayed as a weakness; they are not instructed to rise above it. On the contrary, it is made a part of that which constitutes their true nobility. It is the play of the divine life in their human consciousness. " The resolution to preserve my inward nature intact," says Goethe, " according to its peculiarities, and to let external nature influence me according to its qualities, impelled me to the strange element in which Werther is written."[2]

It is not necessary to claim, here, that Goethe meant especially to justify the practice of suicide, in writing this

[1] Egmont.   [2] Autobiography, Vol. I., p. 470.

work. We may admit what he says in his Autobiography, that Werther "neither approves nor censures, but develops sentiments and actions in their consequences."[1] Undoubtedly he was not conscious of any didactic aim. Perhaps he did not even see that Werther grew logically out of his philosophical views. Yet that it is a work which pantheism legitimates no one can deny; nor can the influence of it, on a person of morbid or suicidal temper, be at all doubtful. Goethe himself says of it, "My friends were led astray by my work; for they thought that poetry ought to be turned into reality; that such a moral was to be imitated, and that, at any rate, one ought to shoot himself. What had first happened here among a few afterwards took place among the larger public."[2] A great many cases of self-murder came to Goethe's notice, in which the victims attributed their rash act to the influence of Werther. He was overwhelmed with letters from persons meditating suicide, and he made journeys into various parts of the country to dissuade poor sufferers from such a step. Yet his interest in these unfortunates was mainly artistic. For the most part, he studied their disease, not to cure it, but for the sake of that culture which he sought in every phase of human experience. "I think it is as absurd to say that a man who destroys himself is a coward, as to call a man a coward who dies of a malignant fever," are words which he puts into the mouth of Werther. The morbid yearning for death is inevitable; it works like a fever in the veins. The great spirit of nature, revealed in the consciousness of the victim, impels him forward till the deadly shot is fired.

Its influence.

[1] Autobiography, Vol. I., p. 513.   [2] Ibid., Vol. I., pp. 511, 512.

Goethe confesses that Werther is mainly himself. The work describes a morbid experience which he went through, and which came near proving fatal. He became ardently attached to a young woman, and was made wretched by learning that she had been already betrothed to one of his friends. Her womanly firmness, in refusing his attentions, drove him to despair. He even contemplated suicide. "Among a considerable collection of weapons," says he, "I possessed a handsome, well-polished dagger. This I laid every night by my bed, and before I extinguished the candle, I tried whether I could succeed in plunging the sharp point a couple of inches into my heart."[1] But while he was in this state, it happened that another young man, of his circle, did commit suicide under a disappointment precisely like his own. This gave Goethe his chance. He began to laugh at his own melancholy, which he saw reflected in the act of his friend. It is greatly to be regretted that he did not imitate Cervantes, and conceive his Werther in the ludicrous vein of Don Quixote; for then he might have saved others, while cleansing his own bosom of its perilous stuff. But he chose rather to turn his friend's fate into sympathetic narrative and glowing eulogy. The young man thus suddenly cut off by his own hand was widely known and admired. His death, in the circumstances, caused a deep sensation. There was a romance in his fate which every one wished to know. Goethe, seeing this double opportunity, resolved at once to cure himself by turning the whole affair into a story. Hence the book, and the eagerness of people to read it. He

Origin of the work.

[1] Autobiography, Vol. I., pp. 508, 509.

says, speaking of himself and his readers, "Tortured by unsatisfied passions, by no means excited from without to important actions, with the sole prospect that we must adhere to a dull, spiritless citizen-life, we became — in gloomy wantonness — attached to the thought, that we could at all events quit life at pleasure. This feeling was so general, that Werther produced its great effect precisely because it struck a chord everywhere."[1] He saw the train laid for him, that is; and, quick as he ever was to see the popular craving, he applied his lighted match. The blaze was prodigious, so long as the material which fed it lasted. The glow of composition, and public applause, wrought a cure in his own case. But in thus freeing himself he put a poisoned cup into other hands, the deadly effects of which cannot be now computed.

Goethe had made free use of the names of his best friends in Werther. Greatly to their surprise, they found a very undesirable notoriety thrust upon them. They received many letters of sympathy on account of this usage, and were obliged to avoid the curious gaze of the public. A deep stain rested on Goethe's honor, and he was made aware of their honest displeasure. Strange to say, he neither denied the charge nor felt sorry for it. It seemed to him to be no occasion for a breach of friendship. All had been done in the interest of art, for which every one should be glad to suffer. His friends should regard themselves as a sacrifice on that high altar to which he also was devoted. Thus had they helped him in his wonderful achievement; and they were wanting in artistic spirit if now disposed to

Complaints of his friends.

[1] Autobiography, Vol. I., p. 507.

complain. The apology did not suffice. Even if honestly meant, which seems hardly possible, it was taken as insult added to injury. It is not much of a privilege to be dissected alive, even though some new truth of physiology should thereby be shown. It was one thing to the painter, and quite another to his blooming wife, whom he had just married, when he exclaimed, in the excess of his rapture at her beauty, "Into paint will I grind thee, my bride."

It is important to notice here one other of Goethe's works, the Wilhelm Meister, — which shows the working of the law of spontaneity in social and domestic relations. If he made pantheism break the bonds of civil order in Goetz, and of probation itself in Werther, in Wilhelm Meister it dissolves all family ties, and confuses our notions of intercourse between man and man. Great as Goethe is, and admirable in the handling of noble subjects, we cannot approve, but must earnestly condemn, while we see him so applying his theory as to place vice and virtue on the same pedestal, and throw the garb of innocency around crime. His doctrine of abandonment to art may have satisfied his own conscience in this; but even art has its limit, — a thus far and no farther, — which it should sacredly heed. If it be true, as Goethe has said, that the writer can describe only what he has experienced, no one can envy him his preparation for Wilhelm Meister. But he gave the word "experience" a broad sense, including that sympathy with nature, and with other men, which we feel, and which, aided by the imagination, enables us to share in all the life about us. Whatever we may think of some of the events and

Marginal note: Wilhelm Meister.

characters in the work, therefore, and though much of it recalls what Goethe has told us of his own wild doings, yet we need not infer that he really went through such a life as he depicts to us. He experienced it artistically, for the sake of the culture which was his aim. There is one Book in Wilhelm Meister, entitled the Confessions of a Fair Saint, which the most exacting may read with pleasure. The subject of the story is a Moravian, in her religious faith; and Goethe, while tracing the course of her outward and inward life, makes most charming use of his knowledge of the Moravians, some of whom were among his dearest friends. Yet he seems to value their faith purely for artistic purposes, and he accounts for it in a wholly natural way, just as for any other social phenomenon, whether pleasing or repulsive. He intimates that the saint-like lady, whose story he is telling, is not altogether of a sane mind; that he learned the facts in her history from a physician, who had treated her for mental disease; that she had been unusually gay in early life; from which she was turned, by a bitter disappointment in love, to seek solace in prayerful retirement.[1] And thus it turns out at last that the piety of the Moravians is good only as a charming story can be made out of it; and that that story properly finds a place in the same volume with those of mere pleasure-seekers, since it was due to natural causes that the subject of it came to be so much unlike them. There is really the same defect in her as in those characters of the work which most offend us: it is the want of a clear ethical basis of conduct, — which was not a fault in

The Fair Saint.

[1] Wilhelm Meister (Bohn's edition), p. 326. Autobiography, Vol. I., p. 290.

Goethe's eye, as indeed it could not be, since his naturalism did not recognize it as possible. Morality is but a part of nature; and what men call conscience, and right and wrong in human conduct, are chiefly due to artificial rules and a false education.

As Goethe's best characters are not ethically good, so his worst characters are never artistically bad. Even Philina is a creation that pleases us while we shut our eyes to the moral law. She is modelled on the theory that human beings are like the fowls of the air, and may live the same free life as they. Her conduct has no regard to external rules or proprieties, but springs wholly out of the unchastened impulses of her own heart. She is playful, generous, entertaining, sympathetic, not without genius, equal to any exigency; yet she loves just when and how she will, and acts out every impulse of her nature, with no compunctions or regrets. She is a creature without a conscience, and flies from one pleasure to another, never shamed by her past follies, or having in view any object but present enjoyment. The Decalogue and Sermon on the Mount are no more a law to her, than to the bobolink which sings in the meadow. Mignon, all heart and soul, and whose poor little body so trembles in the storm of her own feelings, wins us. Yet she, too, seems wholly destitute of an ethical nature. Her life is purely spontaneous, the evil in her working as freely as the good; and the story of her parentage makes that to be natural and inevitable, which our marriage laws and our conscience brand as infamous. The same may be said of nearly all the characters in Wilhelm Meister,—Mariana, Aurelia, Lothario, the Melinas, Serlo,

Friedrich, the Countess. They have noble traits, and some of them have many; yet no difference is put between the noble and the base in them. That which offends our moral sense is allowed the same freedom as that which we approve. The higher nature is no more sacred than the lower, and works itself out no more spontaneously, irrespective of established laws or maxims. The work on Elective Affinities is, philosophically, a part of Wilhelm Meister; and there the law of spontaneity, freeing men from positive restraints, and giving a loose rein to everything in their nature, overwhelms the loving Ottilie with a fatal sorrow, destroys the domestic peace of Edward and Charlotte, and turns the most delightful of friendships into a ghastly tragedy. If men and women were angels, it might do for them to hold that all their "affinities" are divinely right, and should have free course. But conscious as they are of tendencies which if indulged would result in a moral and social chaos, they need another law, — the law which warns them to put down the inward motions of sin, and look on the glory of Christ till changed into the same image. The noblest character in Wilhelm Meister, Natalia, has this fault — she never regards vice from the ethical point of view. And the same is true of Theresa. They follow the higher tendencies in humanity, yet seem to regard as equally innocent those who follow the lower. Wilhelm himself, who has been one of this latter class, Natalia receives as her husband, and adopts his child as her own, though aware of the wild life he has led, and which he is slow to abandon. Nothing in her conduct shows that she is

Other characters.

Elective Affinities.

Natalia and Wilhelm.

ruled by her moral nature. She is wholly æsthetic. Wilhelm and his roving friends are not objects of blame to her. They have followed their own bent, just as she has followed hers. Their doings were different from hers, owing to a difference in natural endowments and surroundings. Even the Abbé, Goethe's ideal of a clergyman, regards the past life of Wilhelm as a wholesome schooling, through which he was fated to pass. He has acted as he felt impelled to, and is no more blameworthy than the robins, who choose their mates, and pillage, and sing, in the farmer's orchard. He has done nothing to sorrow over with a godly sorrow. Joined to Natalia, whose stronger nature will control him, the verdict of the Abbé is, " You will never repent nor repeat your follies; and this is the happiest destiny which can be allotted to man."

From this notice of the works of Goethe I pass to the man himself. Did his pantheistic spirit bear the same fruit in his life as in his writings? To ask the question is to answer it, for his writings confessedly grew out of his life. He is Werther, he is Faust, he is Wilhelm Meister. No doubt it was his wish to be read purely as an artist. But we cannot distinguish between him and his works, as we do between Raphael and the Transfiguration or Last Supper. He casts a roseate light upon sinful deeds. He makes a mode of life which is shamefully wrong, look beautiful and inviting. He brings vice forward in such bewitching forms as to tempt the susceptible reader. Multitudes have accepted his works, not as art, but as the true philosophy of life. Such they were to himself. He held that his nature

Goethe's theoretical views in his own life.

was wholly divine; that each one of his impulses contained its own law; that no external rule could judge him. This faith he dared to practise; and we need, for our own admonition, to see some of the evils into which it led him. *His faults not to be passed over.* This is my reply to those who say that the faults of Goethe should be covered up and forgotten. A writer in one of the English periodicals seems to me to speak justly, where he says, " A certain school of philosophers has even become indignant with anybody who searches into the moral character of the illustrious dead, to see whether or not they conformed strictly to the Ten Commandments. Surely, they hint, men of genius are not to be tested by the Ten Commandments. No heresy, however, can be so mischievous as that which teaches that there is, for different degrees of genius, a different moral code. Moral distinctions are a barrier erected by society between itself and danger, and are assiduously cultivated by educators and legislators to that end; and this barrier is nowhere needed more than in the case of great genius. Great intellectual or material strength, unaccompanied by moral sensibility, is an enemy to mankind's happiness, quite as much as a wild beast is to the repose of an African village."[1]

In noticing the faults of Goethe, which his views of life helped to develop, that which was noble and pleasing in him should not be kept out of sight. He had kind impulses; he gave liberally of his means to the needy; he visited the wretched, and sought to make them forget their trouble; he aided *Noble traits.*

[1] Saturday Review, 1868.

poor students with his advice and money; he counselled young authors, gave them friendly criticism, recommended them to publishers. Such was the culture which he bestowed on the better side of his nature. Thus did the more amiable tendencies in him blossom out and ripen, under the law of spontaneous action. But his culture was not limited to this sphere. It was as broad as his whole humanity. It embraced other tendencies not so admirable. He had, for instance, a natural dread of hardship, and loved a quiet, peaceful life. This trait he cherished; and it was more sacred to him than popular rights, or the honor of his nation. He disliked to see the Germans rising in arms for their liberty, since the peaceful pursuit of culture would thereby be interrupted. He declared that he was unconscious of such a sentiment as love of country. In trying to be a patriot, he should be a hypocrite. All governments are only artificial devices; one was just as bad as another, to him who made nature his rule; and all he asked of any was, to leave him free to act as he pleased. "When we have a place in the world where we can repose with our property," said he, "a field to nourish us, and a house to cover us, have we not there our fatherland? and have not thousands upon thousands got this? and do they not live happy in their limited sphere? Wherefore, then, this vain striving for a sentiment we neither have nor can have, — a sentiment which only in certain nations, and in certain periods, is the result of many concurrent circumstances." These words were addressed to the people of Germany, the object being to dissuade them from making war on Napoleon, who was then moving to over-

Want of patriotism.

throw their nation. The argument is, that nature had not destined them for political dominion. Let them, therefore, quietly enjoy what happened to be theirs, indifferent to the civil power over them, which was no part of nature. But where were human liberty to-day, we may well ask, if such a doctrine had swayed the hearts of all men? Patriotic Germans have not yet forgiven Goethe for accepting the flatteries of Napoleon, and favoring his claims, even while the French army was laying their country waste; and they have proved, by their achievements under William and Bismarck, securing to them an empire, and placing France at their mercy, that they were not vain in their aspirations, while the peace-loving poet was utterly mistaken. Mr. Lewes, apologizing for Goethe as he best can, says, " Without interest in political affairs, profoundly convinced that all salvation could come only through inward culture, and dreading disturbances mainly because they rendered such culture impossible, he was emphatically the 'child of peace,' and could at no period of his life be brought to sympathize with great struggles." [1] Every high sentiment in us agrees with the Christian poet, when he says, —

> "Great truths are greatly won. Not found by chance,
> Nor wafted on the breath of summer-dream,
> But grasped in the dread struggle of the soul,
> Hard buffeting the adverse wind and stream;
>
> " Wrung from the troubled spirit, in hard hours
> Of weakness, solitude, perchance of pain,
> They spring like harvest from the well-ploughed field,
> And the soul feels it has not wept in vain."

[1] Life and Works of Goethe, Vol. II., p. 168.

But Goethe's method of culture calls forth from us no such response. The way which he prefers goes around the Gethsemanes and Calvarys of life. Though a prince of moral disorder, he loves repose, — that soft and dreamy peace which no outward trouble disturbs, while it allows free play to each fond desire.

Shrinking, as he thus did, from all hardship and pain, Goethe could not carry the law of spontaneity out thoroughly in his life. His own peace of mind obliged him to repress some of his impulses, and to regulate even those which he indulged.

<small>Goethe not consistent with his theory.</small>

He often held his natural sympathy in check; says, "I carefully avoided seeing Schiller, Herder, the Duchess Amalia, in the coffin." The feeling of indignation which springs in every heart at the sight of wrongdoing he sought to overcome. "He who hates vices hates men," was one of his strange maxims. We are to love all things just as they are, however bad. Nothing should excite our hatred or pity, but only our joy. "He who rightly knows that all things follow from the necessity of the divine nature, and come to pass in conformity with the eternal laws of nature, will never meet with anything worthy of hatred or contempt; neither will he commiserate any one."[1] Thus taught Spinoza, and Goethe aimed to live out the precept. He made new friends, forsook old friends, moved from place to place, both gave and broke the tenderest pledges, as his plans or present comfort seemed to require. "The most lovable heart," he said, "is that which loves most readily; and that which easily loves also easily forgets." At one time he was

---

[1] Spinoza's Ethics, Part IV., Prop. I., Scholium.

attracted to the society of the Moravians; but finding their piety irksome to him, and their morals too strict for his habits of life, he withdrew from them.[1] "It had become a standing custom with me, whenever I read missionary intelligence to Fraülein von Klettenberg, which she was very fond of hearing, to take the part of the pagans against the missionaries, and praise their old condition as preferable to their new one." He went through a special course of training, that he might school himself to bear, without pain, unpleasant sights and sounds. He attended surgical lectures, with the view, he says, of freeing himself "from all apprehension as to repulsive things. I have actually succeeded so far that nothing of this kind could ever put me out of my self-possession. But I sought to steel myself, not only against these impressions of the senses, but also against the infections of the imagination. And in this also I went so far, that when a desire came over me once more to feel the pleasing shudder of youth, I could scarcely force it in any degree."[2] It will be seen, therefore, that his repression of nature did not grow out of a high moral purpose, but from the wish to avoid pain. He did not always repress what was evil in him, but often that which was good, and thus tried to give the evil unhindered sway. It was not as a Christian, but as an epicurean, that he sought to regulate the law of spontaneous action. He had not the courage to carry out, on all sides, the doctrine which he puts into the mouth of Faust:

"The scope of all my powers henceforth be this,
To bare my breast to every pang, — to know
In my heart's core all human weal and woe,

[1] Autobiography, Vol. II., p. 33.   [2] Ibid., Vol. I., pp. 321, 322.

To grasp in thought the lofty and the deep,
Men's various fortunes on my breast to heap,
To theirs dilate my individual mind,
And share at length the shipwreck of mankind."

Yet too little inconsistent. It is greatly to be regretted that Goethe was not even more inconsistent with his theory than we have now seen. If he had put down some of the impulses which he freely indulged, his life might not have been, in some of its aspects, the sad picture which it is. No respectable critic, however friendly to him, has attempted to justify his domestic and social life. Even Dr. Hedge, in his Prose Writers of Germany, says, "Unquestionably he was no saint. His wildest admirers have sought no place for him in the Christian calendar. In reading Goethe we do not feel, as when reading Dante or Milton, that we are conversing with a pure and lofty spirit." His habit of trifling with maidenly but susceptible hearts was formed in early youth, and he defended the habit on purely subjective grounds, contending that the usages of society were artificial, and had no right to interfere with the action of nature. He refused all legal sanction to his marriage, except so far as might be necessary for the entailment of his name and wealth. His view of the position and rights of a wife are given where he says, "A wife should manage her household properly, and not censure every little fancy of her husband, but always depend on his return."[1] It is certain that this large indulgence of husbands, which he thus recommends to every wife, he took for granted in his own. Her life had but little acknowledged union with his. He was seldom seen

[1] Wilhelm Meister, p. 431.

with her in the company of other persons. Her sad life wore on in seclusion. Other "fancies" were continually leading him abroad; and into his house came the gay and aspiring, almost daily, to enjoy caresses which he denied to her. This manner of life caused Goethe no self-reproaches, for it grew logically out of his philosophical views. It was not wrong, but right, he would claim. It was the spirit of the universe coming to consciousness in him, and to let it act freely was obedience to the highest law. All the impulses of humanity are divine, was the major premise of his conduct; and he carried the reasoning out into his practice, in the direction now shown, even to old age. This appears in the story of Bettine, who came to Weimar while yet a child. Goethe's fame attracted her. She felt the spell of his intellectual greatness; to be his friend was the summit of her ambition. He saw to what her enthusiasm was carrying her, yet encouraged her love of his now superannuated person. He luxuriated in her affection for him, neither checking it nor seeking to elevate and chasten it, though it was wearing away the foundations of her moral nature. No sigh escaped him, but he smiled only the more blandly, while her brilliant but unschooled nature was breaking from its early moorings, and drifting far out from the lights of Christian faith, where the storm which no one rules beat down upon her. It was Mrs. Browning, with her pure woman's heart, who had pity on the young girl, loving so unwisely, and who, in her poem bewailing Bettine's fate, exclaims, —

> "The bird thy childhood's playing
> Sent onward o'er the sea, —
> Thy dove of hope, — came back to thee
> Without a leaf ! Art laying

> Its cold wing no sun can dry,
> Still in thy bosom secretly."

Allowance to be made to art. It is said that something should be pardoned, in Goethe's life, to his artistic spirit. His adventures were studies preparatory to the exercise of his literary function. He needed to experience all those human feelings which he would describe. He held the maxim of the ancient artist, who said that one cannot paint a horse without first becoming a horse. It would be a relief to know that some of Goethe's doings were for this object, and not simply for the gratification of his natural desires; that they were experienced only in sympathy, by the help of his imagination, though told as facts in his history. If we could grant this, then we should use it to explain what is noblest in his conduct as well as that which offends us. Thus his whole life becomes purely histrionic. When he is generous, when he gives to the poor and visits the wretched, just as when he trifles with the too confiding, he is not moved by a benevolent purpose, but is simply gathering material for the next story, play, or poem. He must become a suicide, in order to write Werther; must go into the woods, and live like a robber, in order to do the character of Goetz full justice; must become a stage-manager, and know actors and actresses intimately, in order to describe their rivalries, and jealousies, and quarrels. This artistic zeal made him partial to all the amusements of the theatre. He wrote many plays for the court-theatre at Weimar, and he aided in them as an actor, not only at home, but in the country around. The impression all along, in Wilhelm Meister, is that men may get their best schooling in the experiences of a theatrical career. Not in the sense of Shakespeare, but literally and seriously, he would have all the world a stage, and men and women merely players. Even though this be not the general rule, he at least is an artist, whose business is to paint life in all its phases; and what he would paint, he must somehow first make a part of himself.

But we join issue with Goethe on this definition. It is not the function of art, but of history and criticism, to deal with actual life. He who portrays life to us should discriminate between the bad and good; should make his representations honor the right always, and condemn whatsoever is wrong. Thus only is he a trustworthy teacher, guarding us against evil, and begetting in us a love of what is pure, and true, and of good report. The ideal realm is that which belongs to art, and its moral purpose should be the same as that of criticism and history, — the ennobling of our better nature. It is therefore bound to avoid all subjects which are low, vile, or degrading in their nature, and to give us only such representations as shall appeal to our upward and godlike tendencies. Here it was that Goethe sadly failed. He puts before his readers, painted in colors wholly sympathetic, scenes which stimulate what is most grovelling in human nature. To his deep dishonor it must be said, that he does not teach us to abhor the vices of society; he does not limit his studies to what is worthy of imitation in life; he does not take what is best in man, lift it up into the ideal realm, make it the material of his conceptions, and clothe it with especial charms, so as to draw us away from all that is vile and sinful, towards that life of pure and holy

The obligations of the artist.

love which is the glory of the Father of our spirits. The artist is false to his great mission, and commits one of the darkest of crimes when he puts us face to face with that which stimulates the evil in our natures. It is his sacred duty to put all such temptations behind our backs; to make us see the gates of the city of love, and admire the beauty of its shining towers, and hear the bells ringing out their joyful peals, till our souls shall long to be there.

The adequate theory of culture. The subjective theory of morals, growing out of pantheism, and adopted by Goethe in his writings and practice, is a half-truth. That which is absolutely right in us, making our life so far forth one with the life of God, is a law unto itself. It should be allowed to act itself out freely. But even in its spontaneous action, it does not cease to be subject to authority. It recognizes the moral law as its counterpart, as the outward embodiment of its own ideal. This law, awful as Sinai and lovely as Tabor, is the externization of itself. Subject as it is to disturbances, to the stormy nights which so often issue from our lower nature, this higher nature in us is glad to sail by the light of the constellations; those eternal stars of truth, hung out by the good God in our moral heavens, and ever reflected in the still depths of conscience, which hold us to our course through all the Euroclydons of life, while we watch for their unchanging signals. The true culture of man is therefore not single, as Goethe held, but a twofold process. It is daily a death and a resurrection from the dead. There is evil in us to be crucified, in order that what is best in us may live. Only as our man which is earthly dies, can our man which is heavenly be renewed. No one but Christ, who is our divine ideal, has ever taught us a doctrine of culture adequate to our case. It is as we bear about daily his dying, that his life also is manifest in our mortal body.. That which is from beneath must decrease, while that which is from above takes increase. That is sown in weakness, while this is raised in power; that is sown a natural body, while this is raised a spiritual body; that is sown in dishonor, while this is raised in glory. Who has not many times sat upon the rocks at eventide, and watched the ships sailing away into the setting sun? Before them all was bright, behind them their own dark shadows lay upon the water. Some of their sails were so set as to be pure and glistering in the light, others so turned away from it as to show a darkened surface; yet all were alike helping to bear the ships onward. Such is the process, not single but twofold in aspect, by which man achieves his noblest culture.

> "There was a soul, one eve autumnal, sailing
>   Beyond the earth's dark bars,
> Towards the land of sunsets never paling,
>   Towards heaven's sea of stars.
> Behind there was a wake of billows tossing,
>   Before a glory lay;
> O happy soul! with all sail set, just crossing
>   Into the far away;
> The gloom and gleam, the calmness and the strife,
> Were death before thee, and behind thee life.
>
> "And as that soul went onward, sweetly speeding
>   Unto its home and light,
> Repentance made it sorrowful exceeding,
>   Faith made it wondrous bright;

Repentance dark with shadowy recollections
    And longings unsufficed,
Faith white and pure with sunniest affections
    Full from the face of Christ.
But both across the sun-besilvered tide
Helped to the haven where the heart would ride."

LECTURE VI.

PANTHEISM IN THE FORM OF HERO-WORSHIP.

THE topic of this lecture suggests the name of Thomas Carlyle more naturally, perhaps, than that of any other man. Whether a pantheist or not, it is sure that the tendency to deify and worship great men has in him an earnest advocate, — its most conspicuous and eloquent champion in modern times. The subject could not be adequately treated apart from his writings; and it is in this relation, and with this purpose, that he is here introduced. I do not propose to consider Carlyle, so much as a certain doctrine which he represents. As in the case of Goethe, it is not the man himself, but the speculative views embodied in his writings, with which I am primarily concerned. In this undertaking I shall make large use of the works of Carlyle, quoting them verbatim as often as I conveniently can.[1] This certainly will be much fairer to him, and much more satisfactory, I hope, to those who would know his views, than any account of him which I might give purely in my own words. Nor does it seem to me

The representative name.

Method of treatment.

---
[1] To save space and repetitions, detached passages, both in this lecture and others, have been sometimes brought together as one quotation, and single words here and there dropped or changed; but in no case has this liberty been taken where it would do violence to the author's meaning.

that I need to make any apology for this method of treatment; since every author knows how much easier it is to write about a person than to present him faithfully in his own language, — especially if the work be candid and conscientious, and so done as to preserve the progress and consecutiveness of the thought, at all of which I shall steadily aim.

The name of Thomas Carlyle holds a place second to but few in the English literature of the last generation. Notwithstanding the cry of outlandishness raised against his style, whether by intelligent critics or stupid Philistinism, he yet has a thorough knowledge of the mother tongue; and, when he chooses to do so, he can write with a classic elegance and power of expression which our best authors might well covet. His disregard of accepted rules and standards is not due to ignorance, so much as to his moods of mind. He knows what he is doing, quite as well as any of his critics, when he casts contempt upon the great models in composition; and a close scrutiny of his most characteristic coinage of words and phrases often reveals an amazing fitness and vitality in them. Though unconventional to the verge of lawlessness, his sentences show themselves the true servants of his ideas and feelings. Whatever violence they may do to the laws of composition, it is clear that he utters them unaffectedly, eager only to be relieved of the host of thoughts in him which struggle for expression. These idiosyncrasies of style are the more remarkable in view of his fondness for Goethe, whose writings are among the best models of the literary art. It was in admiration of this German master, indeed, that Carlyle's career as a man of letters began. His education had been planned with a view to the clerical office in the Scotch church. But he recoiled from what seemed to him the narrowing duties of that office, when he had once drunk at the stream of free thought, then bursting forth so boldly on the continent. The draught intoxicated him. He felt that he had found the door to a new world; a fresh and living world, where intellectual freedom was the only law, not that stale and conventional world to which he had been used. He resolved to explore this foreign literature, beside which the standard literature at home seemed to him so dead. And he threw himself into the undertaking with great spirit; too full of enthusiasm to consider whether it was all truth which he followed, or perhaps judging that that could not be false which so exhilarated and emboldened him.

Such were the impulse and first joyous experience, which led Carlyle, yet a young man, to yield himself up to the influence of Goethe. The decisive step was taken. His mind came into communication with the pantheism of the day, and, in all its future workings, embodied more or less of the spirit of that error. Not that he lost his individuality. His genius was too original and persistent for that. He is always himself, though freely appropriating other men's thoughts, and though his style was greatly affected by his German studies. His philosophizing, if such it may be called, reminds us of the crystals we sometimes see in nature, — cast in the mould which their inherent laws make for them, but stained or clouded by the infusion of foreign matter. If the genius of Goethe was mainly æsthetic, that of Carlyle inclined to be ethical.

One is as true to the Scotch bias as the other to the German. By instinct Carlyle was a moralist; and therefore, to whatever matter he applied himself, instead of treating it simply as an artist, he handled it in the spirit of a critic and reformer. If Goethe held that it was the whole function of literature to paint life, Carlyle even more stoutly held that literature should concern itself with the relations of life, and their adjustment between man and man. It was with this reformatory bent of mind that he set out in his literary career. And we are now to see whither it carried him after he had broken loose from his early moorings; when he no more turned to the Father of his spirit for guidance into all truth, but committed himself to the stream of his own reasonings and intuitions.

Ethical tendency.

Though fundamentally at one with Goethe, and making Goethe's works his main study for years, he yet chose an entirely different sphere in which to labor. The German was devoted to poetry, science, and fiction, and to society; the Scotchman gave himself mainly to politics, — the term "politics" being used in its highest and broadest sense, inclusive of all that enters into questions of statesmanship and government. Nor has this political reformer, so far as appears, fallen into those more vicious habits which Goethe contracted while yielding to the æsthetic bent of his genius. That Carlyle regarded political reform as the field in which his life-work was cast, is clear from the very titles of his chief works : the French Revolution, Past, Present, and Chartism, Cromwell, Frederick the Great, and New Essays in which he discusses Model Prisons, Downing Street, the Stump-Ora-

A political reformer.

tor, Parliaments, and kindred subjects. The Heroes and Hero-worship, though a course of lectures ostensibly literary, yet betrays the fact all along, that he subordinated literature to questions of government. The only works in which this aim does not stand prominent are Sartor Resartus, and some of his earlier essays, written before he had fairly settled himself to his more especial purpose. His Life of John Sterling may also be an exception; but this was written not of choice so much as from a regard for the wishes of his lost friend. His criticisms of the American war under Lincoln, and of the measures for national reconstruction which followed it; his interest in General Eyre while trampling on the rights of England's West India subjects; and his utterances respecting the extension of the franchise among his own countrymen, show, however much to his discredit, that his ruling passion is political. As the opinions and sympathies of an old man, they also confirm the proverb, that the ruling passion is strong in death.

Let us go back a little now, and look at the foundation on which Carlyle built up the temple of his thought. I have not found in his writings any explicit avowal of pantheism as the philosophical and religious basis of his speculations. He has, indeed, so late as the year 1870, denied the charge of pantheism, so often brought against him. Yet his way of doing it shows <small>Was he a pantheist?</small> that he cares little about the matter, in any case; nor does he even define what he means by pantheism? Very likely he could in truth repel many of the charges of his critics; yet he leaves the question so indeterminate, and his opponents are so numerous and persistent, that the case must be settled by a careful study of his writings, rather than by any single denials or avowals. Categorical answers are not to be trusted, where the questioner and the person questioned have different notions of the subject-matter between them. The intelligent student knows pantheism by its looks, wherever found, and whether falsely named or nameless: it need not be labelled for his information, any more than a plant in order to be known by the botanist. Carlyle was totally indifferent to names, which he looked on as only the changing "clothes," and no·part of the permanent essence of philosophy. That he was perfectly content to be known as a pantheist is clear from the fact that he has never seriously, but only now and then satirically resented the charge. It is a point which he always managed to evade when urged by his friends, favoring them with replies too flippant, or too scornfully brief, to be at all satisfactory. It should be said, however, that his ambiguity here, as in many other places, may have been due to a certain grim humor, which he loved to indulge on all occasions. He rather enjoyed the impression of his friends that he was a sort of reckless and impious Titan,— holding theories utterly subversive of the present order of society, though angrily refusing to tell just what they were. But pure philosophy was not his province. It does not appear that he had any immediate knowledge of Spinozism, or of the leading thinkers who revived the doctrines of Spinoza in Germany. He imbibed the essence of that philosophy rather, as it was filtered through the works of a more popular class of authors. He drank it in espe-

Not in the dogmatic sense.

cially from the works of Goethe; nor was its influence upon him weakened, but rather strengthened, by his familiarity with the writings of Heyne, Werner, Richter, Novalis, Lessing. He is not a champion of pantheism, nor even a teacher of it, except incidentally. His distinctive work is in the field of political reform. Yet everywhere we may detect, and that quite easily, the pantheistic infiltration.

Take, for instance, the following view of the history of the human race in Sartor Resartus: "Generation after generation takes to itself the form of a body; and forth-issuing from Cimmerian night, on heaven's mission, APPEARS. What force and fire are in each he expends: one grinding in the mill of industry; one, hunter-like, climbing the giddy Alpine heights of science; one madly dashed in pieces on the rocks of strife, in war with his fellow: — and then the heaven-sent is recalled; his earthly vesture falls away, and soon even to sense becomes a vanished shadow. Thus, like some wild-flaming, wild-thundering train of heaven's artillery does this mysterious MANKIND thunder and flame, in long-drawn, quick-succeeding grandeur. through the unknown deep. Thus, like a God-created, fire-breathing spirit-host, we emerge from the inane; haste stormfully across the astonished earth; then plunge again into the inane. But whence? O Heaven, whither? Sense knows not; faith knows not; only that it is through mystery to mystery, from God and to God."[1] *His idea of history.* Now, this is a most vivid description of the collective life of man, it must be owned, whether correct or

Proofs of a pantheistic spirit.

---

[1] Sartor Resartus (Harpers, New York, 1858), pp. 208, 209.

not; though it has too many double words, and shows more passion than is desirable. But the spirit and tone of it cannot be mistaken. It is thoroughly morbid, and manifestly pantheistic in its morbidness. Nothing in Werther could teach more clearly that our true wisdom is in committing suicide. We may admit, as Carlyle, no doubt, thought while writing the passage, that it is "grand;" but we are constrained to add that it is "gloomy and peculiar." One would not like a friend, in a melancholy state of mind, to read much of that sort of sentimentalizing. It makes us " such stuff as dreams are made of," in a sense not intended by Shakespeare. Its God, the beginning and end of the whole "appearance," is not a living Father, whose hand we may grasp in sweet hope when we step off the stage, but simply the "inane," — the pantheist's blank and dark immensity. That human history, considered as a single movement, is divine so far as it has any reality, seems to be assumed in the following: "The life-tree Igdrasil, wide-waving, many-toned, has its roots down deep in the death-kingdoms, amongst the oldest dead dust of men, and with its boughs reaches always beyond the stars; and in all times and places it is one and the same life-tree."[1] There is but one life, that is, by which all the parts of the universal frame are forever filled.

But Carlyle finds this one absolute essence in the individual man, as really as in the race. "The highest God dwells visibly in that mystic, unfathomable visibility which calls itself *I* on the earth. 'Bending before men,' says Novalis, 'is a reverence

<small>Of the individual.</small>

---

[1] Past, Present, and Chartism (Harpers, 1858), p. 36.

done to this revelation in the flesh. We touch Heaven when we lay our hand on a human body.'"[1] Speaking of the man of letters, Carlyle says, " His life is a piece of the everlasting heart of nature herself: all men's life is, — but the weak many know not the fact, and are untrue to it, in most times; the strong few are strong, heroic, perennial, because it cannot be hidden from them. The unspeakable divine significance, full of wonder and terror, that lies in the being of every man, of every thing, is the presence of God who makes every man and thing."[2] "I find it written. within, and not without, the order of nature; and that all things, like all men, are blood-relations to one another."[3] "In this point of view I consider that, for the last hundred years, by far the notablest of all literary men is Goethe. To that man there was given what we may call a life in the divine idea of the world; vision of the inward divine mystery; and strangely, out of his books, the world rises imaged once more as godlike, the workmanship and temple of God."[4]

In his views of nature, too, of which he thus makes every man a part, Carlyle shows the same pantheistic habit of thought. "All nature and life are but one garment, a living garment, woven and ever a-weaving in the loom of time."[5] "Then sawest thou that this fair Universe, were it in the meanest province thereof, is in very deed the star-domed city of God; that through every star, through every grass-

Views of nature pantheistic.

[1] Past, Present, and Chartism (Harpers, 1858), p. 123.
[2] Hero-worship (John Wiley, New York, 1859), pp. 139, 140.
[3] New Essays (Phillips, Sampson & Co., Boston, 1855), p. 416.
[4] Hero-worship, p. 141.
[5] Sartor Resartus (Harpers, New York, 1858), p. 158.

blade, and most through every living soul, the glory of a present God still beams. But nature, which is the time-vesture of God, and reveals him to the wise, hides him from the foolish."¹ "Beautiful, nay solemn was the sudden aspect to the wanderer. He gazed over those stupendous masses with wonder, almost with longing desire; and never till this hour had he known nature, that she was one, that she was his mother and divine. And as the ruddy glow was fading into clearness in the sky, and the sun had now departed, a murmur of eternity and immensity, of death and life, stole through his soul; and he felt as if death and life were one, as if the earth were not dead, as if the spirit of the earth had its throne in that splendor, and his own spirit were therewith holding communion."² "The world of nature for every man is the fantasy of himself; this world is the multiplex 'image of his own dream.'"³ "There is one God, in and over all. He is the reality. We and all things are but the shadow of him; a transitory garment veiling the eternal splendor."⁴ "This so solid-looking material world is at bottom in very deed nothing; is a visible and tactual manifestation of God's power and presence, a shadow hung out by him on the bosom of the void infinite; nothing more."⁵ "What is the mystery of the universe — Goethe's 'open secret,' seen almost by none? that divine mystery which lies everywhere in all beings, from the starry sky to the grass of the field, which is but the vesture, the embodiment that renders it visible? This divine mystery *is*, in all times and places; veritably is. In most times and places it is greatly overlooked, and the

---

[1] Sartor Resartus, p. 207.   [2] Ibid., p. 120.
[3] Hero-worship, p. 23.   [4] Ibid., p. 50.   [5] Ibid., p. 62.

universe, definable always in one or the other dialect, as the realized thought of God, is considered trivial, inert, commonplace matter, — as if, says the satirist, it were a dead thing, which some upholsterer had put together."[1] "Creation lies before us like a glorious rainbow; but the sun that made it lies behind us, hidden from us. Then, in that strange dream, how we clutch at shadows as if they were substances; and sleep deepest while fancying ourselves most awake. Which of your philosophical systems is other than a dream theorem; a net quotient confidently given out, whose divisor and dividend are both unknown? What are all your national wars, with their Moscow-retreats, and sanguinary hate-filled revolutions, but the somnambulism of uneasy sleepers? This dreaming, this somnambulism is what we on earth call life; wherein the most indeed undoubtingly wander, as if they knew right hand from left; yet they only are wise who know that they know nothing."[2]

If Carlyle means what these latter sentences plainly imply, then why, in the name of that wisdom which he so strangely defines, has he spent all his life trying to tell kingdoms, and republics, and society in general, how much he *knows* about their true nature and the best ways of perpetuating them? Some of his voluminous advice is of so absurd a nature as to go no little way towards establishing his theory of universal nescience, though it certainly excludes him from his own category of the "wise," who, knowing that they know nothing, are precluded from any attempt to teach. I will give but one other quotation under this head, showing that Carlyle, in full sympathy

[1] Hero-worship, p. 72.   [2] Sartor Resartus, p. 41.

with pantheism, looked on all things as making up a single and living whole. "Detached, separated! I say there is no such separation: nothing hitherto was ever stranded, cast aside; but all, were it only a withered leaf, works together with all; is borne forward on the bottomless, shoreless flood of action, and lives through perpetual metamorphoses. The withered leaf is not dead and lost; there are forces in and around it, though working in inverse order, else how could it rot? Despise not the rag from which man makes paper, or the litter from which the earth makes corn. Rightly viewed, no meanest object is insignificant; all objects are as windows, through which the philosophic eye looks into infinitude itself."[1]

The fatalism of the pantheist, as well as his unreality of history, of the individual, and of nature, appears in Carlyle. He speaks of "the ring of necessity whereby we all are begirt;" and adds, "happy he for whom a kind heavenly sun brightens it into a ring of duty, and plays round it with beautiful prismatic diffractions; yet ever, as basis and as bourn for all our being, it is there."[2] Carlyle shows a pantheistic habit, too, in his treatment of the subjects of space and time. He does not regard them as objective realities in his metaphysics, but as purely subjective notions, which the mind imagines in certain processes of thinking. "Think well," says he, "thou too wilt find that space is but a mode of our human sense, so likewise time; there is no space and no time: we are we know not what, — light-sparkles floating in the æther of Deity."[3] "Is the past annihilated, then, or only past? is the future

His doctrine of necessity.

Of space and time.

[1] Sartor Resartus, p. 56.   [2] Ibid., p. 78.   [3] Ibid., p. 42.

non-extant, or only future? Those mystic faculties of thine, memory and hope, may answer: already, through those mystic avenues, thou the earth-blinded summonest both past and future, and communest with them, though as yet darkly, and with mute beckonings. The curtains of yesterday drop down, the curtains of to-morrow roll up; but yesterday and to-morrow both are. Pierce through the time element, glance into the eternal. Believe what thou findest written in the sanctuaries of man's soul, even as all thinkers, in all ages, have devoutly read it there: that time and space are not God, but creations of God; that with God as it is a universal Here, so it is an everlasting Now." [1] He even presses the language of the Scriptures into his service, in stating this doctrine. "Well sung the Hebrew Psalmist: 'If I take the wings of the morning, and dwell in the uttermost parts of the sea, there thou art with me.' Thou, too, O cultivated reader, who probably art no Psalmist, but a prosaist, knowing God only by tradition, knowest thou any corner of the world where FORCE is not?" [2] And so, not only do the Scriptures agree with Carlyle, but the God of the Old Testament is no living Father of men — only an almighty and omnipresent force.

But let us follow Carlyle a little into the proper domain of religion. Here he applies the pantheistic solvent to all forms of faith, recognizing no supernatural inspiration, but finding one and the same divinity, whether in Paganism, Christianity, or Mohammedanism. He puts the Bible in the same category with the Koran, quoting with approbation the saying of Novalis,

Religious views.

[1] Sartor Resartus, p. 205. [2] Ibid., p. 55.

that "the highest problem of literature is the writing of a Bible."[1] "To each nation its believed history is its Bible: not in Judea alone, or Hellas and Latium, but in all lands and all times."[2] "All history is an inarticulate Bible; and, in a dim and inarticulate manner, reveals the divine appearances in this lower world."[3]

<small>Bibles.</small>

"Is there no 'inspiration,' then, but an ancient Jewish, Greekish, Roman one? Quench not, I advise thee, the monitions of that thrice-sacred gospel, holier than all Gospels, which dwells in each man."[4] "Moses and the Jews did not make God's laws; no, indeed; they did not even read them in a way that has been final or satisfactory to me. In several respects I find said reading decidedly bad, and will not, in any wise, think of adopting it."[5] This is quite dogmatic, it must be confessed, for the man who only knows that he knows nothing; and it is probable that, on the whole, the Christian world will persist in preferring Moses to Carlyle. Still further defining his ideas of religion, our author says, "The first man who, looking with open soul on this august heaven and earth, this beautiful and awful, which we name nature, universe, and such like, the essence of which remains forever unnamable; he who first, gazing on this, fell on his knees awe-struck, in silence as likeliest, — he, driven by inner necessity, had done a thing which all thoughtful hearts saw straightway to be an expressive and altogether adoptable thing."[6] Here, then, we have all religion defined as essentially nature-worship; and it is rendered, not

<small>Origin of worship.</small>

---

[1] New Essays, p. 358. [2] Ibid., p. 410.
[3] Ibid., p. 412.   [4] Ibid., p. 386.   [5] Ibid., p. 419.
[6] Past, Present, and Chartism, p. 129.

of choice, but spontaneously and of necessity. To the
same effect Carlyle says, "The essence of the Scandinavian, as indeed of all pagan mythologies, we found to
be recognition of the divineness of nature; sincere communion of man with the mysterious invisible powers
visibly seen at work in the world around him."[1] Again
he says that condemnable idolatry is insincere idolatry. Because we all admire sincerity, and abhor hypocrisy, he
seems to think that he carries his point in saying, "Mahomet's creed we call a kind of Christianity;
and really, if we look at the wild rapt earnest- Sincerity the only essential.
ness with which it was believed and laid to
heart, I should say a better kind than that of those miserable Syrian sects, with their vain janglings about Homo-
ousion and Homoiousion, the head full of worthless noise,
the heart empty and dead."[2] But does our author mean
to say that those "Syrian sects" are not one thing, and Christianity quite another? We grant him the right to define
all religion as at bottom a pantheistic sentiment, if he
chooses to do so; but why should one who prides himself
on his love of truth, and who has so·much intellectual
modesty withal,.resort to the stale trick of confounding
Christian truth with the men who hold its forms while
denying its power? That he believes in the divinity of
all religions alike, is plain from the following: "Are not
all true men soldiers of the same army? All fashions of
arms, the Arab turban and swift scimeter, Thor's strong
hammer smiting down Jotuns, shall be welcome. Luther's
battle-voice, Dante's march-melody, all genuine things are
with us, not against us. We are all under one captain,

[1] Hero-worship, p. 27.   [2] Ibid., p. 56.

soldiers of the same host."[1] In his famous Inaugural Address, spoken before a university audience, using words often quoted since, Carlyle defines religion as "reverence for what is below us." This definition, so thoroughly pantheistic, is not original with him, however, but is taken entire from Goethe. Here are Goethe's words; and no words could more clearly show the position of both master and pupil, as also their theory that Christianity even, so far as true, is but a form of pantheism: "But now we have to speak of the third religion, grounded on reverence for what is under us. This we name the Christian, as in the Christian religion such a temper is most distinctly manifested: it is a last step to which mankind were destined and fitted to attain. But what a task was it not only to be patient with the earth, and let it lie beneath us, we appealing to a higher birthplace; but also to recognize humility and poverty, mockery and despite, disgrace and wretchedness, suffering and death, as divine; nay, even to look on sin and crime as not hinderances, but to honor and love them as furtherances of what is holy."[2] Here we are let into the innermost secret of Goethe's glorification of vice and crime; into the innermost secret of Carlyle's eulogies of American Slavery, the Southern Rebellion, and the oppressive measures of General Eyre. Carlyle honors and loves these embodiments of wickedness. They are manifestations of the divine essence of all things; feeble manifestations, so that he has the keenest religious faculties who is able to recognize them as truly divine. The amount of religion

Accepts Goethe's definition of religion.

[1] Hero-worship, p. 108.
[2] Essays (Phillips, Sampson, & Co., Boston, 1858), p. 87.

in a man, that is, is greater as the object of his worship is less manifestly worthy. To call evil good, and darkness light, and adore them as such, is the sublimest act of man's religious nature. We do not touch the high-water mark of our manhood, till we believe in the divinity of crime, and are able to say unto sin itself, "Thou art my God."

<small>Result.</small>

Turning now from these quotations, which seem to me to make clear the pantheistic spirit of Carlyle, let us see how that spirit flows up, and out, into all his writings on political history and reform, giving them their attitude, their shape, their tone.

<small>How his pantheism affects his practical views.</small>

It is in assailing the corrupt governments of Europe, and lampooning their stupid conventionalisms, that Carlyle shows what real strength is in him. Herein, as with Goethe, lay the secret of his power over the masses of the people. He seemed to them to be their champion while, with eloquent and merciless sarcasm, he lashed and laughed to scorn their oppressive rulers. We wonder that a writer who finds divineness in everything, and who worships what is below him, should so denounce the European monarchies; but he is not the first instance of a pantheist crossing his own track in the heat of controversy. He forgets his theory in eagerness to assail "the powers that be;" like that Universalist in the loyal army, who believed in Hell as a military necessity, while any rebels were abroad. Yet Carlyle would probably say that he is philosophically consistent; for he does not regard what he assails as any real thing. Inanities, shams, unrealities, simulacra, are the names he loves most to apply to the objects of his scorn.

<small>Makes him revolutionary.</small>

Take, for example, his work on the French Revolution, which I think the ablest and humanest of all his works. It was written in the freshness of his years, before the pantheistic spirit had soured into misanthropy. His pity for the royal family, for the heirs of great estates, and especially for the beautiful and pious Marie Antoinette, is genuine and touching. His whole soul seems to mourn on account of the woes about to overwhelm the French government. Yet those woes must come; for the Bourbon dynasty, notwithstanding the merits of individual supporters, has become a sham, a cheat, an unreality. It is no longer a revelation of God. That divinity which is the essence of all things has gone out of it; therefore it is untrue, without use or meaning, and cannot but pass away — if not quietly, then with much smoke and noise. "Before those five-and-twenty laboring millions could get that haggardness of face, in a nation calling itself Christian, and calling man the brother of man, what unspeakable, nigh infinite dishonesty (of *seeming*, not *being*) in all manner of rulers, and appointed watchers, temporal and spiritual, must there not, through long ages, have gone on accumulating! It will accumulate: moreover it will reach a head; for the first of all gospels is this, that a lie cannot endure forever."[1] In this strain it is that he speaks of all governments which have become feeble, and which the oppressed masses dare defy. They *are* not, but only seem to be; are not powers any longer, but merely the simulacra of departed strength. He contrasts

[1] French Revolution (Harpers, 1861), Vol. I., p. 35.

these enfeebled governments, which rest on the blind loyalty of the people, with those of a pagan age, sighing for a return of the times in which Thor and Odin were worshipped. "What a world was that old sunk one," he says, "real governors governing it; shams not yet recognized as tolerable in it."[1] And he adds, "A truer time will come for the nations; authorities based on truth, and on the silent or spoken worship of human nobleness, will again get themselves established."[2] "This is a reflection sad but important to the governments now fallen anarchic, that they had not spiritual talent enough. They were not wise enough; the virtue, heroism, intellect, or by whatever other synonymes we designate it, was not adequate."[3] The trouble with these governments, according to Carlyle, is that they are based on law and compacts, not on the inherent and acknowledge ability of the men administering them. And it will be noticed that by "ability" he means sheer strength to govern, of whatever sort. He sees only "synonymes," where the Christian moralist is wont to make distinctions. Anything is right which is able. "It grows late in the day," he says, "with constitutionalism; and it is time for rulers to look up from their Delolme. If the constitutional man will take the old Delolme-Bentham spectacles off his nose, and look abroad into the fact itself with such eyes as he may have, I consider he will find that reform in matters social does not now mean, as he has long sleepily fancied, reform in Parliament alone, or chiefly, or perhaps at all. My alarming message to

Laws and compacts not the basis of a true government.

[1] New Essays, p. 358.   [2] Ibid., p. 183.   [3] Ibid., p. 102.

him is, that the thing we vitally need is not a more and more perfectly elected Parliament, but some reality of a ruling sovereign to preside over Parliament."[1] Carlyle would not do away altogether with constitutional bodies, as they at present exist. They have ceased to have any power to govern. Yet the state of popular feeling gets itself spoken through them; and thus the strong ruler, whom the people fear, is able to adapt his measures to the times. "Of representative assemblies may not this be said? that contending parties do thereby ascertain one another's strength. They fight there, since fight they must, by petition, Parliamentary eloquence, not by sword, bayonet and bursts of military cannon. Why do men fight at all, if it be not that they are yet unacquainted with one another's strength, and must fight and ascertain it? Knowing that thou art stronger, that thou canst compel me, I will submit to thee: unless I chance to prefer extermination, and slightly circuitous suicide, there is no other course for me. That in England, by public meetings, petitions, elections, leading articles, and the jangling hubbub of tongue-fence which perpetually goes on everywhere in that country, people ascertain one another's strength; and the most obstinate House of Lords has to give in before it come to cannonading and guillotinement: this is a saving characteristic of England."[2] Once more, speaking of representative government in Europe, he says, to the same effect, "Beyond doubt it will be useful and indispensable, for the king or governor to know what the mass of men think on questions legislative and administrative; what they will

Function of representative assemblies.

[1] New Essays, p. 297. [2] Past, Present, and Chartism, p. 364.

assent to willingly, what unwillingly; what they will resist with superficial discontents, what with obstinate determination, with riot, perhaps with armed rebellion. No governor can otherwise go along with clear illumination of his path, however plain the load-star and ulterior goal to him; but at every step must be liable to fall into the ditch; to awaken he knows not what sleeping nests of hornets, what sleeping dog-kennels better to be avoided. By all manner of means let the governor inform himself of all this. To which end Parliaments, free presses, and such like, are excellent; they keep the governor aware of what the people, wisely or foolishly, think."[1] An American senator in the year 1861, representing a state which had just seceded from the Union, and defending the right of his state thus to do regardless of any authority of the Congress, rose amid his fellow-senators, and said, "This assembly is not an authoritative body to me, but only a very respectable public meeting." Precisely like that rebellious senator's view, seems to be Carlyle's theory of assemblies of men, met together by election of the people, and under a written constitution, to make laws for the regulation and government of their country.

We have now seen the secret of Carlyle's favor with the struggling masses in Europe. As against the constituted authorities there, he seems to lead them in their arduous struggle. But he is mocking them. If he "keeps the word of promise to their ear," he "breaks it to their hope." This fact has shown itself even in his tirades against constitutional monarchy; but it needs to be more

Hates democracy as much as constitutional monarchy.

[1] New Essays, p. 306.

distinctly noticed. The inference was that one who so lashed existing monarchies must be a lover of democracies. Vain inference! When he glorifies rebellion, in the case of the French led by Mirabeau, of the English led by Cromwell, and of the Americans led by Samuel Adams, it is not because he believes in the liberty they are seeking, but because he can use them for the time being against the more immediate object of his attack. These rebellions, though having but little divinity in themselves, show that the divinity is all gone out of the governments assailed. What could be nobler than his eulogy of the first settlers of Massachusetts? "Hail to thee, poor little ship Mayflower, of Delft-Haven; poor, common-looking ship, hired by common char-

<small>Eulogy of the Pilgrims.</small> ter party for coined dollars; calked with mean oakum and tar; provisioned with vulgarest biscuit and bacon; — yet what ship Argo, or miraculous epic ship built by the sea-gods, was other than a foolish bum-barge in comparison! Golden fleeces or the like these sailed for, with or without effect; thou, little Mayflower, hadst in thee a veritable Promethean spark; the life-spark of the largest nation on earth. They went seeking leave to hear sermon in their own method, these Mayflower Puritans; a most indispensable search; and yet, like Saul the son of Kish, seeking a small thing they found this unexpected great thing! Honor to the brave and true;

<small>Puritanism and Mahometanism put together.</small> they verily, we say, carry fire from heaven, and a power which themselves dream not of. Let all men honor Puritanism, since God so honored it. Islam, with its heart-felt 'Allah Akbar,' was it not honored? There is but one thing without

honor; smitten with eternal barrenness and inability to do or be; insincerity, unbelief. He who believes no thing, who believes only the shows of things, is not in relation with nature and fact at all. Nature denies him; orders him at his earliest convenience to disappear. Let him disappear from her domains, into those of Chaos, Hypothesis and Simulacrum, or wherever else his parish may be."[1] Thus we see that the Pilgrims, though honored, are esteemed no more worthy of honor than the first followers of Mahomet. Ability and fearlessness, in whatever form shown, are the real source of merit; and they are admired just as much in despots as in bodies of men struggling to be free; examples of the latter being extolled only in damaging contrast with the established governments of Europe. In no case is any love shown for governments by the people. When the nation which he recognizes as "the largest on earth," whose seed was wafted in the Mayflower, is in trouble, and asks the countenance of good men throughout the world, while asserting its right to exist, instead of the smallest word of sympathy from Carlyle, it is insulted with outpourings of contempt and scorn. Its purpose to let the oppressed go free is ridiculed under the title of sympathy for "Quashee;" its attempt to carry out its own democratic ideas is called "a shooting of Niagara;" the terrible war which it endures, rather than let the world's last hope of liberty perish, is contemptuously pictured as "the foul chimney burning itself clean." No language could be more scornful than that which Carlyle hurls at the masses of the people, and

No love for free government in either case.

[1] Past, Present, and Chartism, p. 363.

on popular governments of every kind. The law of veracity, the silences, the eternities, or whatever other name he chooses to give his nature-god, is not in them; and therefore, says he, "let them take themselves out of the way."

Carlyle ridicules the efforts of the humane to reform the vicious and criminal classes, thus showing, in its baldest form, his thorough hatred of everything which is too weak to guide and take care of itself. He thinks that every moral and social reform, looking to the recovery of outcasts, should be named a "Universal Sluggard-and-Scoundrel Protection Society." Those outcasts he calls "the elixir of the infatuated among mortals." If we want the worst possible investment of our benevolence, in laboring to save the poor and vicious classes, we "accurately have it." "Nowhere so as here," says he to us, "can you be certain that a given quantity of wise teaching bestowed, of benevolent trouble taken, will yield zero, or the minimum of return. It is sowing of your wheat upon Irish quagmires; laboriously harrowing it in upon the sand of the seashore."[1] "Not brotherhood; in enmity that must last through eternity, in unappeasable aversion, shall I have to live with these! Brotherhood? No, be the thought far from me. They are Adam's children, — alas yes, I well remember that, and never shall forget; hence this rage and sorrow."[2] "If I had a commonwealth to govern," says Carlyle, — as, Heaven be thanked, he has not, — "certainly it should not be these Devil's regiments of the line that I would first

Scorn of moral reforms.

Misanthropy.

[1] New Essays, p. 77.   [2] Ibid., p. 84.

of all concentrate my attention on. With them I should be apt to make rather brief work; to them one would apply the besom, try to sweep them with some rapidity into the dust-bin, and well out of one's road, I should rather say. Fill your threshing-floor with docks, ragweeds, mugworths, and ply your flail upon them, — that is not the method to obtain sacks of wheat. Away, you; begone swiftly, ye regiments of the line." [1]

With such contempt for all efforts to save the abandoned classes, denying them, as he does, the very elements of humanity, declaring that they are not in any degree susceptible of improvement, Carlyle need hardly take the trouble to assure us that he has no faith in popular governments. His political views are a legitimate deduction from his low estimate of human nature. Yet he is at pains to state his political views; and if we do not understand them, it certainly cannot be because his language is not explicit and strong enough. He sees the oppressed people of Europe looking hopefully to the example of America, and he says, "Alas, on this side of the Atlantic and on that, Democracy, we apprehend, is forever impossible. So much, with certainty of loud, astonished contradiction from all manner of men at present, but with sure appeal to the law of nature and the ever-abiding fact, may be suggested and asserted once more. The universe itself is a monarchy and hierarchy; large liberty of voting there, all manner of choice, utmost free-will, but with conditions inexorable and immeasurable annexed to every exercise of the same." [2] Mankind are a worthless set, that is, taken

Origin of his contempt for democracies.

[1] New Essays, p. 74.   [2] Ibid., p. 27.

in the mass; but here and there may be found a single man, worthy to be trusted with such absolute power over his fellows as God exercises on a universal scale! "Democracy is, by the nature of it, a self-cancelling business: and gives in the long run a net result of zero. Where no government is wanted, save that of the parish-constable, as in America with its boundless soil, every man being able to find work and recompense for himself, democracy may subsist; not elsewhere, except briefly, as a swift transition towards something other and further. Democracy never yet, that we heard of, was able to accomplish much work, beyond that same cancelling of itself."[1]

But we will not keep to this negative side of Carlyle's creed any longer. We have seen what power, and what weakness, it lends him before his world-wide audience. Stating his intense disbelief in hereditary monarchies and aristocracies, which are based on written constitutions, the oppressed masses applaud him; and on the other hand those same denounced governments applaud, as he in turn utters his detestation of all popular governments. Republicanism is not better to him than absolutism, but worse, where prescribed forms of law determine the course of affairs. His hatred of constitutional free government is as bitter and fixed as his hatred of constitutional monarchy. He puts them alike into the category of things which are contrary to nature; which are therefore unreal, and without any essence of divinity in them. He denounces them impartially, with such power of expression as he can bring from

Negative side of his political creed.

[1] Past, Present, and Chartism, p. 344.

his ample vocabulary; and then turning from them, as worse than worthless things, he shows *his* " more excellent way." What that way is, we will now proceed to see.

The panacea which Carlyle proposes for all social or governmental evils is Hero-worship. The Millennium will come to the world, and to governments of whatever name, when the masses of the people everywhere bow down, in unquestioning reverence, before a few whom they recognize as great men. Their personal will, unshackled by written constitutions, should give laws to the masses about them; for in them, more than all things else, does the divine soul of nature, which is incapable of error, make itself manifest. "Able men to govern us; that would be the way, nor is there any other remedy for whatsoever goes wrong. There is but one man fraught with blessings to this world, fated to diminish and successively abolish the curses of the world. For him make search, him reverence and follow; know that to find him or miss him means victory or defeat for you in all establishments and enterprises here below."[1] "He is above thee, like a god. Thou, in thy stupendous three-inch pattens, art under him. He is thy born king, thy conqueror and supreme lawgiver; not all the guineas and cannons, and leather and prunella, under the sky can save thee from him."[2] That in men which we call genius, is, according to Carlyle, only the more intensely revealed power of the absolute all-in-all. Jesus of Nazareth had simply the largest amount of religious genius ever enjoyed by a single person; and it is that

His political and social creed positively stated: Hero-worship.

[1] New Essays, p. 137.   [2] Past, Present, and Chartism, p. 291.

which has made him "a god to this hour."[1] "I should say, if we do not reckon a great man literally divine, it is that our notions of God, of the supreme unattainable fountain of splendor, wisdom and heroism, are ever rising higher; not altogether that our reverence for these qualities, as manifested in our like, is getting lower."[2] "The great man is a force of nature; whatever is truly great in him springs up from the inarticulate depths."[3] "To do every one of us what lies in him, that the able man everywhere may be put into the place that is fit for him, which is his by actual right: is not this the sum of all social morality for every citizen of the world?"[4] "Worship, what we call human religion, has undergone various phases in the history of mankind. To the primitive man all forces of nature were divine; either for propitiation or for admiration, many things, and in a sense all things, demanded worship from him. But especially the noble human soul was divine to him; and announced with direct impressiveness, as it ever does, the inspiration of the Highest; demanding worship from the primitive man. Whereby, as has been explained elsewhere, this latter form of worship, *Hero-worship* as we call it, did, among the ancient peoples, attract and subdue to itself all other forms of human worship; irradiating them all with its own perennial worth, which is indeed all the worth they had, or that any worship can have. Human worship everywhere, so far as there lay any worth in it, was of the nature of Hero-worship; this universe wholly, this temporary flame-image of the eternal, was

Hero-worship the source of primitive governments.

[1] Past, Present, and Chartism, p. 292. [2] Hero-worship, p. 75.
[3] Ibid., p. 101. [4] New Essays, p. 330.

PANTHEISM.   255

one beautiful and terrible energy of heroisms, presided over by a divine nobleness and Infinite Hero. Divine nobleness forever friendly to the noble, forever hostile to the ignoble: all manner of 'moral rules' and well 'sanctioned' too, flowed naturally out of this primeval intuition into nature;— which, I believe, is still the true fountain of moral rules, though much forgotten at present."[1]

Not only does Carlyle lay it down as an historical fact, that Hero-worship was the basis of primitive governments, but he contends that such is, and ever must be the only true basis of authority. He is the born ruler, and should be so received, who has the inherent power to make himself master of other men. "In this world there is one godlike thing, the essence of all that ever was or ever will be of godlike in this world: the veneration due to human worth by the hearts of men."[2] In utter forgetfulness of his saying, that "religion is reverence for what is beneath us," Carlyle uses this language, and much more. "Hero-worship; heartfelt, prostrate admiration; submission burning, boundless, for a noblest godlike form of man,— is not this," he asks, "the germ of Christianity itself?"[3] "Hero-worship is the summary, ultimate essence and supreme perfection, of all manner of worship."[4] "It is certain, whatever gods or fetiches a man may have about him, and pay tithes to, and mumble prayers to, the real 'religion' that is in him is his practical hero-worship. Theologies, doxologies, orthodoxies, heterodoxies, are not of moment except as subsidiary towards a good issue in this."[5] "The man Napoleon

Urged as the only real source.

[1] New Essays, pp. 350, 351.   [2] Past, Present, and Chartism, p. 287.
[3] Hero-worship, p. 10.   [4] Past, Present, and Chartism, p. 33.
[5] New Essays, p. 353.

was a divine missionary, though unconscious of it; and preached, through the cannon's throat, that great doctrine, the tools to him that can handle them; which is our ultimate political evangel, wherein alone can true liberty lie."[1] "What is the Bible of a nation, the practically credited God's message to a nation? Is it not, beyond all else, the authentic biography of its heroic souls? This is the real record of the appearances of God in the history of a nation; this it is which teaches all men what the universe, when you go to work in it, really is."[2] "The early nations of the world, all nations so long as they continued simple and in earnest, knew without teaching that their history was an epic and Bible, the clouded struggling image of a God's presence, the action of heroes and God-inspired men."[3] "Human intellect, if you consider well, is the exact summary of human worth;"[4] and "reverence for this intellectual power, loyal furtherance and obedience to it, are the outcome and essence of all true 'religions,' and was, and ever will be."[5] To the man of great intellect, regardless of every other qualification, "belongs eternally the government of the world. Where he reigns all is blessed, and the good rejoice, and the wicked make wail. Where the contrary of him reigns, all is accursed; and the gods lament, and will, by terrible methods, rectify the matter by and by. Have you forbidden this man to rule? Obey he cannot. He will retire rather, into deserts, far from you and your affairs. You and your affairs, once well quit of him, go by a swift and ever swifter road."[6] Carlyle's doctrine of hero-worship,

Great men the real theophany.

[1] Sartor Resartus, p. 138.   [2] New Essays, p. 357.   [3] Ibid., 409.
[4] Ibid., p. 136.   [5] Ibid., p. 135.   [6] Ibid., p. 321.

and the obedience due great men as the ordained rulers of the world, seems to be this: certain fixed and eternal forces, modes of the omnipresent essence of all things, are manifested differently in different men. He who is most vividly conscious of these divine impulses, and who most thoroughly makes himself an instrument for carrying them out to their fated issue, is the true-born master, before whom all others should fall down and worship, letting him do what he will with them and theirs. "God's light," he says, "is human intellect;" and he finds more of that light in Robert Burns than in any other man then on the stage. The poet of Ayrshire, according to him, ought to have been placed at the head of the English government. "Robert Burns," he says, "had not the smallest chance to get into Parliament, much as he deserved, for all our sakes, to have been found there. For the man was a born king of men: full of valor, of intelligence and heroic nobleness; fit for far other work than to break his heart among poor mean mortals."[1] We may go as far as Carlyle in admiration of the wonderful poetical power of Burns; but was that power of just the kind which, in any nation or age, has shown itself able to rule? He who is not master of himself should hardly be allowed to lord it over others in the style which hero-worship enjoins. We could hardly believe that Carlyle is serious, but should suspect him of irony oftentimes, while reading his expositions of his favorite doctrine, did not his evident earnestness forbid. We do not find any man in all history, however great and good and inspired, whom we deem worthy to be clothed with irresponsible power

Carlyle's ideal of a great man.

[1] New Essays, pp. 151, 152.

over other men. What shall be said, therefore, of a doctrine which would give such power to a Burns, a Goethe, the Cromwells, the Fredericks, the Napoleons of the race? Our hearts refuse such homage as he demands, even to the highest possible ideal of a hero; much more do they refuse it to the men he offers us as realizing *his* ideal of human greatness and ability to govern! We are yet to learn that the only hope of the world is its great men. It certainly has breathed freer, oftentimes, when well rid of such; of men, that is, who were great as judged by Carlyle's standard. Spinoza does not persuade our conscience, when he says, "I consider virtue and power one and the same thing;"[1] nor can we any longer consent to the leadership of Carlyle, when he puts before us men great chiefly in their passions and ambitions, as the gods whom we are to obey and worship.

Carlyle seems to suspect that his "political evangel," making the masses of men slaves to here and there a great man, may be unpalatable. He therefore turns special advocate, and endeavors to recommend his theory of government to our favorable notice, arguing for it much as the American slaveholders were wont to argue that slavery is better than freedom for the laboring classes. "The very horse," says he, "that is permanent, how much kindlier do he and his master work, than the temporary one, hired on any hack principle yet known. I am for permanence in all things, at the earliest possible moment, and to the latest possible. Blessed is he that continueth where he is."[2] This reasoning would be well enough touching the organ-

Plea for his theory of government.

---

[1] Ethics, Pt. IV. Def. 8.   [2] Past, Present, and Chartism, p. 280.

ization of human society, if the mass of men have, as seems to be assumed by Carlyle, only an equine nature. What is good for the horse and his owner, is good for men and their rulers, if these rulers be indeed what hero-worship pre-supposes, in relation to those whom they govern. But no such inequality as this can be admitted, while we hold to the unity of the human race, while we recognize freedom, immortality, and the power of self-government in all. It also strikes us oddly, that Carlyle, while holding this theory, should exhort every one to remain where he is. The grand complaint which he makes is, that the great men, who monopolize all the divinity there is in the world, are left so often in obscurity, and not brought forward to be enthroned and worshipped. The "permanence" which he desires is not to begin, therefore, till after this enthronement. When the few "heroes" are clothed with irresponsible power over the rest of mankind, who willingly accept the position of slaves under them, then his millennium will begin. He laments the feudal age of English history, thinking it far happier than the present age of personal liberty. "Gurth's brass collar did not gall him; Cedric deserved to be his master. The pigs were Cedric's, but Gurth would get the parings of them. Gurth had the inexpressible satisfaction of feeling himself related indissolubly, though in a rude brass-collar way, to his fellow-mortals on this earth. He had superiors, inferiors, equals. Gurth is now 'emancipated;' has what we call 'liberty.' Liberty, I am told, is a divine thing. Liberty, when it becomes liberty to die of starvation, is not so divine."[1] It must be confessed that our author faces

[1] Past, Present, and Chartism, p. 212.

this alternative of lordship or serfhood with much show of personal courage. He resigns himself to the decree of fate, in language at least, whether that decree shall assign him to the place of the master or of the slave. "If thou art in very deed my wiser, may a beneficent instinct lead and impel thee to conquer me, to command me. If thou do know better than I what is right, I conjure thee, in the name of God, force me to do it, were it by never such brass collars, whips and handcuffs." [1]

And here we come to the point where Carlyle's doctrine breaks down utterly. It is the point of practical trial; the direct contest, between man and man, which is to decide who shall govern and who submit. The waxen wings by which humanity is to fly clear of all evils melt as soon as the flight is undertaken. The godhead, which is the sum of all reality, dwells in a few great men, who, by virtue of this indwelling divinity, ought to rule over us and ours; but how to place them in position, how to secure them this leadership, so as to inaugurate the golden reign of heroes, is a question before which even Carlyle seems to see that his argument labors. Yet he does not quail. He refuses to accept no logical result of his theory. Never did a reorganizer of human society face a difficulty more boldly, or state it more frankly. "Who is slave, and eternally appointed to be governed; who free, and eternally appointed to govern? It would much avail us to settle this question," says he.[2] "To increase the reverence for human intellect, or God's light, what method is there? Pray that Heaven would please to vouchsafe us each a

The result of the theory is anarchy.

[1] Past, Present, and Chartism, p. 213. [2] New Essays, p. 316.

little of it, one by one! As perhaps Heaven, in infinite mercy by stern methods, gradually will. Perhaps Heaven has mercy too, in these sore plagues that are oppressing us; and means to teach us reverence for heroism and human intellect, by such baleful experience of what issue imbecility and parliamentary eloquence lead to."[1] "What are all popular commotions and maddest bellowings, from Peterloo to the Place-de-Grève itself? To the ear of wisdom they are inarticulate prayers: 'guide me, govern me! I am mad and miserable, and cannot guide myself.' Surely of all 'rights of. man,' this right of the ignorant man to be guided by the wiser, to be gently or forcibly held in the true course by him, is the indisputablest. Nature herself ordains it from the first; society struggles towards perfection by enforcing and accomplishing it more and more. If freedom has any meaning, it means enjoyment of this right, wherein all other rights are enjoyed. It is a sacred right and duty on both sides; and the summary of all social duties between the two. Why does one toil with his hands, if the other be not to toil, still more unweariedly, with heart and head? The brawny craftsman finds it no child's play to mould the unpliant, rugged masses; neither is guidance of men a dilettantism: what it becomes when treated as a dilettantism, we may see."[2]

Thus does the problem present itself to Carlyle's mind; and he is shut up to a single method of solving it. The strongest man must hold the sceptre, the weaker must wear the yoke. Let us not start back from this solution, for he offers no other. "Divine right," he says, "take it on the

[1] New Essays, p. 145.   [2] Past, Present, and Chartism, p. 343.

great scale, is divine might withal." He finds this might in Cromwell, more than in Napoleon; hence he deems the Protector worthy of more homage than the Emperor. This might within him, what Carlyle calls "latent valor and thought, content to lie latent, then burst out as in a blaze of heaven's lightning,"[1] was the basis of his right to revolutionize the English government. But we think that Cromwell himself would have given quite another account of his right in that matter. He asked neither worship nor homage for his own person; nor did he esteem himself strong, save in the devotion of his people with him to a common end, which he sought to secure by just laws representing the national will. "The just thing, in the long run," says Carlyle, "is the strong thing." "Await the issue. In all battles, if you await the issue, each fighter has prospered according to his right. His right and his might, at the close of the account, are one and the same."[2] "The painfullest feeling is that of your own feebleness: to be weak is the true misery."[3] According to Carlyle the Apostle was mistaken when he declared sin to be the great calamity, and when he gloried in his weakness as the occasion of power. His glorying as he did was not a Christian virtue, but a foolish habit of his, since feebleness is "the true misery." And why is man's consciousness of weakness his greatest calamity? Because "mights, I say, are a dreadful business to articulate correctly. Yet articulated they have to be; the time comes for it, the need comes for it, and with enormous difficulty and experimenting it is got done. Call it not succession of rebel-

[1] Hero-worship, p. 212.   [2] Past, Present, and Chartism, p. 11.
[3] Sartor Resartus, p. 128.

lions; call it rather succession of expansions, of enlightenments, gift of articulate utterance descending lower and lower."[1] Thus does the "ultimate political evangel," which was to free the world from hereditary despotisms, from governments by written constitutions, and from elective democracies, and which was to usher in the golden reign of heroes, end in a carnival of riot and red-handed rebellion. A revolutionary spirit, acting itself out to the utmost, is the only way of lifting up to supreme power the few who deserve to rule, and of forcing all others down into proper subjection. It is with men as with oxen, where a trial of sheer strength decides which one shall be the leader of the herd. "I say sometimes," is Carlyle's language, "that all goes by wager of battle in this world; that strength, well understood, is the measure of all worth. Give a thing time; if it can succeed, it is a right thing."[2] "I care little about the sword: I will allow a thing to struggle for itself in the world, with any sword, or tongue, or implement it has, or can lay hold of. We will let it preach, and pamphleteer, and fight, and to the uttermost bestir itself; and do, beak and claws, whatsoever is in it; very sure that it will, in the long run, conquer nothing which does not deserve to be conquered. In this great duel nature herself is umpire, and can do no wrong: the thing which is deepest rooted in nature, which we call truest, that thing will be found growing at last."[3] "The fighting was indispensable, for ascertaining who had the right over whom. By much hard fighting, as we once said, 'the unrealities, beaten into dust, flew off;' and left the

[1] Past, Present, and Chartism. p. 360. [2] Hero-worship, p. 128.
[3] Ibid., p. 55.

plain reality and fact; 'thou stronger than I, thou wiser than I; therefore thou king, and subject I.'"[1]

Verily here is a prospect such as Robin Hood, or Goetz of the iron hand, would have shrunk from contemplating. Ishmael, whose hand was against every man, is our nearest example of Carlyle's true hero. He delivers the world over to a perpetual scene of conflict, each man for himself and against all others; and the whole dominion is his, who for the time being manages to keep uppermost. No wonder that our author, in view of this "dreadful business of getting the mights articulated into rights," exhorts men to fling away fear. "It is an everlasting duty," he says, "the duty of being brave. Valor is still value. The first duty of a man is still that of subduing fear. We must get rid of fear; we cannot act at all till then. A man's acts are slavish, not true but specious; his very thoughts are false, he thinks too as a slave and coward, till he has got fear under his feet. Odin's creed, if we disentangle the kernel of it, is true to this hour. A man shall and must be valiant; he must march forward, and quit himself like a man, trusting imperturbably in the appointment and choice of the upper Powers; and, on the whole, not fear at all. Now and always, the completeness of his victory over fear will determine how much of a man he is."[2] The madness of poor old Lear, defying the darkness and storm; or of Milton's Satan, braving the terrors of the fiery abyss, was not more audacious in its wildness than Carlyle would beget in each and every man. "What art thou afraid of?" he scornfully says to the man who has an atom of fear for anything in heaven, on earth, or under the earth.

[1] Past, Present, and Chartism, p. 245.   [2] Hero-worship, p. 28

Wherefore, like a coward, dost thou forever pip and whimper, and go cowering and trembling? Despicable biped! What is the sum-total of the worst that lies before thee? Death? Well, death; and say the pangs of Tophet too, and all that the devil and man may, will, or can do against thee. Hast thou not a heart? Canst thou not suffer whatso it be; and, as a child of freedom, though outcast, trample Tophet itself under thy feet, while it consumes thee? Let it come, then; I will meet and defy it."[1]

This will do. Here we take our leave of Carlyle and his ultimate evangel. We trust it is not want of courage, but want of misanthropy, which makes us shrink from the social chaos he invokes, — a chaos which that of old, when the earth was void and darkness rested on the face of the deep, but faintly prefigured. It is not Titanic strength, confusing heaven and earth with its wild rush and battle, but the spirit of God, brooding like a dove on human society, that will bring forth order, and serene beauty and peace. There is a better gospel for the nations than this pantheism, which limits all reality to a few mighty men, for whose use and behoof all things else are, and were, and ever will be. It is with feelings of profound joy that we turn from Carlyle's desperate conclusion to such words as those of Goldwin Smith, where he says, "Of the religion of hero-worship I am no devotee. Great men are most precious gifts of Heaven, and unhappy is the nation which cannot produce them at its need. But their importance in history becomes less as civilization goes on. A Timour or an

Hero-worship contrasted with Christianity.

[1] Sartor Resartus, p. 131.

Attila towers immeasurably above his horde; but in the last great struggle which the world has seen, the struggle of the North American states for their Union, the hero was an intelligent and united nation. And to whatever age they may belong, the greatest, the most godlike of men, are men, not gods. They are the offspring, though the highest offspring, of their age. They would be nothing without their fellow-men. Carlyle prostrates morality before greatness. We might as well bow down before the hundred-handed idol of the Hindoos. To moral force we may bow down; but moral force resides and can reside in those only who obey the moral law. It is found in the highest degree in those at whom hero-worship sneers." [1] Set over against the political ravings of Carlyle, who knows no God, and no government, human or divine, save what he finds in great men, how grandly true are the lines of Wordsworth, in his Sonnets dedicated to liberty, where he says, —

"A few plain instincts, and a few plain rules,
 Have wrought more for mankind, in the disastrous hour,
 Than all the pride of intellect and thought." [2]

Every right feeling in us responds instantly to these noble words. And a Greater than Wordsworth or Goldwin Smith has taught us, in language still sending an inspiration through the ages, that not the lofty, but the lowly-hearted are the light of life to our world. Let the pantheist leave his great men, whom he regards as the

---

[1] Three English Statesmen (Harpers, 1867), pp. 79–81.
[2] I give the lines as usually quoted, though changed from their original form. See Sonnets dedicated to Liberty (English ed., p. 239), Part II., Sonnet 10.

only Shekinah. Let him go back from his hero-worship, through Him who is the living way, till he finds again that Father of his spirit from whom he has wandered, and he shall know the truth. He shall know that truth which breaks the fatal dream of philosophy, and leads her forth into the liberty of the children of God. For it is an everlasting truth, which all history illustrates and every noblest thing in us welcomes, that God chooses not the mighty, but the weak to confound the mighty; that it pleases him to hide from the wise and prudent what he reveals unto babes; and that in the blessed ages to come, when mankind shall be at peace and walk together as brethren, no imperial chieftain, but a little child shall lead them.

LECTURE VII.

PANTHEISM IN THE FORM OF SELF-WORSHIP.

THE pantheist, holding that all objects in the universe manifest its one divine essence, will find that essence more especially amid those investigations to which his energies are devoted. Goethe, with his passion for culture, found it in art, and the æsthetic relations of things. Carlyle, the eager student of history, found it in the great men of the world. But there are other mental peculiarities of pantheists, giving especial form to the common doctrine which they hold. The class of minds <small>Individualism.</small> which naturally tend to individualism in their workings is perhaps as large as the æsthetic or the historic and reformatory. Their tendency is subjective rather than objective; they believe in the ideal, and distrust the so-called real. Where this class of thinkers locate their Shekinah, when under the influence of pantheism, it is important next to consider.

What has already been said of Carlyle in relation to hero-worship may, in relation to this subjective pantheism, be with justice said of Ralph Waldo Emerson. He represents, perhaps better than any other popular <small>Represented by Emerson.</small> author, the introspective tendency in modern thought. The subject could hardly be treated apart from his writings; and we may safely conclude that we are masters of it, not needing to extend our researches, when we thoroughly understand him. Representing this individualism as he does, and carrying it to the point of self-worship under the lead of pantheism, I shall fulfil the task of the present lecture, if I give a faithful account of his philosophy, considered both in its substance and its practical development. And that the account may be faithful, with the least possible chance of misrepresentation by me, I shall, as in the case of Carlyle, allow less space to my own comments than to the words of the author himself. What I give, let me also say, must not be regarded as a full and complete estimate of Emerson. It is in a single relation only that I propose now to examine his writings. He may have many merits which the present inquiry does not especially contemplate, though I shall hope to recognize them all as they incidentally occur. My main object will be gained, if I make clear his philosophical views and their bearings, with a regard to the logical connections and progress of the thought, such as his own pages do not deign to give.

Method of treatment.

It is with feelings of relief that I turn from the works of Carlyle to those of Emerson, for I cannot help the impression that the latter is much the greater man of the two: not a reader of so many books perhaps, nor so accurate and exhaustive a student of history; but higher toned, of a serener spirit, with less in his writings that is ephemeral; central in his thought, and balanced in expression, so as to speak not for a day or generation, but for all time. While the peculiar

Contrasted with Carlyle.

phase of thinking which he represents is in the world, he will be recognized as one of its major prophets; as having at times, I think, surpassed any other writer in uttering the spirit of a subjective and ideal pantheism. Should the present age of materialism pass away, and there be another revival of the a-priori philosophy, as will no doubt be the case, I predict that Emerson will be read, while Carlyle is comparatively forgotten. That energy which Carlyle lets off in stormy passion, Emerson carefully husbands, and puts into the very substance of his thinking. He never raves, like his friend across the sea, but is always self-contained, measured in his statements, well-poised and calm. The poet Lowell is hardly less just than witty where he says, speaking of the two men, —

> "To compare him with Plato would be vastly fairer;
> Carlyle's the more burly, but E. is the rarer:
> He sees fewer objects, but clearlier, trulier;
> If C.'s an original, E.'s more peculiar:
> That he's more of a man you might say of one,
> Of the other, he's more of an Emerson;
> C.'s the Titan, as shaggy of mind as of limb,
> E. the clear-eyed Olympian, rapid and slim." [1]

His excellent temper.

It is easy to see, while reading Emerson, that he is a person of very great sensitiveness; that he has felt keenly the sharp antagonism of early friends. But though this longing for the love of good men, and pain at the absence of it, appear in many places, I have looked in vain for any weak word of complaint. There is but little that looks like recrimination anywhere in his writings. Few authors, so roughly criticised as he,

[1] Fable for the Critics.

show so little vindictiveness. Even those who ignorantly and stupidly abuse him, he treats with good-natured condescension rather than hard contempt. So free are his pages from the spirit of controversy, that as you read on the comment you make is, "This man does not seem to know how severely the views he is here stating have been denounced." It is a fact, I believe, that he has never formally replied to any of his critics. Certainly a man so without enmities, and whom any one may assail feeling that he will not retaliate, should be resisted only in the interest of truth, and with a spirit more generous, if possible, than his own. In all that I am now about to offer I shall not speak against him, nor affect to speak for him; but, as just intimated, shall the rather permit him to speak for himself. I have already shown what pantheism, in its last analysis, is; and if he is in full sympathy with that doctrine, both he and his friends ought to desire that his readers should know the fact.

Having compared Emerson with Carlyle, to the disadvantage of the latter in some respects, I wish also to say that, to my view, he stands on a higher plane than Goethe even. By this I do not mean that his intellectual range is broader than Goethe's. He has no such knowledge of natural science as Goethe had; is not, like him, at home in all the literatures of the world; but he more uniformly speaks to what is noblest and best in us. There is far less in his pages to offend our conscience and self-respect. One feels, all along, that he is reading a man whose thoughts and life are pure. However dangerous the underlying theory, yet, by a charming inconsistency, the immediate appeal is to our

Of purer tone than Goethe.

honor, our love of the good, our sense of right. Being less true than Goethe to his main speculation, he is more true to the moral convictions of mankind. I quote with pleasure his own judgment against Goethe, as showing, however his theory may tally with the German poet's, that his New England blood will not let him indorse that theory, when it is practically carried out to all the results. Emerson says, "I dare not say that Goethe has ascended to the highest grounds from which genius has spoken. He has not worshipped the highest unity. He is incapable of self-surrender to the moral sentiment. There are nobler strains in poetry than any he has sounded. There are writers poorer in talent, whose tone is purer, and more touches the heart. Goethe can never be dear to men. His is not even the devotion to pure truth; but to truth for the sake of culture."[1]

In one respect it is not so hard to enucleate the pantheism of Emerson as that of Goethe and Carlyle. He rarely loses sight of his major premise. His writings, whatever the occasion or immediate purpose, seem always to be instinct with the spirit of Spinozism. That is the string on which they are all strung together; their one logical connection, if they have no other. I am confident that any one, assuming this to be the clew to his writings, would find but little difficulty in tracing their harmony,—nay, even their monotony. I shall follow this thread only a little way, omitting much that is strictly pertinent, and keeping to his more elaborate essays, in the present inquiry. It is true that we

Monotony.

[1] Representative Men (Boston, Phillips, Sampson, & Co., 1850), pp. 278, 279.

shall not find, even in these essays, frequent allusions to Spinoza, or to his doctrine under its proper designation. Emerson is shy of names; and though he has a confession of faith, he is careful not to give it to his readers in any formulated shape. Nor is it necessary to say, as some of his critics have, that he thus avoids the well-known and abhorred phraseology because he wishes to deceive his readers, imbuing them with the principles of pantheism while they are off their guard. He is no such zealot. He cares little for the reception his doctrine gets in other minds. It is not to any taint of Jesuitism, but to the purely literary bent of his genius, that this impatience of technical terms is due. We need not be misled, however, though failing to find the usual superscription on the coin; the ring of the metal tells us, more clearly than any image could, what is its nature. Very often where Emerson uses the words "soul," "spirit," "mind," "intellect," we shall find, when we understand him, that he does not refer to anything individual or personal, but to an all-surrounding, all-filling substance, which he calls divine, and regards as constituting the whole of reality. "Soul," or "the soul," seems to be his favorite designation of this essence, which Spinoza calls substance, Schelling the subject-object, and Hegel the absolute idea; as where he says, "the universe is the externization of the soul."[1] But he uses other terms, such as "life," "light," "God," "the Holy Ghost," "Pan," "Fortune," "Minerva," "Proteus." He has added one term to the vocabulary of pantheism, which merits particular notice. "All the universe over," says he, "there is

Nomenclature.

[1] Essays (Boston, Phillips, Sampson, & Co., 1858), Vol. II., p. 19.

but one thing, this old Two-Face, creator-creature, mind-matter, right-wrong, of which any proposition may be affirmed or denied."[1] Old Two-Face, forsooth!

"Old Two-Face." We fancy that at such a designating as this of the absolute and sole reality, even Hegel's hair would have bristled. But the speculative views of Emerson will not be obscure, I think, as we go forward in our inquiry, whatever may happen to be his phraseology.

I shall, in the first place, present passages from Emerson's writings which lay down the doctrine of
Comprehensive statements of pantheism. pantheism in its more generic forms. What words, for instance, could utter the doctrine of Spinoza more decisively than these? "Under all this running sea of circumstance, whose waters ebb and flow with perfect balance, lies the aboriginal abyss of real Being. Essence, or God, is not a relation, or a part, but the whole. Being is the vast affirmative, excluding negation, self-balanced, and swallowing up all relations, parts and times within itself. Nature, virtue, truth, are the influx from thence."[2] Or we might take this: "The philosophical perception of identity through endless mutations, makes man know the Proteus."[3] Or the following might be confidently relied on to sustain our position: "The ultimate fact we reach on every topic, is the resolution of all into the ever-blessed ONE. Com-
All things are God. merce, husbandry, hunting, whaling, war, eloquence, personal weight, are somewhat; and engage my attention as examples of its presence and action."[4] In his essay on History Emerson says, "There

[1] Essays, Vol. II., p. 236. [2] Ibid., Vol. I., p. 109.
[3] Ibid., p. 28. [4] Ibid., pp. 61, 62.

is one mind common to all individual men. Whoever hath access to this universal mind is a party to all that is or can be done, for this is the only and sovereign agent."[1] And the poetical motto, prefixed to that essay, is,— *History.*

> " There is no great and no small
> To the soul that maketh all ;
> And where it cometh all things are,
> And it cometh everywhere."

Again he says, "I am much struck in literature by the appearance that one person wrote all the books; there is such equality and identity both of judgment and point of view in the narrative, that it is plainly the work of one all-seeing, all-hearing gentleman. When I read Proclus it is not Proclus, but a piece of nature and fate that I explore. It is a greater joy to see the author's author, than himself."[2] The discovery that the author of Proclus, and of every other writer, is a "gentleman," hardly equals in sublimity the announcement of the ancient sage that "God is a geometer," but it certainly leaves us in no doubt as to the speculative views of our modern philosopher. Emerson further says, "Virtue is the incoming of God himself, or absolute existence."[3] "God is the all-fair. Truth, and goodness, and beauty, are but different faces of the same all."[4] "Cause and effect are two sides of one fact."[5] "The soul strives amain to live and work through all *Literature.* *God a gentleman.*

[1] Essays, Vol. I., p. 3.   [2] Ibid., Vol. II., pp. 224, 225.
[3] Ibid., Vol. I., p. 109.
[4] Miscellanies, (Boston, Phillips, Sampson, & Co., 1858), p. 22.
[5] Essays, Vol. I., p. 285.

things. It would be the only fact."[1] "The true doctrine of omnipresence is, that God reappears with all his parts in every moss and cobweb."[2] Emerson's theory of love, with all the charms of social and domestic life to which it gives birth, is purely pantheistic. It is the omnipresent divinity in the two sexes, which, revealed as the positive and negative poles of a resistless magnetism, draws them together. Why does man involuntarily love a beautiful woman? Because she "suggests to him," says our author, "the presence of that which is within the beauty. Beholding the traits of the divine beauty, the lover ascends to the highest beauty, to the love and knowledge of the divinity."[3] He gives a definition of prayer equally novel, and equally faithful to his constant doctrine: "Prayer is the contemplation of the facts of life from the highest point of view. It is the soliloquy of the beholding and jubilant soul. It is the spirit of God pronouncing his works good."[4] This language is a perfect rendering of the meaning of Spinoza where he says, "The intellectual love of the mind towards God is part of the infinite love wherewith God loves himself."[5] Prayer, as thus strangely defined, is not the offering of petitions by man to his Maker; it includes all action of whatever form. "The prayer of the farmer kneeling in his field to weed it, the prayer of the rower kneeling with the stroke of his oar, are true prayers heard throughout nature."[6] It is not a person, but the impersonal soul of the universe, which prays; and

Marginal notes: Love. Prayer.

[1] Essays, Vol. I., p. 93. [2] Ibid., p. 91.
[3] Ibid., pp. 164, 165. [4] Ibid., p. 68.
[5] Ethics, Pt. V., Prop. XXXVI. [6] Essays, Vol. I., p. 68.

what we call our consciousness of praying is but the talking of that soul to itself.

This definition of prayer leads me to notice what the author has to say on the subject of personality. His views here are perfectly at one with those of the most famous pantheists. "I wish to speak with all respect of persons," says he, "but sometimes I must pinch myself to keep and preserve the due decorum. They melt so fast into each other, that they are like grass and trees, and it needs an effort to treat them as individuals. Though the uninspired man certainly finds persons a conveniency in household matters, the divine man does not respect them: he sees them as racks of clouds, or a fleet of ripples which the wind drives over the surface of the waters."[1] "We learn that God is; that he is in me; and that all things are shadows of him. The idealism of Berkeley is a crude statement of the idealism of Jesus; and that is a crude statement of the fact, that all nature is a rapid efflux of goodness executing and organizing itself."[2] "From within or from behind, a light shines through us upon things, and makes us aware that we are nothing, but the light is all."[3] "Let us go for the universal; for the magnetism, not for the needles. Human life and its persons are poor empirical pretensions. A personal influence is an *ignis fatuus*. The great gods of fame fade before the eternal."[4] "This deep power in which we exist, and whose beatitude is all accessible to us, is not only self-sufficing and perfect every hour, but the act of

What Emerson has to say of personality.

An ignis fatuus.

[1] Essays, Vol. II., p. 227.   [2] Ibid., Vol. I., p. 281.
[3] Ibid., p. 246.   [4] Ibid., Vol. II., p. 221.

seeing and the thing seen, the seer and the spectacle, the subject and the object, are one." [1] "The larger experience of man discovers the identical nature appearing through them all. Persons themselves acquaint us with the impersonal. In all conversation between two persons, tacit reference is made, as to a third party, to a common nature. That third party, or common nature, is not social; it is impersonal, it is God." [2] "I clap my hands in infantine joy and amazement, before the first opening to me of this august magnificence, old with the love and homage of innumerable ages, young with the life of life, the sunbright Mecca of the desert." [3]

God impersonal.

It is sufficiently clear, in the light of these extracts, that I do Emerson no wrong in ranking him with the disciples of Spinoza. On the contrary, should I not be doing him a most palpable injustice did I deny to him the pantheistic doctrine which he so plainly and earnestly professes? Our respect for him as a thinker should lead us to yield him the position he has so distinctly taken, and which he defines almost in the exact terms of the most famous teachers of pantheism. A writer who declares that persons are "poor empirical pretensions," ripples on the ocean of real being; who says that subject and object, the seer and the thing seen, are one; who affirms that the personal brings us to the impersonal, which is God, or the sole reality, — this writer must be set down as a pantheist, or language may mean just the opposite of what it plainly asserts, and Hegel himself was not a Hegelian, nor Spinoza a Spinozist.

But one conclusion possible.

But the nature of Emerson's doctrine will be even more

[1] Essays, Vol. I., p. 245.   [2] Ibid., p. 252.   [3] Ibid., Vol. II., pp. 73, 74.

manifest, as we go forward, in the second place, to consider his method. Is this subjective or objective? Where does he find the one absolute reality he so firmly believes in? So far as this question goes, he is more true, I think, to the subjective and transcendental method, than either Goethe or Carlyle. He finds the absolute essence of things, not in society, with the German; nor in great men, with the Scotchman; but in each individual consciousness. In this respect he is nearly, if not quite, on the same ground as Fichte. True, there is at times a gush of hero-worship, reminding one of Carlyle; but he looks steadily within for the primary advent of divinity. The divineness of the outward is but secondary, the shadow of the true God. It is reflected deity, either conscious or unconscious. "Plants are the young of the world," says he, "vessels of health and vigor; but they grope ever upward towards consciousness; the trees are imperfect men, and seem to bemoan their imprisonment, rooted in the ground. The maples and ferns are still uncorrupt; yet no doubt, when they come to consciousness, they too will curse and swear."[1] "Every animal of the barn-yard, the field, and the forest, of the earth and of the waters that are under the earth, has contrived to get a footing and to leave the print of its features and form in some one or other of these upright, heaven-speaking faces."[2] Such remarks, occurring in various places, show that Emerson holds to the doctrine of identity, as taught by Schelling; but he has chosen not to state that doctrine, for the most part, in the Schellingian form. His method

<small>Emerson's method.</small>

<small>Consciousness the way to all truth.</small>

---

[1] Essays, Vol. II., p. 177.   [2] Ibid., Vol. I., p. 20.

is subjective and ideal. His private consciousness is the door through which he passes to the universal fact. That personality with which we flatter ourselves, is an illusion while considered as the self. It is an efflux of the Eternal One; and to recognize it as such is to behold, at a glance, all that is, or was, or ever can be. "Standing on the bare ground," says our author, "my head uplifted into infinite space, all mean egotism vanishes. I become a transparent eye-ball; I am nothing; I see all; the currents of the universal being circulate through me; I am part or parcel of God."[1] Thus it appears that the charge of egotism, which ignorant readers have so often made against Emerson, is thoroughly unjust and false. The object of his adoration is not the empirical self, but the transcendental, — by which "self," as ordinarily understood, is swallowed up. All his egotism is an entire absorption of the finite ego into the eternal.

<small>No mean egotism.</small>

Man, according to our author, is nothing real and substantial, but only a passing phenomenon, the form in which the universal fact is for the time being self-conscious. "Within man is the soul of the whole; the wise silence; the universal beauty, to which every part and particle is equally related; the eternal ONE."[2] It is Spinoza who says, "We feel and are persuaded that we are eternal;" and the language of Emerson, oftentimes, is but an echo of these words. "The soul in man is an immensity not possessed, and that cannot be possessed,"[3] says he. "The heart in thee is the heart of all; not a valve, not a wall, not an intersection is there anywhere in nature, but one blood rolls uninterrupt-

<small>Definition of man.</small>

---

[1] Miscellanies, p. 8. [2] Essays, Vol. I., p. 245. [3] Ibid., p. 246.

edly in endless circulation, through all men; as the water of the globe is all one sea, and, truly seen, its tide is one."[1] "Of this pure nature every man is at some time sensible. Language cannot paint it with his colors. It is too subtle. It is indefinable, unmeasurable, but we know that it pervades and contains us. We know that all spiritual being is in man."[2] "The soul's communication of truth is the highest event in nature, since it then does not give somewhat from itself, but gives itself, or passes into and becomes that man whom it enlightens; or, in proportion to the truth he receives, it takes him into itself."[3] As the soul, which is the divine and universal fact, is present in all persons, making them whatsoever they are, "so it is in every period of life. It is adult already in the infant man. In my dealing with my child, my Latin and my Greek, my accomplishments and my money stead me nothing. If I am wilful he sets up his will against mine; but if I renounce my will, and act for *the soul,* setting that up as umpire between us two, out of his young eyes looks the same soul."[4]

But the view of individual man, which we find in Emerson's works, is no more pantheistic than his definition of genius. He argues that any unusual elevation of spirit, religious or artistic, is purely an influx of the divine essence in the form of what we call our mind. Such is all inspiration; that of Paul, of George Fox, of Swedenborg, of Michael Angelo. "The revivals of the Calvinistic churches, the experiences of the Methodists," he says,

<small>The varieties of genius forms of the divine consciousness.</small>

[1] Essays, Vol. I., p. 267. [2] Ibid., p. 247.
[3] Ibid., p. 255. [4] Ibid., p. 254.

"are varying forms of that shudder of awe and delight with which the individual soul always mingles with the universal soul."[1] The natural genius of these Calvinists and Methodists, that is, is religious. They have a special aptitude for receiving the divine substance in that form which constitutes pious enthusiasm. Their mistake is in believing that God is outside of themselves, and that their excitement is anything more than a transient shadow of him. His going forth into self-consciousness is what makes the "revival," as it makes all that we admire, or love, or wonder at in human achievement. "When we have broken our God of tradition, and ceased from our God of rhetoric, then may God fire the heart with his presence. It is the doubling of the heart itself; nay, the infinite enlargement of the heart with a power of growth to a new infinity on every side."[2] "An individual is an enclosure. Time and space, liberty and necessity, truth and thought, are left at large no longer. Now, the universe is a close or pound. All things exist in the man tinged with the manners of his soul."[3] "Each man has his vocation. The talent is the call. This talent and this call depend on his organization, or the mode in which the general soul incarnates itself in him."[4] "The maker of all things and all persons stands behind us, and casts his dread omniscience through us over things."[5] "The wit of man, his strength, his grace, his tendency, his art, is the grace and presence of God."[6] Any fresh generalization of philosophy "is always a new influx of the divinity into the mind." And "Empedocles undoubtedly spoke a truth of thought,"

---

[1] Essays, Vol. I., p. 257. [2] Ibid., p. 266. [3] Ibid., Vol. II., p. 97.
[4] Ibid., Vol. I., p. 126. [5] Ibid., p. 255. [6] Miscellanies, p. 186.

says Emerson, "when he said, 'I am God.'"[1] Not while we go searching abroad, but while we stay at home, keeping the door of consciousness open, the great spirit of the universe not only comes in, but makes that into which it comes; not only sups with us, but is that with which it sups. He constitutes our private thought, in the depths of which he is manifested. "God enters by a private door into every individual;"[2] and this melting of subject and object into a single consciousness, is a blessed experience, which words must forever labor in vain to utter. "Ineffable is the union of man and God in every act of the soul. The simplest person, who in his integrity worships God, becomes God; yet forever and ever the influx of this better and universal self is new and unsearchable."[3]

Having seen that Emerson's God is the same as Spinoza's, and that, like Spinoza, he finds it in his private consciousness, let us, in the third place, see what he has to say of its evolution or "becoming." What is the law of this evolution? Does the noumenon mirror itself in phenomena freely, choosing whether it will or not, or under conditions of the sternest necessity? Here also, as we might expect, our author teaches the pantheistic fatalism. He does not believe in a freedom of will involving the power of alternate choice. The law of man's action is, to his view, the same as that of nature, — spontaneous and inevitable. Whatever we do, we cannot do otherwise. Any theory of a moral government which involves accountability, and which is sustained by penalties and rewards, he regards as chimerical, — a fancy

Teaches the pantheistic fatalism.

[1] Miscellanies, p. 190. [2] Essays, Vol. I., p. 297. [3] Ibid., p. 265.

of certain sects in theology. The only liberty is spontaneity; and the perfection of this automatic activity is in its absolute necessity. The universe is but one, and forever acts and reacts upon itself, compassed in the folds of an eternal fate. This necessity of action, whose endless coil lies at the centre of our being, is the freedom which, when joyfully yielded to, makes us free indeed.

But on this topic, as on others, I shall not assume to present Emerson in my own words, so much as in the language which he himself has largely used. In his essay on fate he says, "We trace fate in matter, mind, and morals. A part of fate is the freedom of man."[1] "The day of days, the great day of the feast of life, is that in which the inward eye opens to the unity of things; to the omnipresence of law; sees that what is must be, and ought to be, or is the best."[2] He quotes with approbation the stanza of the Mohammedan poet, —

<blockquote>
"On two days it stands not to run from thy grave,
The appointed, and the unappointed day;
On the first neither balm nor physician can save,
Nor thee, on the second, the universe slay."[3]
</blockquote>

All things subject to fate.

"A man's power," says he in the same essay, "is hooped about by a necessity, which, by many experiments, he touches on every side, till he learns its arc."[4] "A breath of will blows eternally through the universe of souls in the direction of the right and the necessary."[5] "Let us build altars to the blessed unity, which holds nature and souls in perfect solution, and compels every atom to serve

---

[1] Conduct of Life (Boston, Ticknor & Fields, 1860), pp. 18, 19.
[2] Ibid., p. 21.   [3] Ibid., p. 3.   [4] Ibid., p. 16.   [5] Ibid., p. 23.

an universal end. Let us build altars to the beautiful necessity, which secures that all is made of one piece; that plaintiff and defendant, friend and enemy, animal and plant, food and eater, are of one kind."[1] A severe critic might be tempted to infer, from the way in which the doctrine of unity is here carried out, things not a little shocking to our author's sensibilities. If animal and plant, food and eater are one, our horror at the deed of the cannibal, who slays his guest and makes a meal of the victim, is wholly out of place. We all are continually living upon some form of the blessed unity, either vegetable or animal; nor can we destroy any life, in any realm of nature below us, save by a kind of murder and suicide. There is not one flesh of men and another of birds, as Paul thought, but all creatures are the same flesh, and beast and herb are one; and altars should be built to the beautiful necessity which secures this eternal fact.

Everything being what it is by that inevitable fate which rules the undivided whole, no person, according to Emerson, is in the last analysis responsible for his own character. The case of politicians, who change their principles as the influences brought to bear on them change, is adduced; and their inconsistencies are accounted for purely on the ground of natural and irresistible laws. "The rabid democrat," says our author, "as soon as he is senator and rich man, has ripened beyond the possibility of sincere radicalism, and unless he can resist the sun, he must be conservative the remainder of his days."[2] Could any doctrine be more comforting than this to the outlawed rebel,

No one can do otherwise than he does.

[1] Conduct of Life, pp. 41, 42.   [2] Essays, Vol. II., p. 236.

who has sought to destroy the government of his country? Though he stood high in the confidence of the public, and was the trusted servant of the nation, so that his treachery drew immeasurable ruin after it, yet he has no occasion to reproach himself; he was ripened into the wickedness as apples are ripened. "The only sin," says this apologist for wrong-doing, "is limitation."[1] At times he seems almost to regret the fatalism in which he so firmly believes, as where he says, "I would gladly be moral, and keep due metes and bounds, which I dearly love, and allow the most to the will of man; but I have set my heart on honesty, and I can see nothing at last in success or failure but more or less of vital force supplied from the eternal."[2] "Character is nature in the highest form."[3] "The same law of eternal procession ranges all that we call the virtues, and extinguishes each in the light of a better."[4] "What avails it to fight with the eternal laws of mind, which adjust the relations of all persons to each, by the mathematical measure of their beings and havings."[5] "We talk of deviations from natural life, as if artificial life were not also natural. The smoothest-curled courtier in the boudoirs of a palace has an animal nature, rude and aboriginal as a white bear, omnipotent to its own ends, and is directly related there, amid essences and billets-doux, to Himmalch mountain-chains and the axis of the globe."[6] "As children in their play run behind each other, and seize one by the ears and make him walk before them, so is the spirit our unseen pilot. All art is a portion of history; a stroke drawn in

All life natural.

[1] Essays, Vol. I. p. 279. [2] Ibid., Vol. II., p. 71. [3] Ibid., p. 106.
[4] Ibid., Vol. I., p. 285. [5] Ibid., p. 134. [6] Ibid., Vol. II., p. 177.

the portrait 'of that inevitable fate, perfect and beautiful, according to whose ordinations all beings advance to their beatitude."[1]

Now, if Emerson were wont to deal in tropes and rhetorical flourishes, we might abate somewhat from the palpable force of his words. But he is a literalist. He contends, as we have already seen, that those who believe in a personal God, and hold that they might act otherwise than they do, are deceived by their rhetoric. Even his poetry, he claims, is the exact language of philosophy. When he says, "Every one must act after his kind, be he asp or angel," he can mean nothing less than universal fatalism. The passages I have quoted from him on this subject are not to be taken figuratively, but literally. We are to understand him as meaning just what his words plainly imply, when he says, "I have been floated into this thought, this hour, this connection of events, by secret currents of might and mind; and my ingenuity and wilfulness have not thwarted, have not aided to any appreciable degree."[2] The author shows a desire to see his views adopted by other persons. And here it is, as we see the case, that his doctrine of fatalism presses. For why attempt to make disciples, we say, of beings whom an iron necessity rules in every act? But he anticipates our criticism, saying, "If you say, 'the acceptance of the vision is also the act of God,' I shall not seek to penetrate the mystery; I admit the force of what you say."[3] His utterances of doctrine, and all his conduct, are alike the forthputtings of an eternal fate, and he

Emerson's use of words not rhetorical.

Even fate a mystery.

[1] Miscellanies, p. 201. [2] Essays, Vol. I., p. 298. [3] Miscellanies, pp. 212, 213.

has only this account to give of them. His struggle to make others believe as he believes is unnatural, since God himself is in every instance both master and disciple; and this pantheism, which he offers as a substitute for our traditional faith, is at last confessed to be as inexplicable as anything in Calvinism! A part of fate are his writings and all his wise sayings. "The universal nature, too strong for the petty nature of the bard, sits on his neck, and writes through his hand; so that when he seems to vent a mere caprice and wild romance, the issue is an exact allegory."[1] "By virtue of this inevitable nature, private will is overpowered, and, maugre our efforts or our imperfections, your genius will speak for you, and mine for me. That which we are, we shall teach, not voluntarily, but involuntarily. Thoughts come into our minds by avenues we never left open, and thoughts go out of our minds through avenues we never voluntarily opened."[2]

Having seen what the fundamental doctrine of Emerson is, in its substance, method, and law, let us next consider some of the conclusions to which it leads him, within the two great realms of nature and history. The soul of all things, found primarily in his own consciousness, and forever acting within the ring of necessity, mirrors itself forth, through him, under the forms of mind and matter. Here we have, with hardly a shade of difference, Spinoza's infinite attributes of thought and extension. History and nature are not radically distinct. They are, the one more, and the other less, vivid manifestations of the absolute essence of all

The objective world in the light of Emerson's philosophy.

[1] Essays, Vol. I., p. 30.   [2] Ibid., p. 260.

things. In human history the universal soul is still self-conscious; whereas in everything below the plane of history its reflex is too faint to produce consciousness. History is God conscious; nature is God struggling towards consciousness. All our study, in these two departments of knowledge, is God looking at himself; beholding as it were his own image reflected to him in a mirror. All recorded science, and the annals of the ages, are his autobiography; the naturalist, or historian, being but the pen with which he traces a record of his own action and reaction, in one or more of the successive *stadia*. Our author might therefore, in strict conformity to his doctrine, bring the whole objective world under a single treatment. But he has chosen to treat nature and history separately; and hence in giving his views I shall regard the distinction.

Taking up first his view of history, we find that he holds it to be simply a conscious reflex of the universal soul. "The soul," he says, "looketh steadily forward, creating a world before her, leaving worlds behind her. She has no dates, nor rites, nor persons, nor specialties, nor men. The soul knows only the soul; the web of events is the flowing robe in which she is clothed."[1] "Everything the individual sees without him corresponds to his states of mind. The primeval world I can dive to in myself, as well as grope for it in catacombs, libraries, and the broken reliefs and torsos of ruined villas."[2] "There is no age, or state of society, or mode of action in history, to which there is not somewhat corresponding in each man's life. He is greater than all the geography and all the governments in the

History absorbed into the soul.

---

[1] Essays, Vol. I., p. 249.   [2] Ibid., p. 21.

world. I can find Greece, Asia, Italy, Spain, and the Islands, — the genius and creative principle of each and of all eras in my own mind."[1] "A man shall be the temple of fame. I shall find in him the fore-world, the age of gold, the apples of knowledge, the Argonautic expedition, the calling of Abraham, the building of the temple, the advent of Christ, the dark ages, the revival of letters, the Reformation, the discovery of new lands, the opening of new regions and new sciences. He shall be the priest of Pan, and bring with him into humble cottages the blessing of the morning stars and all the recorded benefits of heaven and earth."[2] "The advancing man discovers how deep a property he has in literature, in all fable as well as in all history. His own secret biography he finds in lines wonderfully intelligible to him, dotted down before he was born. One after another *he* comes up in his private adventures with every fable of Æsop, of Homer, of Hafiz, of Ariosto, of Chaucer, of Scott, and verifies them with his own head and hands."[3] "Of the universal mind each individual is one more incarnation. All its properties consist in him."[4] "All literature writes the biography of each man. Books, monuments, pictures, conversation, are portraits in which he finds the lineaments he is forming. The silent and the eloquent praise him and accost him, and he is stimulated wherever he moves as by personal allusions."[5] "History is an impertinence and an injury, if it be anything more than a cheerful apologue or parable of my being and becoming."[6]

All literature the biography of each man.

[1] Essays, Vol. I, pp. 7, 8, 9. [2] Ibid., p. 35. [3] Ibid., p. 27.
[4] Ibid., p. 4. [5] Ibid., p. 7. [6] Ibid., p. 58.

"I am owner of the sphere,
Of the seven stars and solar year,
Of Cæsar's hand and Plato's brain,
Of Lord Christ's heart and Shakespeare's strain."[1]

"How easily these old worships of Moses, of Zoroaster, of Menu, of Socrates, domesticate themselves in the mind! I cannot find any antiquity in them. They are mine as much as theirs."[2] "Civil and natural history, the history of art and literature, must be explained from individual history, or must remain words. There is nothing but is related to us, nothing that does not interest us, — kingdom, college, tree, horse, or iron shoe, the roots of all things are in man. The priestcraft of the east and west; of the Magian, Brahman, Druid, and Inca, is expounded in the individual's private life. He finds Assyria and the mounds of Cholula at his door, and himself has laid the courses."[3]

Such is history, according to Emerson: the essence of deity or reality projected forward in actual events, under the forms of each man's private consciousness. If this theory of the subjective essence of all facts be true, the author has acted very foolishly when he has visited different parts of the world, and read tedious volumes of antiquarian lore, to get a knowledge of mankind in present and former times; for he held within him, all the while, everything which he sought. Fireside travels are as good as any, and as literal, though they be but dreams, if the roots of all things are in man. It sometimes happens that persons cursed with a prodi-

A practical result.

[1] Motto to Essay on History. [2] Essays, Vol. I., p. 23.
[3] Ibid., pp. 16, 25, 26.

gious vanity, or with that defect of memory which consists in remembering too much, illustrate our author's doctrine in their conversation and public discourse, — recounting experiences which they never passed through, and describing scenes in parts of the world which they never visited. They are simply reducing the Emersonian theory to practice; yet sensible people feel constrained to regard such talk as *lying*, and those who have fallen into the habit of thus retailing ".impersonal" experiences are held to be candidates for the jail or the madhouse. A pantheist once pressed this subjective theory of history on the attention of Nathanael Emmons. "Doctor," said he, "I was with Adam and Eve in the garden at the eating of the apple." "Yes," was the quick reply of the theologian, "I have always understood that a *third* person was present." The justice of this reply is equal to its wit, for the pronoun *I* cannot refer to an impersonal existence; if we know and are persuaded that we are eternal, as Emerson and Spinoza teach, we are bound to have a distinct and personal remembrance of that eternity.

But let us also look at the theory of nature, which our author holds on the basis of his general doctrine. Nature is the universal soul projected beyond the sphere of self-consciousness. God is the great light whose rays, constantly going out and returning, make all things. When they return from points so near as to awaken consciousness, they make history; but when from points more remote, so that the eternal centre is not conscious of the reflection, they make nature. This doctrine will easily appear, from Emerson's own words. "The world," he says, "proceeds from the same spirit as

<small>Nature an evolution of the soul.</small>

man. It is a remoter and inferior incarnation of God, a projection of God in the unconscious."¹ "We see the world piece by piece, as the sun, the moon, the animal, the tree; but the whole, of which these are the shining parts, is the soul."² "I am somehow receptive of the great soul, and thereby I do overlook the sun and the stars, and feel them to be the fair accidents and effects which change and pass. More and more the surges of everlasting nature enter into me. Revering the soul, man will come to see that the world is the perennial miracle which the soul worketh. The soul calls the light its own; and feels that the grass grows and the stone falls, by a law inferior to, and dependent on, its nature."³ "Genius detects through the fly, through the caterpillar, through the grub, through the egg, the constant individual; through countless individuals, the fixed species; through many species, the genus; through all genera, the steadfast type; through all the kingdoms of organized life, the eternal unity. Nature is a mutable cloud, which is always and never the same."⁴ "Nature is the opposite of the soul, answering to it part for part. One is seal, and one is print. Its beauty is the beauty of his mind who is conscious of the soul. Its laws are the laws of his own mind. Nature then becomes to him the measure of his attainments. So much of nature as he is ignorant of, so much of his own mind does he not yet possess."⁵ "Build, therefore, your own world. The advancing spirit shall create its ornaments along its path, and carry with it the beauty it visits, and the song which enchants it."⁶ "Man filled nature with his overflowing

¹ Miscellanies p. 62.   ² Essays, Vol. 1., p. 245.   ³ Ibid. p. 260.
⁴ Ibid., p. 12.   ⁵ Miscellanies, p. 83.   ⁶ Ibid., p. 74.

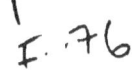

currents; out from him sprang the sun and moon. The laws of his mind, the periods of his action, externized themselves into day and night, into the year and the seasons."[1] "The world is a divine dream, from which we may presently awake to the glories and certainties of day."[2]

Emerson represents nature as the soul or God yet asleep; God only dreams till he awakes to consciousness in the mind of man. Man, however, is not real save as he is an inlet of the divine essence. It is not the empirical, but the transcendental man; the absolute cause, not the effect, that he means when he says, "A man's genius determines for him the character of the universe."[3] "Not in nature, but in man, is all the beauty and worth he sees. The world is very empty, and is indebted to this gilding, exalting soul for all its pride."[4] "Out of the human heart go, as it were, highways to the heart of every object in nature. A man is a bundle of relations, a knot of roots, whose flower and fruitage are the world."[5] "Man carries the world in his head, the whole astronomy and chemistry suspended in a thought."[6] "Let man, then, learn that the sources of nature are in his own mind."[7] "I am present at the sowing of the seed of the world. With a geometry of sunbeams, the soul lays the foundations of nature."[8] "Nature is the incarnation of a thought, and turns to a thought again, as ice becomes water and gas. The world is mind precipitated. Man crystallized, man vegetative, speaks to man im-

The world man externized.

---

[1] Miscellanies, p. 69. [2] Ibid., p. 60. [3] Essays, Vol. I., p. 129.
[4] Ibid., p. 132. [5] Ibid., p. 32. [6] Ibid., Vol. II., p. 178.
[7] Ibid., Vol. I., p. 267. [8] Ibid., p. 314.

personated."[1] "The great Pan of old, who was clothed in leopard skin to signify the beautiful variety of things and the firmament, — his coat of stars, — was but thee, O rich and various man! thou palace of sight and sound, carrying in thy senses the morning and the night, and the unfathomable galaxy; in thy brain the geometry of the city of God."[2]

Now let us pause and breathe a moment, and consider whereto the author has brought us in these extracts. If what he has been saying be true, as we must believe that he holds it to be, since he is not a rhetorician, but states things precisely as they are to his view, then it is plain that all our knowledges and our philosophy need to be reconstructed for the most part, whatever may be the case of his own. The old fable of a man in the moon, pales before this declaration that the moon is in every man. And not only this, but the sun and stars, and other very formidable objects, quite too numerous to mention, are a part of the original furniture of the human mind. We do not have to "stretch" our minds at all, as good Dr. Watts thought, to take in sea and shore; for all nature is ours before we are born, and we carry it about with us eternally in our thoughts, knowing it to the same extent that we know ourselves. The kingdom of heaven within us is not peace and joy in the Holy Ghost, as the Apostles wrote; it is, literally, the firmament and its galaxies, with the earth and other planets, and empty regions between, and unmeasured spaces beyond. The microcosm contains the macrocosm. The universe lives, and moves, and has its being in man,

Knowledge of nature but self-knowledge.

[1] Essays, Vol. II., p. 190.   [2] Miscellanies, p. 197.

and is the stupendous miracle which he works day by day.

It is but just to call attention here to that form of idealism which Emerson holds, in order that his views, as now given, may be credited with such rationality as they have.

Emerson's theory of nature that of every subjective idealist.

He sees no absurdity in the theory of nature just presented; for nature is to him not real. He denies the existence, or at least assumes the non-existence of an objective world. He is an idealist, as every consistent pantheist is at last forced to be. Pure idealism cannot be other than subjective, while it rests on demonstration. "Before the revelations of the soul," says Emerson, "time, space, and nature shrink away."[1] "I have no hostility to nature, but a child's love. I expand and live in the warm day, like corn and melons. Children, it is true, believe in the external world. The belief that it appears only, is an after-thought; but with culture this faith will as surely arise as did the other."[2] "Whether nature enjoy a substantial existence without, or is only the apocalypse of the mind, it is alike useful and alike venerable to me. Be it what it may, it is ideal to me, so long as I cannot try the accuracy of my senses. A noble doubt perpetually suggests itself, whether nature outwardly exists."[3] "Perhaps these subjective lenses have a creative power; perhaps there are no objects. Once we lived in what we saw; now, the rapaciousness of this new power, which threatens to absorb all things, engages us. Nature, art, persons, letters, religions,— objects, successively, tumble in, and are, in their turn, its ideas. Nature and literature are subjective phenomena; every

---

[1] Essays, Vol. I., p. 249.   [2] Miscellanies, pp. 56, 57.   [3] Ibid., pp. 46, 45.

evil and every good thing is a shadow we cast."[1] "Let us no longer omit our homage to the efficient nature, *natura naturans*, the quick cause, before which all forms flee as the driven snows; itself secret, its works driven before it in flocks and multitudes."[2] Man, whose eye and step fate is ever turning outward, —

> " Sees full before him, gliding without tread,
> An image with a glory round its head;
> This shade he worships for its golden hues,
> And makes, not knowing, that which he pursues."

The pantheism of Emerson, the main features of which have now been presented, involves other doctrines more specific, and entering more directly into the daily conduct of life, which are still to be considered. *Practical teaching.*

He teaches, as one legitimate consequence of his philosophy, the duty of self-reverence. This is not vulgar egotism, or self-conceit. In the popular sense of the term, no one is less an egotist than Emerson. The self, regarded as an effect, a person, is, upon his theory, absorbed into the one universal soul which fills all things. For the sake of convenience he retains the name, but only the name; meaning, by it, the impersonal divinity which rises into consciousness under this fleeting form. The reverence enjoined in the Bible involves the being of a personal God, and guards sacredly the personality of the worshipper; but that enjoined by Emerson annihilates the worshipper, and leaves, to be worshipped, only an impersonal force, besides which there is no reality. *Duty of self-reverence.*

[1] Essays, Vol. II., p. 77.   [2] Ibid., p. 174.

This is the underlying doctrine when he tells us that "nothing is at last sacred but the integrity of our own mind."[1] "It demands something godlike in him who has cast off the common motives of humanity, and has ventured to trust himself for a task-master. High be his heart, faithful his will, clear his sight, that he may in good earnest be doctrine, society, law to himself."[2] "A man is the word made flesh; and the moment he acts for himself, tossing the laws, the books, idolatries, and customs out of the window, we pity him no more, but thank and revere him."[3] Since man is wholly a manifestation of the divine essence, Emerson admonishes us never to use words of self-reproach, but to reverence ourselves at all times. "It is the highest power of divine moments," he says, "that they abolish our contritions also;"[4] — words which remind us of Spinoza's saying, that "repentance is not a virtue, or does not arise from reason, but he who repents of any deed he has done is twice miserable."[5] "I accuse myself of sloth and unprofitableness day by day; but when these waves of God flow into me, I no longer reckon lost time."[6] "Let a man know his worth, and keep things under his feet. Let him not peep or steal, or skulk up and down with the air of an interloper, in the world which exists for him."[7] If questioned as to the propriety of reverencing a thing, which is neither subject nor object, but the impersonal essence of both forever acting under fixed laws of fate, our author has nothing to say. There is in the self the impulse to worship a somewhat which there makes

---

[1] Essays, Vol. I., p. 44. [2] Ibid., p. 65. [3] Ibid., p. 67.
[4] Ibid., p. 287. [5] Ethics, Part IV., Prop. LIV.
[6] Essays, Vol. I., p. 288. [7] Ibid., p. 54.

itself known; and this impulse should be joyfully obeyed.

Emerson urges, as involved in his general doctrine, the duty of self-reliance, — still using the term "self" in a transcendental sense. He has an entire essay on this duty, the motto of which is, *Ne te quæsiveris extra* — Seek nothing but yourself. "Trust nothing but thyself: great men have always done so, betraying their perception that the absolutely worthy was seated at their heart, working through their hands, predominating in all their being."[1] "Entire self-reliance belongs to the intellect. One soul is a counterpoise of all souls, as a capillary column of water is a balance for the sea."[2] "Obey thyself. That which shows God in me, fortifies me. That which shows God out of me, makes me a wart and a wen."[3] "Only by coming again to themselves, or to God in themselves, can men grow forevermore."[4] "The true Christianity, a faith like Christ's in the infinitude of man, is lost. Once leave your own knowledge of God, your own sentiment, and take secondary knowledge, as St. Paul's, or George Fox's, or Swedenborg's, and you get wide from God with every year."[5] "The reformers summon conventions, and vote and resolve in multitude. Not so, O friends, will the God deign to enter and inhabit you, but by a method precisely the reverse. It is only as a man puts off all foreign support, and stands alone, that I see him to be strong, and to prevail. He is weaker by every recruit to his banner. Is not a man better than a town? Ask nothing of men, and

Self-reliance.

[1] Essays, Vol. I., p. 41.   [2] Ibid., p. 312.   [3] Miscellanies, p. 127.
   [4] Ibid., p. 128.   [5] Ibid., p. 140.

in the end thou, only firm column, must appear the upholder of all that surrounds thee. He who knows that power is inborn, that he is weak because he has looked for good out of him and elsewhere, and so perceiving, throws himself unhesitatingly on his thought, instantly rights himself, stands in the erect position, commands his limbs, works miracles."[1] "Let us not rove; let us sit at home with the cause. Let us stun and astonish the intruding rabble of men and books and institutions, by a simple declaration of the divine fact. Bid the invaders take the shoes from off their feet, for God is here within."[2] "Great is the soul, and plain. It is no flatterer, it is no follower; it never appeals from itself. Before the immense possibilities of man, all mere experience, all past biography, however spotless and sainted, shrinks away."[3] Now this is pantheism carried out to the last degree. It is the being and non-being of Hegel put into a didactic form, and made to each man the rule of his daily life. The self is nothing, and there is nothing but the self; and all is a necessary deduction from the postulate that the known God, as defined by Hegel and Emerson alike, "is that of which everything may be affirmed and everything denied." The religion of Christ was self-worship; and we shall be Christs, in the same sense that he was, when we find the sum of all that is real and divine where alone it exists for us, — within the compass of our own thoughts.

Another practical deduction, which Emerson finds in his subjective pantheism, is the duty of self-assertion.

Self-assertion. "This one fact the world hates," says he, "that the soul *becomes;* for that forever degrades the

[1] Essays, Vol. I., p. 78. [2] Ibid., p. 62. [3] Ibid., p. 268.

past, turns all riches to poverty, all reputation to shame, confounds the saint with the rogue, shoves Judas and Jesus equally aside."[1] Here, as we perceive, the "becoming" of Hegel's logic is made the basis of a rule for our everyday life. Self-assertion, by which we understand forwardness, aspiring, pushing for place, personal ambition, self-consciousness, a bustling sense of one's own importance, and the like, our author regards as God coming out of non-being into being; and therefore the more of it we have, the more will God be manifested. And the sinner should be just as earnest as the saint, in this becoming; for God is the essence of them both. Emerson admits that this doctrine, if carried out in all its consequences, legitimates the social chaos of Goethe, and the political lawlessness of Carlyle. Yet he offers no other creed, while he urges this upon every man. "I appeal from your customs. I must be myself. I cannot break myself any longer for you, or you. If you can love me for what I am, we shall be the happier. If you cannot, I will still seek to deserve that you should. I will not hide my tastes or aversions. I will so trust that what is deep is holy, that I will do strongly before the sun and moon whatever inly rejoices me, and the heart appoints."[2] "A man may have that allowance he takes. Take the place and attitude which belong to you, and all men acquiesce. The world must be just. It leaves every man, with profound unconcern, to set his own rate. Hero or driveller, it meddles not in the matter. It will certainly accept your measure of your doing and being, whether you sneak about and deny your own name, or whether you see your work produced to the concave sphere of the

[1] Essays, Vol. I., p. 61.   [2] Ibid., p. 64.

heavens, one with the revolution of the stars."[1] "Speak your latent conviction, and it shall be the universal sense; for the inmost in due time becomes the outmost,—and our first thought is rendered back to us by the trumpets of the last judgment."[2]

Still another injunction, which Emerson finds in his general doctrine, and which he lays on us all, is that which bids us seek the law of our duty within. All trustworthy rules for the conduct of life are of subjective origin; and they alone are the standard by which to judge those pretending to come from any outward source. If this inward law were simply the voice of conscience, that higher law of our moral nature by which Christ teaches us to regulate our practice, it would be well. But it is far other than that. It is the total tendency of the man, the resultant of all his energies in free exercise. The moral imperative is no more sacred to him whose ethical nature predominates, than the animal imperative to him whose appetites predominate. "No law can be sacred to me," says our author, "but that of my own nature. If I am the devil's child, I will live from the devil. Good and bad are names very readily transferable to this or that; the only right is what is after my constitution, the only wrong what is against it. A man is to carry himself, in the presence of all opposition, as if everything were titular and ephemeral but he."[3] "It is of no use to preach to me from without. If a man do not speak from within the veil, where the word is one with that it tells of, let him lowly confess it."[4] "What your heart thinks great is great. The soul's emphasis is al-

The moral law wholly subjective.

[1] Essays, Vol. I., p. 136. [2] Ibid., p. 39. [3] Ibid., p. 44. [4] Ibid., p. 261.

ways right."[1] "No love can be bound by oath or covenant to secure it against a higher love. No truth so sublime but it may be trivial to-morrow in the light of new thoughts. People wish to be settled; only as far as they are unsettled is there any hope of them."[2] Our author admits that the law thus enunciated confounds all established notions of social order, but he retracts nothing. "The bold sensualist," he says, "will use the name of philosophy to gild his crimes, but the law of consciousness abides."[3] "One man thinks justice consists in paying debts, and has no measure in his abhorrence of another who is very remiss in this, and makes the creditor wait tediously. But that second man has his own way of looking at things."[4] Let each obey his tendency, is Emerson's admonition to them both, and in neither case shall any real injustice be done, but the highest ethical perfection be indifferently attained by the two diverse courses of action. He proceeds in a similar strain, seeming to feel the dangerous nature of the ground he is on, yet pressing boldly forward, in the line of his fundamental theory: "I hear some reader say, you have arrived at a fine Pyrrhonism, at an equivalence and indifferency of all actions, and would fain teach us that our crimes may be lively stones, out of which we shall construct the temple of the true God! I am not careful to justify myself. I own that I am gladdened by seeing that unrestrained inundation of the principle of good into every chink and hole that selfishness has left open, yea; into selfishness itself; so that no evil is pure, nor hell itself without its extreme satisfac-

---

[1] Essays, Vol. I., p. 130. [2] Ibid., p. 290.
[3] Ibid., p. 65. [4] Ibid., pp. 286, 287.

tions."[1] The ultimate fate of the wicked, that is, will be a source of blessedness to them, as truly as the destiny of the righteous will make them forever content. Judas, in going to his own place, went to a place which satisfied him, no less than the Lord of glory himself. The conclusion is certainly somewhat startling, yet it grows logically out of the Emersonian philosophy. The optimism of that philosophy is all-encompassing, absolute. To whatever any being, angel or devil, is brought by the largest outcome of all that is in him, it cannot but be to him a state of perfect blessedness. It may be called "perdition," and by many other hard names; and "the Book" may paint its terrors in blackness and fire; nevertheless, it is not an evil, but a good, and, to those who bravely meet it, full of "extreme satisfactions."[2] The words which exhort us to make to ourselves friends who shall receive us when our earthly tabernacles fail, is here broadened into a precept which confounds holiness and sin; which makes it a matter of indifference whether we choose this or that alternative, so long as we are in the path to which the "emphasis" of our nature impels us.

Another duty involved in the pantheistic creed of Emerson, and which he does not omit to press, is that of self-isolation. All true life rests at last on a basis of pure individualism. Intercourse with men, and devotion to mere affairs, render us forgetful of that in which all true greatness consists. The secret doors, by which the soul of all things comes into us, are

Duty of self-isolation.

[1] Essays, Vol. I., p. 288.
[2] For a fine statement and criticism of this view of evil, see Müller's Christian Doctrine of Sin, Book II., chap. IV.

not kept open. We no longer feel the charm of the eternal; but its spell is broken, and we fall away into the temporal. We cease to be, and only seem. From all this seeming we must withdraw ourselves, and retire into the solitude of our own thoughts. Thus alone is it that we feel the impulses of the universal soul; as the rivers, by pouring themselves into the sea, are filled out of its depths through all their courses. "If a man would know what the great God speaketh," our author says, "he must 'go into his closet and shut the door,' as Jesus said. God will not make himself manifest to cowards. One must greatly listen to himself, withdrawing himself from all the accents of other men's devotion. Even their prayers are hurtful to him, until he have made his own. He that finds God a sweet enveloping thought, never counts his company. When I sit in that presence who shall dare to come in?"[1] "The poor mind does not seem to itself to be anything, unless it have an outward badge; some wild contrasting action, to testify that it is somewhat. The rich mind lies in the sun and sleeps, and is nature."[2] To be wholly self-absorbed the highest blessedness. He whose mind is in a perpetual doze, and all whose life comes nearest to the idea of natural vegetation, is, according to this language, the man blessed with the largest measure of intellectual wealth. Contentment with idle reverie is the characteristic of genius; and they are greatest whose blessedness consists with doing nothing.

Urging this duty of self-isolation, and entire satisfaction with one's inward life, Emerson says, "I like the silent church before the service begins better than any preaching.

[1] Essays, Vol. I., p. 268.   [2] Ibid., p. 146.

How far off, how cool, how chaste the persons look, begirt each one with a precinct or sanctuary. So let us always sit."[1] "Let us not be too much acquainted. We should meet each morning as from foreign countries, and, spending the day together, should depart at night as into foreign countries."[2] "Men descend to meet. In their habitual and mean service to the world, for which they forsake their native nobleness, they resemble those Arabian sheiks wHo dwell in mean houses, and affect an extreme poverty, to escape the rapacity of the Pacha, and reserve all their display of wealth for their interior and guarded retirements."[3] Now this solitary and lofty self-sufficiency, which is a duty if pantheism be true, certainly ought not to claim any affinity with the spirit of Him who went about doing good, teaching us that only as we humble ourselves are we exalted, and that we must "wash one another's feet" if we would be great in his kingdom. "Your isolation must not be mechanical, but spiritual; that is, must be elevation. At times the world seems to be in conspiracy to importune you with important trifles. Friend, client, child, sickness, fear, want, charity, all knock at the gate of the closet door, and say, 'Come out to us.' But keep thy state; come not into their confusion."[4] And this man is an oracle to not a few philanthropists of to-day.

"Men descend to meet."

Misanthropy.

Do those who regard him as a safe guide in ways of loving service to mankind really apprehend the spirit of his writings? Undoubtedly there are those who imagine themselves in sympathy with his views,

---

[1] Essays, Vol. I., p. 63. [2] Ibid., Vol. II., p. 135.
[3] Ibid., Vol. I., p. 253. [4] Ibid., p. 63.

while they are dealing their bread to the hungry, and striving to break every yoke. Yet nothing can be clearer, in the light of the words now quoted, than that the path which they follow is not his, but "the more excellent way" in their own hearts. They do good despite of his teachings. They are not swerved from their loving-heartedness and charity, though charmed by the sweet-voiced dream. Their protection against the unloving tone of much that Emerson has written consists partly in the fact that they are too good to comprehend it, and partly in the fact that his own practice gives the lie to his theory.

It is a little surprising that Emerson, after putting so low an estimate as he does on the Christian Scriptures, should endeavor to show that they accord, in some of their teachings, with his doctrine. Why should he claim the indorsement of a volume whose authority he has disowned? Seeing how manifestly the Bible is against him in its whole drift, he seems to me to wrest its free language in a quite extraordinary way. He broadly intimates that the account of the fall of man, in the first chapter of Genesis, is simply an exposition of his theory, as held by Moses, or whoever wrote the book; that it is an allegory, picturing to us the human family, who in the main have ceased to commune with the great spirit of nature revealed in them, and are living in that objective world which he regards as unreal.[1] "Christianity," he says, "is rightly dear to the best of mankind; yet was there never a young philosopher whose breeding had fallen into the Christian church,

<small>Attitude towards the Bible and Christianity.</small>

---
[1] Essays, Vol. II., p. 174.

by whom that brave text of Paul's was not specially prized: 'Then shall also the Son be subject unto him who put all things under him, that God may be all in all.' Let the claims and virtues of persons be never so great and welcome, the instinct of man presses eagerly onward to the impersonal and illimitable, and gladly arms itself against the dogmatism of bigots with this generous word out of the book itself."[1] "The dogmatism of bigots" is a rather tart phrase for so amiable a writer as Emerson to apply to those whose only bigotry is, that they do not with him find pantheism, but monotheism in the writings of the apostles. But let the harsh utterance stand. Our author has read the story of the Pilgrim Fathers. "What a debt is ours," he says, "to that old religion which, in the childhood of most of us, still dwelt like a Sabbath morning in the country of New England, teaching privation, self-denial and sorrow! A man was born not for prosperity, but to suffer for the benefit of others, like the noble rock-maple which, all around our villages, bleeds for the service of man."[2]. When Emerson has found, in all the pantheism of the ages, any such flowering as this into holy and sacrificial lives, it will be time for him to characterize an earnest Christian faith as "the dogmatism of bigots," and to quote the words of the Son of God as confirming his own speculative views. "Jesus Christ," he says, "belonged to the true race of prophets. He saw with open eye the mystery of the soul. One man was true to what is in you and me. He said, in this jubilee of divine emotion, 'I am divine. Through me, God acts; through me,

Insinuates that Christ was a pantheist.

[1] Essays, Vol. I., p. 284. [2] Miscellanies, p. 211.

speaks. Would you see God, see me; or, see *thee*, when thou also thinkest as I now think.'"[1] To the view of Emerson, therefore, Christ is not an exceptional person among men. He is one of a class; those, namely, who have lived and spoken from the soul which dwells consciously in us all. "When the gods come among men, they are not known. Jesus was not; Socrates and Shakespeare were not."[2] But this classification will not stand. For no exegesis can make out the religion of Christ to be only self-worship, or the God of the Christian Scriptures to be the same as that of Emerson and Spinoza. We have seen, in noticing Emerson's attitude towards all reforms and charities, to what opposite results the doctrine of Christ and that of the pantheist logically come. The God whose will Christ came to do is a Father, with the father's heart of pity and tenderness towards all his children; the God whom the pantheist would set up in his place, and persuade us to worship, is an eternal fate, which devours all things up. Emerson says, Believe in the god within yourself, and you shall live; Christ says, Whosoever believeth in me shall never die. Emerson says, Obey your own tendency and you shall be led into all truth ; Christ says, I am the way, and the truth, and the life. Emerson says, Accept my speculation and it shall unsettle you in all things; Christ says, Take my yoke upon you and ye shall find rest to your soul.

Spirit of the two contrasted.

But some one may accuse me of injustice in representing that the spirit of Emerson's doctrine is just the opposite of the spirit of Christ; that he would unsettle and bewilder us, rather than lead us in a plain path, where our

[1] Miscellanies, p. 125.   [2] Essays, Vol. I., p. 28.

Emerson would unsettle all things. souls shall be at peace. Yet here are his words, fully justifying all that I have said: "Lest I should mislead any when I have my head and obey my own whims, let me remind the reader that I am only an experimenter. Do not set the least value on what I do, or the least discredit on what I do not, as if I pretended to settle anything true or false. I unsettle all things. No facts to me are sacred; none are profane; I simply experiment, an endless seeker, with no past at my back."[1] Unlike Him who declared that he was the light of the world, Emerson here announces that he is a planet yet uncertain of its own orbit, and which rushes on, in obedience to an inward impulse, regardless alike of the past and the future.

It may seem to some that I misrepresent Emerson, in saying that he is not a philanthropist, but, so far as consistent with his theory, a despiser of all acts of charity and beneficence among men. His own language shall decide whether I have misrepresented him or not. "I tell thee, thou foolish philanthropist, that I grudge the dollar, the dime, the cent, I give to such men as do not belong to me, and to whom I do not belong. Your miscellaneous popular charities; the education at college of fools; the building of meeting-houses to the vain end to which many now stand; alms to sots; and the thousandfold relief societies; though I confess with shame I sometimes succumb, and give the dollar, it is a wicked dollar, which by and by I shall have the manhood to withhold."[2] As if these words were not enough, he again says, in one of his later works, "Leave

No philanthropist.

---

[1] Essays, Vol. I., p. 289. [2] Ibid., pp. 45, 46.

this hypocritical prating about the masses. Masses are rude, lame, unmade, pernicious in their demands and influence, and need not to be flattered, but to be schooled. I wish not to concede anything to them, but to tame, drill, divide and break them up, and draw individuals out of them. The worst of charity is, that the lives you are asked to preserve are not worth preserving. Masses! the calamity is the masses. I do not wish any mass at all, but honest men only; lovely, sweet, accomplished women only; no shovel-handed, narrow-brained, gin-drinking, million stockingers or lazzaroni at all. If government knew how, I should like to see it check, not multiply the population. When it reaches its true law of action, every man that is born will be hailed as essential. Away with this hurrah of masses, and let us have the considerate vote of single men, spoken on their honor and their conscience. In old Egypt it was established law, that the vote of a prophet be reckoned equal to a hundred hands. I think it was much underestimated."[1] Certainly, this burst of misanthropy almost rivals Carlyle. It is as undemocratic as the most violent aristocrat could desire. It savors not of philanthropy, but of that spirit of caste which would do a Brahman's heart good. It is, in fact, whether consciously or not to the author, a passionate rendering of Spinoza's language, where he says, as one of the inferences from his pantheistic system, "The man who lives by reason endeavors as much as possible not to be touched by pity or compassion."[2]

In asserting, as I have, that Emerson confounds the

[1] Conduct of Life, pp. 218, 219.   [2] Ethics, Pt. IV., Prop. L., Coroll.

No moral distinctions. bad with the good in morals, and sees only the same kind of sacredness in men as in the meanest animals, it may be said that I wrong him. But his own words shall judge between us. "I talked to-day with a pair of philosophers: I endeavored to show my good men that I love everything by turns, and nothing long; that I loved the centre, but doted on the superficies; that I loved man, if men seemed to me mice and rats; that I revered saints, but woke up glad that the old pagan world stood its ground, and died hard; that I was glad of men of every gift and nobility, but would not live in their arms."[1] The same soul of nature, that is, which gives understanding to men, reveals itself in the small burrowing creatures; paganism is as good as Christianity while earnestly cultivated; the warrior who desolates a continent, may claim the same homage as the enlightener of a nation. A Cæsar and a Paul are alike noble, as judged by that philosophy which sees God in all action; but Emerson himself, whom this nobility fills with joy, is greater than all, and disdains familiar intercourse with that which he so admires, since the most sacred revelations of God cannot be from without, but are always from within.

Now a stranger, who should visit Emerson after canvassing the views which I have given, would expect to find him the veriest wild creature that was ever caged. But how agreeable, how exhilarating the surprise!
Emerson better than his theory. He is the kindest, gentlest, simplest of men. These bad and hard utterances are not characteristic of him. They belong to the system he has em-

[1] Essays, Vol. II., p. 239.

braced, as he is forced to see; but the New England blood in him is too pure to welcome them. He for the most part avoids that side of pantheism which looks towards lawlessness and vice, and keeps rather to its spiritual side, which permits him to discourse so like a Christian mystic, if not in the exact language of Christianity. In nearly all his utterances he is benevolent, and true to our love of the beautiful and just in morals, owing to this great inconsistency. His practice is not in agreement with his theory, and therefore the two do not walk together. That theory, whose realized ultimate would be a social chaos, does not destroy in him a certain high-toned virtue, bred in the ancestral stock, which makes him the friend of order, of domestic purity, and of every grace of character that adorns either public or private life. Possibly some of those who feel the greatest repugnance to Emerson's doctrine, and who believe in a personal God, and one Master, even Christ, are quite as inconsistent with their creed as he, — and that, too, far less to their credit, since they are made worse by that which makes him better. It is not honorable to men to disregard in practice a wise system of faith, but in view of Emerson's faith we certainly esteem him the more for saying, "A foolish consistency is the hobgoblin of little minds, adored by little statesmen and philosophers and divines. With consistency a great soul has simply nothing to do."[1] When Spinoza's landlady came to him, asking him to teach her his doctrine, he advised her to be content with the Christian faith, in which she had been bred up. And Emerson, as though valuing a spirit of sincere piety more

Inconsistency recommended.

[1] Essays, Vol. I., p. 50.

than his own speculations, says to his disciples, "In your metaphysics you have denied personality to the Deity; yet when the devout motions of the soul come, yield to them heart and life, though they should clothe God with shape and color. Leave your theory, as Joseph his coat in the hand of the harlot, and flee."[1] Certainly we are inclined to judge in the most favorable light possible one who thus insists on right action whatever may become of theory; but it is the theory, and not the man, with which we have been especially concerned in this inquiry; nor do we grant that it is indifferent what a man's speculative views may be, if he tries to make his practice right, since in the great majority of cases the speculative views do, sooner or later, determine the practice. Hypocrisy is never to be encouraged, even where it makes men seem better than their honest convictions. We naturally carry our creeds out into our lives. This is the tendency, and it must ultimately prevail, as external hinderances, and the restraints of education and birth, are taken away. While gladly recognizing all the virtues to which our author may lay claim, and admitting that it is not hypocrisy, but goodness of nature, which makes his life so much more pleasing than his creed, I still insist that no word, in which I have set forth the spirit and drift of his teachings, should be taken back, or qualified, or in any respect explained away. He does not lay a foundation for society, for government, or for personal development such as our circumstances, and our knowledge of what we are, demand. Our own self, looked at from the transcendental point of view, and including all its

The good man forced to be a hypocrite.

[1] Essays, Vol. I., p. 50.

weaknesses and exposures to evil, is the only sacred thing. This we are to worship; for this we are to live; in this are the springs and the law of all that is, or was, or ever shall be.

Upon rising from this examination, the same question confronts us as when we rose from the examination of Spinoza. Are the conclusions which Emerson has reached, both as to the substance of truth and the conduct of life, a warning to us to beware of the a-priori philosophy? Not by any means. The danger of the great mass of mankind has always lain just the other way. The popular thought of the world ever looks outward and down, — away from ideas to facts, from spirit to matter, from the kingdom of God to questions of food, raiment, shelter, temporal thrift. *Transcendentalism not to be judged by Emerson.* That thought would be far nobler, and far more ennobling, if it could be trained to a steady love of those truths which transcend the sphere of the senses, and which we reach only as the inner doors of the soul are open to our consciousness. We may count here and there one, among transcendentalists, who, though a star of the first magnitude, has wandered out of the orbit of truth, and become lost in the blackness of darkness. Yet we are at the same time permitted to look on a host of others, of the same school of thought, whom no such fate has overtaken. They are the brightest names in the Christian church, and in that literature which never grows old, shining forth in calm splendor on the ages God would lead and enlighten. All these safely travelled the high circuit which Emerson too self-reliantly essayed, held to their course, as he was not, by that central Luminary which is the light and the life of

Christ the grand safeguard. men. If the flight proved too hard for him, and we must sorrowfully own that he fell like the son of the morning, yet his overthrow cannot be imputed to the form of philosophy which he held in common with them. They have not been shaken, though members of the same starry host to which he belonged. They have kept their first estate. No shock has been able to hurl them from their sphere. They shine on with undiminished lustre, and as the brightness of the firmament, trusting not to that force which is in themselves, but to Him who holdeth the stars in his right hand.

LECTURE VIII.

THEISM WITH A PANTHEISTIC DRIFT.

IT would be a serious defect, in any account of modern free-thought, to omit the speculations of Theodore Parker. Perhaps the name of no religious theorist of the last generation is more widely known. To the public generally, however, he is known more as an earnest political reformer, and bitter opponent of the existing institutions of Christianity, than as the teacher of a positive system of religious belief. But he had elaborated such a system, even before he emerged from the comparative obscurity of his early manhood; a system which he claimed as peculiarly his own, and which he professed to hold unchanged to the very close of his life. And if I should not succeed in trying to make clear just what his views and position were, I shall hope at least to preserve a spirit of candor and calm inquiry, such as I have often failed to discover in him.

Parker always felt it a hardship, as his friends still feel it to be, that he was classed with infidels by the popular verdict. Yet it is rather to the odium associated with the word "infidel," than to the doctrine which that word marks, that objection has been made. I do not now use it for the sake of the odium, but

<small>Theodore Parker.</small>

<small>Disliked to be called an infidel.</small>

as a descriptive term, which, however abused, has a well-defined meaning. If the word "infidel" were an honorable term, having lost its odium as the once odious word "Christian" has, I would use it all the same. Those who refuse to call Christ their master, or who, after having once bowed to his authority, turn from him to trust in something else as the final arbiter, are at liberty to make their action as honorable to themselves as they can. They are not charged with absolute infidelity, but only with infidelity to Christ the Lord. The term is accurately employed. It describes just what they have done. They should glory in it, as some try to do, if there be a religious authority for them superior to that of Christ.

Did not bow to Christ as the final authority in religion.

Let us then, in the first place, see the proof that Parker did not own the authority of Christ as supreme in matters of religious faith; the proof that he revolted from under that authority, and set up for himself another religious oracle. This evidence will not be hard to find. It is so abounding, and so acknowledged by both himself and his friends, that I may be thought to do a superfluous work in adducing it. But we must go step by step; taking the first for the sake of the second, if indeed for no other reason.

In his chapter on the "limitations of Jesus," Parker says, "It is apparent that Jesus shared the

Affirms that Jesus was profoundly in error on many subjects.

erroneous notions of the times respecting devils, possessions, and demonology in general; respecting the character of God, and the eternal punishment he prepares for the devil and his angels, and for a large part of mankind. If we may credit the

most trustworthy of the Gospels, he was profoundly in
error on these important points, whereon absurd doctrines
have still a most pernicious influence in Christendom. But
it would be too much to expect a man 'about thirty years
of age' in Palestine, in the first century, to have outgrown
what is still the doctrine of learned ministers all over the
Christian world. He was mistaken in the interpretation
of the Old Testament, if we may take the word of the
Gospels. But if he supposed that the writers of the
Pentateuch, the Psalms, and the prophecies spoke of him;
if he applied their poetic figures to himself, it is yet but a
trifling mistake, affecting a man's head, not his heart. It
is no more necessary for Jesus than for Luther to understand all ancient literature, and be familiar with criticism
and antiquities; though with men who think religion rests
on his infallibility, it must indeed be a very hard case for
their belief in Christianity."[1] Now, in this extract it is
noticeable, that Parker accepts the orthodox exegesis
respecting future punishment, a personal devil, and Messianic prophecies; that he rejects the exegesis which prevails,
on those topics, among Unitarians and Universalists. He
also expresses a doubt as to the claim of the New Testament, not merely to divine authority, or special inspiration,
but to the trustworthiness of ordinary history. And he
very graciously apologizes for the errors of Jesus, attributing them to youthful enthusiasm, inexperience, and limited
advantages for culture. But the point to be especially
noticed is, that he finds no element of authority in Christ
as a religious teacher; he has a feeling of pity for all, of
whatever shade of belief, who hold to the infallibility of

---

[1] Discourse of Religion (Little & Brown, Boston, 1856), pp. 276, 277.

Jesus. He says in another place, speaking of modern theology, it "has two great idols, the BIBLE and CHRIST."[1]

Calls Christ and the Bible idols.

The Unitarian body is denounced by Parker for still recognizing the authority of the Son of God. That party, he says, " differs theoretically from the orthodox party in exegesis, and that alone ; like that, is ready to believe anything which has a thus-saith-the-Lord before it; its Christianity rests on the authority of Jesus; that on the authority of his miracles; and his miracles on the testimony of the Evangelists. The old landmarks must not be passed by, nor the Bible questioned as to its right to be master of the soul. Christianity must be rested on the authority of Christ."[2] Such, he alleges, is the doctrine of conservative Unitarians; and from it he earnestly dissents, as being " too narrow for the soul." The fact that Christ claims this authority he does not deny, but considers it one of the mistakes into which Christ's enthusiasm led him.

Unitarians denounced for retaining them.

Parker more usually calls his own system or speculation the Absolute Religion, though not always. In one place, distinguishing it from the prevailing theology, he calls it spiritualism; and says it teaches that " God is immanent in spirit and in space." Here we have, at the very threshold, a statement which is strictly pantheistic in form. This spiritualism, the author goes on to say, "believes that God is near the soul; hears him in all true Scripture, Jewish or Phœnician; stoops at the same fountain as Moses or Jesus. It sees in Jesus a man living man-like, highly gifted, though not without

What Parkerism finds in Christ.

[1] Discourse of Religion, p. 453. [2] Ibid., p. 439.

errors. He lived for himself; died for himself; worked out his own salvation, and we must do the same, for one man cannot live for another more than he can eat and sleep for another. The divine incarnation is in all mankind."[1] So high is the throne of judgment on which Parker seats himself. Nor is it easy to see how the statement, that all mankind are the incarnation of God, differs from the most distinctive utterances of Spinozism. But waiving this point for the present, and still tracing the plain marks Parker has left of his estimate of Jesus, we find him saying, in an account of his early experiences, " I had no belief in the plenary, infallible, verbal inspiration of the whole Bible, and strong doubts as to the miraculous inspiration of any part of it. I could not put my finger on any great moral or religious truth taught by revelation in the New Testament, which had not previously been set forth by men for whom no miraculous help was ever claimed."[2]

Of the Old Testament Parker says, " The legendary and mythological writings of the Hebrews have no more authority than the similar narratives of the Phœnicians, the Persians, and the Chinese."[3] He thinks that many things in those ancient writings were relatively true, and of use, to the people to whom they were spoken. But humanity, which is ever moving forward in religious ideas as in other matters, has long since outgrown them, and left them, as cast-off garments, far behind on its path. " Hebraism, Heathenism, Christianism are places where man halted in his march towards the promised land, encampments on his pilgrimage.

The Old Testament long since outgrown.

[1] Discourse of Religion, pp. 444, 449.
[2] Experience as a Minister (Boston, 1859), p. 37.
[3] Discourse of Religion, p. 111.

He rests a while; then God says to him, Long enough hast thou compassed this mountain; turn and take thy journey forward. Lo! the land of promise is still before thee."[1] As to the nature of this religious progress, our author does not leave us in doubt. It is an endless "becoming," a continuous unfolding of the absolute religion in new and better forms. It delivers evermore from the power of the past, and from all authority external to the soul itself. The present emphasis of each man's religious consciousness is his guide for the time being. In that he learns to trust, and to reject every other oracle, as he grows truly wise concerning his own faculties and destiny. "There must be a better form of religion," he says. "It must be free, and welcome the highest, the proudest, and the widest thought."[2] Whoever seeks this nobler form "bows to no idols, neither mammon, nor the church, nor the Bible, nor yet Jesus. Its redeemer is within, its salvation, and its heaven and oracle of God."[3] "Protestantism delivers us from the tyranny of the church, and carries us back to the Bible. Biblical criticism frees us from the thraldom of the Scriptures, and brings us to the authority of Jesus. Philosophical spiritualism liberates us from all personal and finite authority, and restores us to God, the primeval fountain."[4] Not only, therefore, is the true God impersonal, according to Parker, but the gospel of Christ, and all the forms of Christianity, are each a despotism, whose sway the human soul rejects, upon coming to a clear knowledge of its own inherent nature.

His idea of religious progress.

---

[1] Sermons of Theism (Boston, Little & Brown, 1856), Introd., p. 74.
[2] Ibid., p. 72. [3] Discourse of Religion, p. 446. [4] Ibid., p. 449.

Having seen what Parker denies on religious subjects, let us, in the second place, see what he undertakes to affirm. I have said that he calls his doctrine the Absolute Religion, Spiritualism, or Philosophical Spiritualism. The first of these designations is that by which his more distinctive views are best known. In some of his later writings, however, the word "theism" seems to be preferred; and he strongly insists that the speculation thus named is something quite other than deism, pantheism, or atheism. Indeed, he labors so hard and often to make out this distinction, that we suspect it was not clear to the minds of his friends, even if he himself had no doubt of its reality. The terms he chose by which to designate his views show that he was ambitious of originality, though the views themselves are in almost no sense original. It is in forms of expression, not in essence of doctrine, that he is unlike some of those from whom he claims to differ. He was unwilling to call any one master, even while freely appropriating the opinions of others. Whether he really believed himself to be the founder of a new religion or not, that was evidently the high character and office to which he aspired, and which he labored all his life long to show that he had attained. But it will appear, I think, that he was not as successful as he thought himself to be; that in large part, unconsciously perhaps, he was a disciple of other men; that even where he most stoutly asserts his independence and originality, he is not the central sun, but rather a secondary orb, in the system to which he belongs. I shall hope to give an intelligible, though condensed statement

The positive side of Parkerism.

Terms used to designate it.

Parker less original than he supposed.

of what Parker calls his Theism, without taking up very much space.

Three factors of Absolute Religion.

The elements which he places at the bottom of the Absolute Religion, and which he traces through all its multitudinous forms, are three in number: the Sentiment, the Idea, the Conception. There is in all men a feeling of dependence: this is the religious sentiment. But the feeling of dependence involves, or is necessarily connected with, an intuition of something on which the dependence rests: that objective something is God, and constitutes the religious idea. And this idea, as it is variously apprehended, limited, and defined, becomes the religious conception. Of these three elements, the first two, the sentiment and the idea, are universal. They are also unvarying in their nature, being a part of the essential furniture of the human mind. Not so, however, the third element. This is the form under which the idea is apprehended. It belongs to the comprehending faculty, and differs with the differing capacities, idiosyncrasies, and culture of men. The conception of God in the mind of a New Zealander, for instance, differs vastly from that in the mind of an educated Englishman; but the sentiment and idea are in both cases the same. These three factors, then, constantly working together everywhere, make the Absolute Religion. This is all the religion there is in the world, or ever was, or will be. Judaism, Paganism, Christianity, Mohammedanism, are but the transient forms of this permanent essence.

The Sentiment.

The Idea.

The Conception.

The conception alone varies.

All religions are substantially one and the same. But

they differ endlessly in form, owing to the variable term, the conception of God. This is purely subjective, and determined, in each individual case, by inherent but constantly changing peculiarities. The religious conception has been in a state of progressive development from the beginning. It has not yet reached its perfect maturity, however near to perfection some marvellously gifted soul, here or there, may perchance have come. Man is a steadily progressive being in religion, as in all the other elements of his nature. This progress the author thinks he has traced in the histories of the various families of men: not traced it as thoroughly as he could desire, since the data are wanting, but sufficiently to persuade him that his main position is correct. He would be glad of certain facts which he does not find, — just as the extreme Darwinists would be, in proving their doctrine of the origin of species. But the large mass of facts which he does find seem to him to make the unfound so probable, that he assumes their existence; and he announces the conclusion to which he comes from such a premise with an air of scientific certainty. Man's original conception of God was in the form of Fetichism. Then, as he emerged from barbarism, and became somewhat civilized, that conception rose to the form of Polytheism, or even to some of the ruder forms of Pantheism. Then, as governments were set up, and nations became rivals of each other, this conception took the shape of a belief in national gods. Hence the Isis and Osiris of the Egyptians, the Indian Brahma and Gaudama; the Greek, and the Roman pantheon, the Scandinavian Thor, the Persian Ormuzd, the

Origin of religious.

Their succession traced.

Phœnician Baal. The Jehovah, of whom we read in the Old Testament, was but the national god of the Hebrews; an imperfect god, as were those worshipped by the other nations; one who loved the Jews, and who was bent on making them the supreme political power among men. But this exclusive national spirit gave way somewhat before the conquests of the Roman empire. A new political era dawned, in which peoples hitherto at strife were brought under a single government. This new state of things led the way to the Christian conception of God; a conception larger and nobler than any which had preceded it, but still imperfect, since even the God of Christianity is a partial being, whose purpose it is to save a part of the human race, and to eternally torture all the others. Plainly, then, the perfect conception is not yet reached. Parkerism, as judged in its own light, must soon perish. It is the duty of all men to struggle for something better yet in store for them. Forgetting the venerable past, and disentangling themselves from the present, they should keep their conception ever enlarging, that it may accord with the growing science, thought, and philanthropy of the world. This doctrine of an endless progress, as all must see, destroys the basis of the author's whole system. For by what right can he claim to speak of an absolute religion, while holding that the very faculties and powers on which man is dependent for all his religious views, are in a constant process of change? That which seems absolute to-day will be seen to be relative to-morrow, if his theory be true. Only a weary eternity of escape from one falsehood to another is before us. If there can be no absolutely perfect

Parkerism to be superseded.

revelation of God to us out of a supernatural sphere, but we can know him only under those forms of our own minds which we are daily outgrowing, the word *truth* is eternally without a fixed meaning; and whatever we may now happen to believe concerning God and our obligations to him, we are sure to reach a point in the future where we shall see that we believed a lie.

There are particular statements in the author's exposition of his theory, with which we might not disagree. Much that he says respecting the religious sentiment, the idea, and the conception in the unaided mind, is, no doubt, true, notwithstanding the suicidal spirit of his scheme as a whole. And besides this fatal feature, even the partial truths which he utters, rest on a theory of progress which the settled facts of history flatly contradict. Those facts were given in a previous lecture.[1] Scientific researches have shown that monotheism existed in the world — in Egypt, China, and elsewhere — before the ages of idolatrous worship. Fetichism is not the most ancient religion of which we have historic record. Archæology proves that a better religion than polytheism preceded polytheism. And the verdict of history is not that there was steady progress, but fearful degeneracy, in man's forms of worship and conceptions of God. There is a solid basis, which no plausible theory can disturb, for our belief that man was, at least religiously, better as God made him than as we find him in the savage state. However he may have improved in other respects, in that spiritual nature which makes him God's child, he has fallen. As a religious being he degenerated into the primeval barbarism, and

Parker's theory of religious progress refuted by history.

[1] Lecture I.

did not grow up into it out of a deeper ignorance of the true God.

Perhaps there is no fact on which Parker insists more strongly, than the infinite perfection of the Creator. Yet he does not seem to see that the biblical doctrine of a fall, and of the religious degeneracy of man, is necessary to sustain this vital fact. That, rather than his own doctrine of progress from a life wholly brutish, is the logical inference from God's infinite perfection. He insists, with great earnestness, that God has a perfect motive, and perfect purpose, and makes a perfect use of the most perfect means in fulfilling that purpose. Now, which being is more worthy of such a God, more worthy of infinite wisdom and love to create as the father of a religious race? Shall the first term in this grand series be a savage, more a brute than a man; one who, by the necessity of his organization, and with no capacity for a less revolting worship, sacrifices his child to the cat which he has defied? Or shall this wondrous creature, made for fellowship with the great Father of men, be such as that Adam who is described to us in Genesis; upright, fashioned after the image of God, searching the heavens with fearless eye, and awaiting the visits of the Infinite One among the trees in the cool of the day? Certainly we should expect such a being, rather than the monster of Parker's theory, to come forth from the divine Artist's hand. There is also a firmer basis of hope for man, more reason to expect that he will rise into communion with God and become a partaker of the divine holiness, if originally endowed with those high powers which the biblical account of his crea-

Obscures the character of God.

Weakens our basis of hope for man.

tion ascribes to him. But those high powers involved the gift of free-will. Man, like the Creator, could determine for himself what course of moral action he would pursue. In the exercise of this freedom, with holiness and sin alike possible to him, he was tempted into the choice of the latter. Thus he forsook the God in whose image he was made, and sank down to the level of superstition where Parker finds him. And hence it follows, that the first great need of man is not progress in his present state, but redemption from it. The whole scheme of a revelation from God, with the purpose of an atonement and restoration, is seen to be rational. Our faith in the goodness of God leads us to expect that he will interpose for the recovery of his children. And that remedial work must have on it the seal of his own divine name and authority, and must be in the hands of a Mediator who is not subject to human limitations. The blind cannot lead the blind. None but a Saviour who has never fallen, and whose nature is such that he cannot be tempted of evil, may hope to avail for us in this sore exigency. *The doctrine of redemption rational.*

I have now sketched the main features of Parker's theism; and have indicated, in brief, the line of refutation to which he is exposed, assuming him to be only a theist, and the leader he has been supposed to be. It may appear, however, as we go on, that this assumption is unfounded, or at least that it but partially states the case; that there was in him, not a conclusion, perhaps, but a tendency towards a conclusion, which forbids us to assign him the place of leadership, and requires that he be set down as the follower of a school of *Parker not simply a theist.*

theorists long known in the history of religious speculation. Had I been told that Parker was a pantheist, before studying him with a view to the settlement of the matter, I should have been strongly inclined to deny the charge; and I still deny it, after carefully reading his works, if the meaning be that he had finally and openly declared himself to that effect. But that the imputation is altogether false, if only the drift and tone of his thinking be meant, no thorough student of him, I am sure, will undertake to maintain.

Let us therefore, in the third place, see if there be any sufficient ground for bringing Theodore Parker within the limits of a treatise on pantheistic thinking.

Was Parker a pantheist?

Here it is important to revert, for a moment, to the position taken in the introduction to these lectures. It was there maintained that there can be but two sources of philosophical infidelity; that all free thought has its logical ultimate in pantheism or positivism: in pantheism when the a-priori or transcendental method of thinking is rigidly adhered to, in positivism when the a-posteriori or empirical method is strictly followed. Any other forms of infidelity are but half-way houses between Christianity and one or the other of these two. The human mind having let go its hold upon God, and not recovering that hold in Christ, gravitates steadily towards Spinoza or Comte. Christ, if I may so speak, stands as it were at the apex of the triangle of religious thought; and whomsoever faith in Christ does not uphold at that point, the same settles steadily downward

A re-statement of the alternative of unbelief.

through the process of speculation, till he reaches the base line; the original bent of his mind having meanwhile, according as it is transcendental or empirical, carried him aside on that line either to the angle occupied by Spinoza, or to that occupied by Comte. Any intermediate positions, such as deism, theism, scepticism, rationalism, naturalism, are but points in the process, where he is held in suspense for a longer or shorter time.

This statement is, if I mistake not, confirmed by the drift of Parker's speculations. Having cast off the authority of Christ, he did not escape the fatal spell which draws all minds downward, either in the direction of pantheism or positivism; not in the direction of positivism in his case, as we shall soon see. The bent of his genius was not empirical, but transcendental. He found the germs of the absolute religion, not in the philosophy of the senses, but in that of consciousness. Had he lived to the present time, when the intuitional philosophy is at a low ebb and the sensational is coming in like a flood, he would logically stand with the retiring rather than the advancing host. *[margin: Parker could not be a positivist.]*

There is one subject on which we need to discriminate with care, or we shall often confound the pantheist with the positivist: it is the subject of development in nature. They both speak of this, sometimes in nearly the same words; but if we consider we shall see that with one it is a development downward, and with the other a development upward. Pantheism is thus made to appear as a kind of a-priori positivism, and positivism as a-posteriori pantheism. According to the pantheist there is an efflux of the divine *[margin: Pantheism may be mistaken for positivism.]*

essence ever farther and farther down, constituting nature, both the conscious and the unconscious. The positivist admits no such divine essence, much less any manifestations of it under natural forms; but, on the contrary, holds that all the reality we can know is centred in nature, and is constantly ascending towards consciousness by the action of inherent forces. We might think that even Emerson is a positivist, when he says that the plants grope ever upward towards consciousness; but he is not, for he elsewhere teaches that it is the going forth of the eternally conscious "soul," ever downward from the higher to the lower forms, that makes nature. The development of nature, however variously expressed, is the divine mind taking its own outgoings back into itself.

Thus, rather than in the atheistic sense, are we to understand Parker when he seems to use the language of positivism or materialism. "I have been into man with my scalpel in my hand, and my microscope, and there is no soul. Man is bones, blood, bowels, and brain. Mind is matter. Do you doubt this? Here is Arnoldi's perfect map of the brain: there is no soul there; nothing but nerves."[1] He puts these words into the mouth of an imagined teacher of materialism, and so far from accepting the doctrine they embody, he utters his strong abhorrence of it. It is true that he often speaks kindly of atheists, especially while contrasting them with orthodox Christians, for whom he has no patience; yet he does not leave us to infer from this that he has any sympathy with atheism. "The Christian world," says he, "has something to learn, at this day, even from the athe-

Parker not a materialist.

[1] Sermons of Theism, p. 10.

PANTHEISM. 333

ist; for he asks entire freedom for human nature, — freedom to think, freedom to will, freedom to love, freedom to worship if he will, not to worship if he will not. And if the Christian world had granted this freedom, then there would have been no atheism. If theology had not severed itself from science, science would have adorned the church with its magnificent beauty. Even the protests against 'Christianity' are oftenest made by men full of the religious spirit. Many of the 'unbelievers' of this age are eminent for their religion; atheists are often made such by circumstances. M. Comte must have a new Supreme, — *Nouveau Grand Etre*, — and recommends daily prayers to his composite and progressive deity."[1] What Parker here says of the duty of the Christian church to admit atheists into its fellowship, my present purpose does not require me to notice; but in denying, as he does, the possibility of atheism, he shows that Denies the possibility of atheism. he is not a disciple of any a-posteriori system of philosophy or religion. No one could speak more earnestly, or more feelingly and indignantly, than he, against speculative atheism. It is in a strain of tearful remonstrance almost, that he exclaims, "Take away my consciousness of God; let me believe there is no infinite God; no infinite Mind which thought the world into existence, and which thinks it into continuance; no infinite Conscience which everlastingly enacts the eternal laws of the universe, no infinite Affection which loves the world, — then I should be sadder than Egyptian night. Yes, I should die in uncontrollable anguish and despair."[2] Our author had been accused of atheism, by some of those who undertook

[1] Sermons of Theism, Introduction, pp. 70, 72.   [2] Ibid., pp. 29, 30.

to criticise his Discourse of Religion. It may be, therefore, that in his Sermons of Theism, preached some years later, he spoke more strongly than he otherwise would, in order to vindicate himself before his own friends, who were firm theists. No doubt, also, he felt lonely in that state of comparative isolation into which his controversies had driven him; and it comforted him, more than at an earlier day, to believe that an infinite Friend was helping him in his hard battles. It is true that his representations of the nature of God are somewhat vague. He seems to confuse the Creator with his works, in saying that God "thinks the world into existence and continuance." Yet even this language, though indicating that his theism has something peculiar in it, strengthens his protest; nor have we any reason to doubt, what he so earnestly avers, that there was no tendency in his thinking, which by any possibility could have carried him on to the errors of positivism.

The charge of vulgar atheism, brought against Parker, may therefore be dismissed as wholly untenable. Nor is evidence wanting that Parker held stoutly back, on the other hand, from what he defines as pantheism. "Two things," he says, "are necessary to render religion possible; namely, a religious faculty in man, and God out of man as the object of that faculty."[1] The phrase "God out of man" seems clear and decisive. We should expect it only from an opponent of pantheism. Speaking of what he calls the infancy of religion, Parker says, "Its highest form was the sublime but deceitful reverence which the old Sabæan paid to the host

Denied that he was a pantheist.

[1] Discourse of Religion, p. 151.

of heaven, or which some Grecian or Indian philosopher offered to the universe personified, and called Pan, or Brahma. God was worshipped in a sublime and devout, but bewildering pantheism. He was not considered as distinct from the universe."[1] Pantheism, then, is one of the earlier forms through which the absolute religion has passed in the process of historical development. Limiting his view to the form only, and assuming that he has given an exhaustive statement of the nature of all pantheism, he may be right in saying that he is not a pantheist. And yet, even with this statement, it is only in the "transient" element of religion that he makes himself to differ from the Brahman. A different culture induces a different form, but the religion itself is in either case the same, being absolute and always unchangeable in essence.

The manifest anxiety of Parker not to be thought a pantheist is at times suspicious. Why should he be so fearful of that of which he is wholly unconscious? This anxiety may account for the narrow and inadequate definition of pantheism which he lays down. One may prove that he differs from any doctrine whatsoever, if allowed to define it as he pleases. Pantheism is not altogether an ancient thing. It has thriven recently, and even now exists; and the question is whether Parker's speculations have anything in common with this modern movement. In one place, after denouncing positivism, he says, " Besides, the pantheists tell us of their God, who is but the sum total of the existing universe of matter and of mind, immanent in each, but transcending neither, imprisoned in the two; blind, planless,

But his definition is inadequate.

[1] Discourse of Religion, p. 53.

purposeless, without consciousness, or will, or love; dependent on the shifting phenomena of finite mind and of finite matter, finite itself; a continual Becoming this or that, not absolute Being, self-subsistent, and eternally the same perfection : their God is only law, the constant mode of operation of objective and unconscious force."[1] We are amazed that any respectable writer should think this a fair view of pantheism. The misrepresentations of Christian thinkers, which Parker published at different times, have long been familiar to us. These we had set down to prejudice, and to that one-sidedness which the heat of controversy is apt to beget. It now appears, however, that the friends of Christianity are not an exception; that Parker misapprehends the system taught by Fichte and Emerson, quite as strangely as evangelical systems; that his inability to treat an opponent candidly, amounted to a constitutional weakness. If the idealistic pantheism of Germany makes God "unconscious," "finite," "not absolute," "dependent on shifting phenomena," then there are no pantheists. Does the theism of Parker require this unfair definition of pantheism, in order that it may continue to be theism? If so, many an earnest follower of Spinoza may claim to be a theist; for probably not one of them would accept the account our author gives of their doctrine. Yet Parker is not wanting in charity towards the leaders of pantheistic thought in modern times. He makes his narrow definition acquit them together with himself. He allows no place to the object of his dread, outside of barbarism. Fichte, Schelling, and Hegel do not teach pantheism; for they do

Acquits Spinoza.

[1] Experience as a Minister, p. 147.

not teach the absurd theory he describes. He assumes them all to be good theists; as he is, judged by his own definition; and even in regard to Spinoza he says, "Pantheism is a word of convenient ambiguity, and serves as well to express the *odium theologicum* as the more ancient word atheism." [1]

But Parker claims to be mainly in agreement with these masters. If he interprets them rightly, what they would call the reflex of the divine consciousness does not differ from what he calls the feeling of dependence in man. And if he knows God by a direct intuition, as manifest in the feeling of dependence, then his doctrine of God cannot be at a great remove from theirs. This similarity of doctrine evidently did not escape him; and therefore, to defend himself, he tries to show that Spinoza and his successors had been misunderstood. He claims that they were no more pantheists than the mystics of the middle ages, or the evangelist John; thus leaving us to infer that such men as Tauler, and the beloved disciple, did not, any more than Hegel, recognize the separate existence and personality of both the Creator and the creature. He says in one place that the question between the pantheist and pure theist is this: "*Is God the immanent cause of the world, or is he not?*" Now, we have already seen, and shall yet further see more positively, that Parker takes the affirmative of this question. He repeatedly speaks, almost in the exact words of Spinoza, who says, "God is the immanent or indwelling, not the transient or outside cause of all things." [2] Clearly, then, he is a Spinozist by his

Admits the thing while disowning the name.

[1] Discourse of Religion, p. 91, note.   [2] Ethics, Prop. XVIII.

own admission, though he refuses to be called a pantheist. How does he escape the odious name? It is, as we have already seen, by resorting to a definition which does not cover all the forms of pantheistic thinking. "Monotheism," he says, "is the worship of one supreme God. He may, however, be supposed to manifest himself in one form, or in all forms, as the Pan and Brahma of the Greek and Indian; for it is indifferent whether we ascribe no forms or all forms to the infinite."[1] But that is a singular species of theism, certainly, which teaches that the Greek polytheism did not differ from monotheism essentially, and which saves itself by asserting that the infinite may be defined under any form, or as being without form. It is amazing, considering how much space our author devotes to the subject, that he succeeds so poorly in freeing himself from the charge of pantheism.

More positive proofs of pantheism.
 I proceed, therefore, to trace some of the more positive indications, in Parker's writings, of a pantheistic drift in what he calls his theism. If I seem to go over ground already traversed in doing this, it will be because even his denials of pantheism do not deny, so much as affirm, what must be regarded as pantheistic doctrine. Let me further say, if I seem to any to do him injustice in this examination, that I shall at least hope to misrepresent him less than he does Christianity. I may fail to discern the tendency of his doctrine; but I can hardly be guilty of such misrepresentation as he utters when he says, "The popular theological idea represents God as finite, limited subjectively by self

[1] See Discourse of Religion, pp. 86-92.

ishness, wrath, and various evil passions, objectively by elements in the world of men which continually prove refractory, and turn out as he did not intend."[1]

Here it is to be observed that the same philosophy which was carried out into pantheism in Germany, gave direction to our author's inquiries after religious truth. He says, "I found most help in the works of Immanuel Kant. If he did not always furnish conclusions I could rest in, he yet gave me the method, and put me on the right road."[2] Kant did for him, that is, the same work as for Fichte, Schelling, and Hegel; started him in his investigations, but did not go far enough to satisfy him. Parker's argument for the existence of God is that of the transcendentalist.: "Now the existence of this religious element," he says, "our experience of this sense of dependence, this sentiment of something without bounds, is itself a proof by implication of the existence of its object,—something on which dependence rests. The belief in God's existence is therefore natural, not against nature. It comes, as the belief in light comes, by using the eyes. The knowledge of God's existence may be called an intuition of reason. Our belief in God rests not on a-priori or a-posteriori arguments; on no *argument;* not on reasoning, but reason. The arguments a-priori and a-posteriori confirm our belief."[3] Thus far some of the foremost of Christian theologians would agree with Parker. It is when he begins to define his theism, when he speaks of the nature of the God he finds in reason, that we cannot go with him. "Specula-

Held the Kantian philosophy.

---
[1] Sermons of Theism, p. 157.   [2] Experience as a Minister, p. 42.
[3] Discourse of Religion, pp. 19, 21, 22.

His definition of God does not exclude pantheism.

tive theism," he says, "is the belief in the existence of God, in one form or another; and I call him a theist who believes in any God. A man may deny actuality to the Hebrew idea of God, to the Christian idea of God, or to the Mahometan idea of God, and yet be no atheist."[1] "A man says, there is no God. But he says, Nature — meaning by that the whole sum-total of existence — is powerful, wise, and good; Nature is self-originated, the cause of its own existence, the mind of the universe, and the providence thereof. Very well. In such cases, the absolute denial of God is only formal, not real. The quality of God is still admitted, and affirmed to be real; only the representative of that quality is called Nature, and not called God. That is only a change of name."[2]

All men theists.

As if this were not enough to make clear the pantheistic drift of his theism, our author says, in close connection, "Spinoza may call God *natura naturans*, but he admits the existence of the thing so diversely entitled. The name is of the smallest consequence."[3] Of the smallest consequence, surely, if, as he says in another place, "There is but one religion, as one ocean; though we call it faith in our church, and infidelity out of our church."[4]

It is difficult at times to make out the entire consistency of Parker. In one connection he condemns the later pantheism of Germany, saying, "That is a fatal error with Hegel, and with his followers in England and America."[5]

---

[1] Sermons of Theism, p. 4. [2] Ibid., p. 9.
[3] Ibid. [4] Discourse of Religion, Introd., pp. 6, 7.
[5] Sermons of Theism, p. 155.

But this criticism is based on a false imputation. It assumes certain errors, which Hegel and his followers, whatever their mistakes, do not hold. Parker here charges upon them that gross pantheism which is all that his own narrow definition allows. He seems to forget his apology for them in another place, where he gives a less inaccurate statement of their views. "There are two classes of philosophers," he says, "often called atheists; but better, and perhaps justly, called pantheists. One of these says, 'There are only material things in existence, resolving all into matter; the sum-total of these material things is God.' That is material pantheism. If I mistake not, M. Comte, of Paris, and the anonymous author of 'Vestiges of Natural History in Creation,' with their numerous coadjutors, belong to this class. The other class admits the existence of spirit, sometimes resolves everything into spirit, and says, 'The sum-total of finite spirit, that is God.' These are spiritual pantheists. Several of the German philosophers, if I understand them, are of that stamp."[1] Evidently our author does not "understand them," if he really believes that they resolve all things into "finite" spirit. By his definition, Hegel himself was not a Hegelian. We are left to infer that Parker had no clear or fixed views of the two grand and conflicting systems of philosophy. He must show not only that he is not a Comtist, and that he rejects the crude theories here imputed by him to Hegel, but that he has no sympathy with what we know to be the *real* Hegelianism, if he would prove that he is not a pantheist. His denial of the imaginary doctrine is so put

[Misrepresents pantheists.]

[1] Sermons of Theism, pp. 154, 155.

as to affirm the actual doctrine taught by Spinoza and his successors. He says that the pantheism he disowns represents God as in a state of progressive development.[1] But this is the doctrine of Comte's positive religion. It is as far from real pantheism as the east is from the west. The later German philosophers held no such doctrine; nor Carlyle, nor Emerson. He does those writers great injustice when he says that they thus believe and teach. They believe in the eternal completeness of God as firmly as he. He confounds the fact with the manifestation, the Being with the Becoming. They say God is Being; only in what we call our knowing him, is he a Becoming. If Parker's definition acquits himself, it acquits Emerson. But it fails to make out a clear case of theism for either, since it does not touch the real ground of distinction.

Having said that he dissents from pantheism as defined by himself, and as he wrongly ascribes it on the one hand to Comte and on the other to Hegel and his followers, Parker goes on to utter words, almost in the next sentence, which harmonize perfectly with the main principles of the pantheists. "There is no point of space, no atom of matter," he says, "but God is there."[2] How can he claim that he holds to a God distinct from the world, after saying, "Finite matter and finite spirit do not exhaust God. He transcends the world of matter and of spirit, and in virtue of that transcendence continually makes the world of matter fairer, and the world of spirit wiser."[3] This is saying that all of God is not yet manifested; but it does not separate him

Identifies God with the world.

---

[1] Sermons of Theism, p. 155.   [2] Ibid., p. 156.   [3] Ibid.

from the world, and make him an independent existence. Wittingly or unwittingly, Parker speaks with the pantheist when he says "There is really a progress in the manifestation of God, but not a progress in God the manifesting."[1] Spinoza could accept that statement, both as to its affirmation and its denial. We think our author is going to proclaim himself a veritable theist, when he says, "God must be different in kind from the world of matter and of man." But in the next breath he changes ground, and speaks of that difference as being only in degree: "They are finite, he infinite; they dependent, he self-subsisting; they variable, he unchanging. God must include both matter and spirit."[2] If the only difference between God and the universe be that one is infinite and the other finite, then are they the same qualitatively. And if the universe be but the progressive manifestation of God, what is there besides God? Schelling could not teach the doctrine of identity in plainer terms. The doctrine that "all difference is quantitative," cannot be pantheism in Germany and good theism in America.

In his efforts to contrast the human and divine, Parker makes no mention of distinct personalities, but says, "Man's consciousness of God and God's consciousness of himself must differ immeasurably. No man can have an exhaustive conception of God,—one, I mean, which uses up and comprises the whole of God."[3] To some even this utterance may not seem to bring our author clearly out on pantheistic ground. But can there be any doubt after the following? "In the self-consciousness of God subject and object are

With God subject and object are the same.

[1] Sermons of Theism, p. 156. [2] Ibid., p. 154. [3] Ibid., p. 153.

the same, and he must know all his own infinite nature."[1] Certainly, if there be no pantheism here, we must conclude with Talleyrand, that words were made to conceal thought, and not to express it. It is a significant fact also, in view of this bold utterance, that Parker, while careful to show how he differs from deism and atheism, forgets his usual caution on the other side, not even alluding to pantheism. His words embody the doctrine of Schelling, almost in Schelling's own terms; yet he nowhere applies to that doctrine the name which would indicate its real nature, but couples that name with a false definition of his own. "I use the word theism," he says, "as distinguished from atheism, the denial of God; from the popular theology, which affirms a finite ferocious God; and from deism, which affirms a finite God without ferocity."[2] Deism is better than Christianity, for its God is "without ferocity," though still "finite." "It starts from the sensational philosophy, and abuts in materialism, leaving out of sight the intuition of human nature."[3] The superiority of Parker's theism, he claims, is that it begins in consciousness, and avoids the finiteness, or, which is the same thing, as we shall soon see, the personality of the God of deism.

The fault of deism.

Parker preached several glowing discourses on the subject of immortality. Here certainly was an opportunity, if he desired it, to state his belief in the personal and conscious existence of men after death, which would have gone far to disprove his alleged sympathy with pantheism. But he made no such use of that opportunity. He goes no further than to

His view of immortality pantheistic.

---

[1] Sermons of Theism, p. 154.   [2] Ibid., p. 152.   [3] Ibid.

say, alluding to those discourses years after, "The instinctive intuition of the immortal, a consciousness that the essential element of man, the *principle* of individuality, never dies," had been a prominent topic in his preaching.[1] Here may be a faith broad enough for fancy and imagination, and wherewith to delight undiscriminating hearers; but surely one must hold to something more than the immortality of "the essential element of man," in order to teach that the future life will be so related to the present that memory may join them together as experiences of the same person,— which is the only idea of immortality at all inspiring, or even intelligible to us. Our bodies are immortal, in the sense that the particles of matter which make them are forever reappearing in other forms. They never perish. Emerson has discoursed of immortality to the edification of Christian worshippers. But what they took for the immortality of the person as now living and conscious, he seems to have meant only for the eternity of the impersonal "soul" which fills all things. There is no valid proof that Parker's doctrine differed essentially from his; and he declares that if we raise the question of the immortality of the conscious individual, looking to the future, and not wholly satisfied with the present, we are "already fallen."

We have seen that Parker, after saying that the question between the pantheist and theist is one of the immanency of God in the world, seems to side with the former. He repeatedly makes statements which go to show, if he did not take that side, that he considered it as differing only by the faintest

God immanent in all things.

[1] Experience as a Minister, p. 42.

shade from the other. In giving his experience as a minister, he says, "I believed in the immanence of God in man, as well as matter, his activity in both."[1] "The infinitely perfect God is immanent in the world of matter, and in the world of spirit; each particle thereof is inseparable from him, while he transcends both. There must be a complete solidarity between God and the twofold universe."[2] Still more decisively he says, in his Discourse of Religion, "The material world, with its objects sublimely great or meanly little, as we judge them; its atoms of dust, its orbs of fire; the rock that stands by the seashore, the water that wears it away; the worm, a birth of yesterday, which we trample under our foot; the streets of constellations that gleam perennial overhead; the aspiring palm tree fixed to one spot, and the lions that are sent out free, — these incarnate and make visible to us all of God their several natures will admit."[3] "God, then, is universally present in the world of matter. He is the substantiality of matter. No atom of matter so despised and little but God, the Infinite, is there. God is immanent in the world, however much he transcends the world. He is the ground of nature; what is permanent in the passing; what is real in the apparent. All nature, then, is but an exhibition of God to the senses. It is the fulness of God that flows into the crystal of the rock, the juices of the plant, the life of the emmet and the elephant."[4] Do not these extracts confirm the view, that all searching after truth, which is independent of divine guidance, must at last come either

"God is the substantiality of matter."

[1] Experience as a Minister, p. 39.
[2] Ibid., pp. 80, 81.
[3] Discourse of Religion, pp. 104, 105.
[4] Ibid., pp. 161, 162, 163.

to the position of Spinoza or to that of Comte? It is not in the power of language to state, if they do not, the identity of God with the world. If God is "the substantiality of matter," I do our author no injustice, but rather state the case in its mildest possible form when I say that there was in his theism a drifting towards pantheism.

On the subject of a person's responsibility for the form of religious faith he may hold, Parker speaks after the manner of Goethe and Carlyle. All the religions of the world are forms of the absolute religion, which manifests itself thus variously by virtue of fixed law. The faiths of men cannot be other than they are. The religion which exists necessarily in all is bearing them on, through whatever temporary forms, to the same blessedness; and this high result is sure to be reached, irrespective of any free volitions they may put forth. He says, "All men are at bottom the same; but as no two nations or ages are exactly alike in character, circumstances, or development, so therefore, though the religious element be the same in all, we must expect to find that its manifestations are never exactly alike in any two ages or nations, though they give the same name to their form of worship. From the difference between men, it follows, that there must be as many different subjective conceptions of God, and forms of religion, as there are men and women who think about God, and apply their thoughts and feelings to life. The phenomena of religion, like those of science and art, must vary from land to land, and age to age, with the varying civilization of mankind; must be one thing in New Zealand, and the first century, and be something

Men not responsible for the religion they hold.

Different religions a necessity of circumstances.

quite different in New England, and the fifty-ninth century. They must be one thing in the wise man, and another in the foolish man. They must vary also in the same individual. The religion of the boy and the man, of Saul the youth and Paul the aged, how differently they appear!"[1] But there are men, intelligent thinkers of the fifty-ninth century, quite able to find out what their own belief is, with no help from Parker, who claim to hold the religious faith of the first century; nor is it at all likely that Paul, whose opinion in the case must be regarded as at least equal to Parker's, was conscious of one way of salvation when he repented at Damascus, and of another when he wrote to Timothy. The Christian religion is the same now that it was in the beginning; nor is there any state of society, however refined or however rude, to which it is not equally adapted. But granting that Parker has the facts of history on his side, the thing to be noticed in what he says is, that a stern necessity has fixed men in their various beliefs, — which beliefs are not essentially different, but at bottom one universal religion. All is the same, and all inevitable; a statement which accords perfectly with the views of acknowledged pantheists. "The religion of each is the same, distinguished only by the more or less."[2] Again he says, after having spoken of fetichism, polytheism, dualism, pantheism, monotheism, "Each of these forms represented an idea of the popular consciousness which passed for a truth, or it could not be embraced; for a great truth, or it could not prevail widely; yes, for all of truth the man could receive at the time he embraced it. We creep before walking. Mankind has

All the same at bottom.

---

[1] Discourse of Religion, pp. 47, 48, 49.   [2] Ibid., p. 99.

likewise an infancy, though it will at length put away childish things.. Each of these forms did the world service in its day."[1]

By his own showing, therefore, Parker's religious theory is not a finality, but a tendency towards something else; and that drift is the result of a force as resistless as that which moves the planets through space. "To censure or approve Catholicism, or Protestantism, is to censure or approve the state of the race which gave rise to those forms. They could not have been but as they were. To condemn them is to condemn the absolute religion; is to condemn both God and man."[2] Orthodox Christians should remember this passage, when suffering under that wrath which Parker so often pours out on their heads. It is only by a figure of rhetoric that they are at all culpable. His scorching invective, provided he spoke from his theory, was not meant for them, but for "the state of the race," which has made them what they are. And why he is so enraged at this, we are still puzzled to know; for the immanent God is in every "atom" thereof, and it is ever opening out, through the necessity of the divine inworking, into the more blessed and more fair. "The history of man's religious consciousness," he says, "seems to be a series of revolutions. What is to-day built up with prayers and tears, is to-morrow pulled down with shouting and bloodshed, giving place to a new fabric equally transient. Prophets were mistaken, and saints confounded. Religious history is a tale of confusion. But looking deeper, we see it is a series of developments, all tending towards one great and beautiful end, the harmoni-

An endless succession of religions.

[1] Discourse of Religion, p. 102. 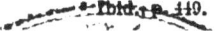 Ibid. p. 449.

ous development of man. The circle of his vision becomes wider continually, his ideal more fair and sublime."[1] We deny that man has reached any fairer religious ideal than grew up in Galilee eighteen centuries ago. But granting this again, we see the pantheistic doctrine of necessity which Parker holds. The everlasting progress of man in religion is not kept up by any supernatural helps, nor by gradually learning to choose good rather than evil, but is all the while only the spontaneous unfold-

The pantheistic fatalism. ing of a religious nature. Speaking of the religious element in man, he says, "In my own consciousness I found it to be automatic."[2] "Each form of religion has grown out of the condition of some people, as naturally as the wild primitive flora of Santa Cruz has come from the state of the island; as naturally as the dependent fauna of the place comes from its flora."[3] After this full statement of the law of necessity, under which Parker makes the religious sentiment eternally act, a necessity as relentless as the pantheist's fatalism, and in appearance the same, we are prepared for his unbounded tolerance. This, however he may forget it in the heat of debate, is fully equal to that of Goethe, who makes even wickedness divine. It admits into its paradise

Absolute toleration. the greatest sinner, with the same abundant entrance as the greatest saint, saying, "Many a savage, his hands smeared all over with the blood of human sacrifice, shall come from the east and the west, and sit down in the kingdom of God, with Moses and Zoroaster, with Socrates and Jesus."[4]

[1] Discourse of Religion, p. 105.
[2] Experience as a Minister, p. 41.
[3] Ibid., p. 86.
[4] Discourse of Religion, p. 107.

The immanency of God in the world, as held by Parker, might not be an evidence of pantheism if he had anywhere clearly asserted the doctrine of second causes. But he denies this doctrine, at least by implication, allowing no real efficiency to man even, and making God the one producing cause of all things. What we call our freedom, he calls "oscillation." " In the world of nature, not endowed with animal life, there is," he says, " no margin of oscillation. In the world of animals there is a small margin of oscillation. But man has a certain amount of freedom ; a larger amount of oscillation, wherein he vibrates from side to side." [1] So far as the final result is concerned, however, it is indifferent whether we say " man has no freedom of will at all," or " some freedom of will." " There can be no absolute evil or imperfection in the world of man, more than in the world of matter, or in God himself." [2] " Creation and providence are but modifications of the same function. Creation is momentary providence ; providence perpetual creation ; one is described by a point, the other by a line. Now, God is just as much present in a blade of grass, or an atom of mahogany, this day and every moment of his existence, as he was at the instant of its creation." [3] Thus providence is the same thing as creation, and creation is the same as emanation, according to our author, for besides this statement he elsewhere says, " There can be nothing in nature which God did not put in nature from himself." [4] " God is responsible for his creation, his world of matter and his world of man ; for mankind

<small>No second causes.</small>

<small>Creation and providence the same.</small>

<small>All the action of nature God's action.</small>

---

[1] Sermons of Theism, p. 167. [2] Ibid., p. 170.
[3] Ibid., p. 160. [4] Ibid., p. 158.

in general; for you and for me."[1] "The immanence of God in nature is the basis of his influence."[2] "The man with pure theism in his heart looks out on the world, and there is the infinite God everywhere as perfect cause, everywhere as perfect providence, transcending all, yet immanent in each; with perfect power, wisdom, justice, holiness, and love, securing perfect welfare unto each and all."[3] "The powers of nature, — that of gravitation, electricity, growth, — what are they but modes of God's action?"[4] These mighty agents have not even an instrumental function in themselves; they are the immanent essence of all things, coming forth in various forms. "All the natural action in the material world is God's action, whether the wind blows a plank, and the shipwrecked woman who grasps it, to the shore, or scatters a fleet, and sends families to the bottom."[5]

There are statements in the writings of Parker which would indicate that he held the mathematical method of proof, as applied by Spinoza to the principles of the Cartesian philosophy. He says, in one place, that the human faculties can "ascertain truth in religious matters, as in philosophical or mathematical matters."[6] And in another place he says, "The truth of the human faculties must be assumed in all our arguments, and if this be admitted, we have the same evidence for spiritual facts as for the maxims or demonstrations of geometry."[7] It would seem, therefore, that

Held to the mathematical method.

---

[1] Sermons of Theism, p. 174.
[2] Theism, p. 179.
[5] Ibid., p. 158.
[3] Discourse of Religion, p. 170.
[4] Discourse of Religion, p. 163.
[6] Sermons of Theism, p. 152.
[7] Discourse of Religion, p. 19 (note).

our author held to this method as the proper guide in the search for religious truth. And if he did believe that all truth can be mathematically proved, he must have known that he was a pantheist. For this method of proof, applied rigidly to the analysis of the religious sentiment, which is the central principle of his system, affords no resting-place short of Spinozism.

I shall adduce but one other fact here, as indicating a pantheistic drift in Parker's speculations,— his view of the divine personality. This subject, if I mistake not, is considered as giving a decisive test to the religious thinker. One definition of pantheism is, that it is the denial of the personality of God. The personality of God is certainly the especial stumbling-block of the pantheist, the shibboleth which he cannot utter. Parker has much to say of the mind, conscience, affection, will of God, which in itself might satisfy any theist; but he uniformly denies personality to God. What the nature of the attributes just named can be, or how God can awaken our love and homage if he be impersonal, we think it would be impossible for the author to explain. It does not clear up the matter to say that personality is the same as anthropomorphism, and that Parker denies to God only what is meant by this latter term. The words have broadly different meanings. It requires no great learning or insight to conceive of persons other than men, persons having for the most part superhuman qualities. To recognize the personal existence of God is a different thing from making him such a one as ourselves. This is an act of irreverence against which the Scriptures warn

God impersonal.

Makes personality the same as anthropomorphism.

us, even while a personal God is the object of worship they reveal. The distinction is one which the untutored intellect may see; nor could our author have overlooked it, though, to break the force of the more pantheistic word, he sometimes joins the two together. In his Discourse of Religion he says, "The feelings, fear, reverence, devotion, love, naturally personify God; humanize the Deity." Thus is God made personal only as any object in nature may be; that is, by personification. It is rhe-

<small>God personal only in a rhetorical sense.</small> torically, by a figure of speech, but in no other way, that God can have personality. The thing is not objective and real, but altogether subjective. "Some rude men require this," he says, but adds, "It must be remembered all this is poetry. This personal and anthropomorphitic conception is a phantom of the brain that has no existence independent of ourselves."[1] "There has been dogmatism enough respecting the nature, essence, and personality of God. It avails nothing. As the absolute cause, God must contain in himself, potentially, the ground of consciousness, of personality, — yes, of unconsciousness and impersonality."[2] This statement certainly identifies God, in substance, with all existence; and also reminds us of Hegel's doctrine that being and non-being are the same. Not only may God be considered

<small>Our conception of him purely subjective.</small> as neither personal nor impersonal, since he is only potentially either one or the other, but we cannot say that he is conscious or unconscious, since in regard to these states there is not the actuality, but only the ground or possibility. It is just as true that God is impersonal and unconscious, as that he is personal

---

[1] Discourse of Religion, pp. 156, 157.   [2] Ibid., p. 154, 153.

and conscious. In another place, as we saw, Parker spoke of the importance of "a God out of man." Here he seems to consider it a matter of no importance at all. "The greatest religious souls that have ever been," he says, "are content to fall back on the sentiment and idea of God."[1] "God is nowhere in particular, but everywhere in general, essentially and vitally omnipresent. Denying all particular form, we must affirm of him universal being."[2]

<small>God is universal being.</small>

I have now stated the evidence, found in Parker's writings, which convinces me that I do him no wrong by bringing him within the limits of a treatise on pantheistic thinking. His religious theorizing may not have come to its logical conclusion, even in his own view; but its tendency was the same as that of Spinoza, Hegel, Emerson. He was sailing the same voyage, and would have reached the same port by keeping on. The fact that his ship went down in mid-ocean does not prove that it was headed some other way. That he is to be judged by his tendency, rather than the conclusions he had clearly reached, seems evident from his own words. He said, near the close of his life, that one of his deepest regrets in dying was, that he must leave his system incomplete. "The will to live," he writes from Santa Cruz, "is exceedingly strong; more vehement than ever before, as I have still much to do, — some things to begin upon, and many more now lying half done, that I alone can finish; and I should not like the little I have done to

<small>Parker to be judged by his tendency.</small>

---

[1] Discourse of Religion, p. 154.　　[2] Ibid., p. 158.

perish now for lack of a few years' work."[1] Undoubtedly it will be better, in replying to the views of Parker, whether as stated by himself or his disciples, not to impute to them decided and intentional pantheism. He, and those who more especially represent his views, have chosen to be called THEISTS. Let them bear the name they have assumed. I indicated, near the beginning of this lecture, the line of refutation to which they are open while holding to that theistic ground, and teaching an absolute religion forever in a state of progressive development. If called pantheists, they will flatly deny the charge; and they can show much that will seem, to the view of the undiscriminating, to make good their denial. In his popular discourse, therefore, let the Christian minister grant them the theism to which they lay claim. Then, besides overturning their professed theory, it will be easy to show that their thought has not yet ultimated itself; that they are not established, but drifting; that there is in their theism a tendency towards pantheism, — unless perchance it be towards positivism, owing to the fact that they are empirical, rather than transcendental, in their turn of mind.[2]

The school of theism.

Several things conspired to keep Parker from pushing his speculation to its logical ultimate. He was a sympathetic student of all the modern systems of free religious thought; so sympathetic as to show the influence upon him of the last author

His real tendency held in check.

[1] Experience as a Minister, pp. 26, 27.
[2] The Rev. O. B. Frothingham, of New York, speaking of the impression made on himself and others by Mr. Parker's preaching, said, "We were forced to man the life-boat, to save ourselves from the floods of pantheism." — *Lecture before the Parker Fraternity* (Boston).

he had read. His settled and vehement hostility to everything evangelical threw him unresistingly into the arms of the opposite class of writers. Thus he was embarrassed by the amount and variety of his learning; not mastering his materials, so much as seeming to be mastered by them; neither an independent thinker, who knew just what he believed, and could clearly state and consistently defend it, nor a sturdy adherent of some other master; a multifarious rather than accurate student, having partial knowledge of many systems, but knowing no one thoroughly; and loving all authors who strengthened him in his fight with orthodoxy, so that he did not care to discover how widely they differed from himself and each other.

<small>Character of his scholarship.</small>

Parker claimed to be a consistent Unitarian to the end of his life. But to make good this claim he did not plant himself on any doctrinal belief of Unitarianism, so much as on its postulate of the supremacy of reason in the search for religious truth. Accepting this postulate in the absolute sense in which it is held by the advocates of Free Religion, — in other words, finding the only source of religious truth in the soul of each man, — he found himself forced to disown the authority of the Bible altogether, as well as the right of Jesus to be called Master and Lord. For this heresy, the "new protestantism" of the free religionists, he was cast out of the Unitarian body; and he claimed that the Unitarians, in excommunicating him, had stultified themselves. At any rate, whether or not he had misstated their cardinal principle, the cry of persecution arose; and a number of persons in Boston, professing a desire to see "fair play,"

<small>Relation to the Unitarians.</small>

secured for him an opportunity to be heard. Besides this nucleus, composed chiefly of Unitarians, others soon began to flock around him;— attracted by his zeal in the reforms of the day, for devotion to which they were suffering much discomfort in the older churches and conservative circles throughout the country. The influence of this audience upon the preacher was probably quite as great as his influence upon them. Multitudes of them clung to their evangelical faith, and heard approvingly only his reformatory views.[1] He knew the settled reverence of the New England mind for the Scriptures and for Christ; and it was only from the vantage-ground of his position as a reformer, that he could succeed at all in his efforts to undermine or shake it. I cannot resist the feeling that there was a strong Christian sentiment in the friends he most loved, to say nothing of the instincts of his own heart, which was a constant check to his speculative tendency. He was too dearly attached to those who had rallied to his support in the hour of need, to press forward in a course of thinking which, except as veiled from their comprehension, must have done violence to their long-cherished convictions. The time for earnestly undertaking such a work as this, for devoting himself to it with any hope of success, he did not live to see. It was easy enough for him to lash the Unitarians for their inconsistency, as he believed, in opposing him; to lash the Orthodox for their treachery to the spirit of the New Testament, in upholding slavery and kindred wrongs; and it was his merciless doing of this, not his

Some of his strongest supporters disowned his theology.

---

[1] "Mine is the old faith of New England. On those points he and I rarely talked."— *Address of Wendell Phillips*, at the funeral services for Theodore Parker in Boston.

theological notions, but this in spite of them, which made him in some respects a leader and guide to other minds.

It is an instructive fact, that the fullest and clearest statements we have of his speculative views are contained in a volume mainly written before he was much known to the public. Had the germs contained in that volume been allowed to unfold and mature, he could have hardly failed, even during his not very long ministry, to come out distinctly and avowedly on pantheistic ground. But his speculative tendency, for such reasons as those just named, seems to have been checked. His theological bias was held in suspense. Devotion to reforms, and regard for the feelings of those who stood by him in adversity, blocked the wheels of his logic, so that he never clearly and openly reached the goal at which alone he could legitimately stop. It is significant, as showing that I do not misjudge him, that the pantheistic leaning is more apparent in the early treatise to which I have alluded, the Discourse of Religion, than in later works. It was after he had been laboring for years with the earnest New England reformers, that he preached his Sermons of Theism, — in which the name *Theism* is given to his system, and the attempt made to distinguish between himself and pantheists, atheists, and deists. To what shifts of false statement and definition that attempt led, at least in the case of pantheism, we have already seen. It is a fact, of which he was aware all through his ministry, that his preaching was more liked the nearer it came to evangelical ground. However important his peculiar views seemed to himself, he could not

[margin: The early statements of his views most decided.]

[margin: His most scriptural preaching best liked.]

preach them, save negatively and indirectly, with any hope of persuading the mass of his more intelligent hearers. Hence those views remained in the undeveloped form of the early treatise, to find lodgment here and there in a few scholarly but ill-balanced minds, who, now that he is no more, seem to be completing in themselves the process which was begun in him;—trying, that is, to hold by a position which is not a position, but a tendency; and falling away one after another into pantheism or positivism, according to the original bias of their thinking, where they have not fortunately received divine strength to flee backward, and regain the only sure foundation, which is laid in Jesus Christ.

Weightily true, and nobly solemn in counsel to us all, are the words of Tholuck, spoken in view of the fate of all human thinking which is divorced from faith in the Son of God: "Philosophy can never remain stationary. Aristotle expressed the hope, as Cicero says in the Tusculan Questions, that philosophy would be perfected in a short time. Kant also, in modern times, has said, 'My philosophy will bring eternal peace to the world.' And yet the progress of philosophy is onward, ever onward, without delay. The truths which are recognized by one system are discarded by another. From this mutability of philosophical dogmas, however, is the truly Christian theology exempt. This teaches us to rely on one single MAN, who has laid claim to infallibility. So soon as we acknowledge that the absolute truth is revealed by Jesus, then have we such a ground of confidence as can never be shaken."[1] In all his efforts to raise up

The fate of philosophy when bereft of faith in Christ.

---

[1] Bibliotheca Sacra, Vol. I., p. 207.

the fallen, and promote justice between man and man, Parker could draw no inspiration from his peculiar system of religious thought. As his arm is lifted higher to smite down great iniquities, and sympathy for the wretched breathes more tenderly through his words, he draws nearer and nearer to the burden of the teachings of Christ. Eighteen hundred years of human speculation have made no difference. All that is best, even in the utterances of this denier of Christ's lordship, is an unconscious testimony to the wisdom of the fisherman, — who, when others were forsaking his Master, exclaimed only the more ardently, and with an overflowing faith, "Lord, to whom shall we go? Thou hast the words of eternal life."

_{The Rock of Ages.}

LECTURE IX.

THE STRENGTH AND WEAKNESS OF PANTHEISM.

I HAVE now gone over the ground especially marked out in this course of lectures. The point taken at the beginning of the discussion, and briefly explained and defended, was that all systems of religious error have their genesis in the estrangement of men from God; and that from this original source two main streams of speculation have flowed forth, owing to those opposite mental tendencies, either transcendental or empirical, which characterize all thinkers.[1] It is the errors of religious thought in which the first of these two tendencies may be chiefly traced, that I have thus far considered. The subject, therefore, to which my inquiries have been limited, was the source and development of pantheism; since it is in pantheism, as I endeavored to show, that all a-priori thinking which is not kept by Christian faith must find its legitimate stopping-place. An examination of ancient authors made it appear that pantheism, at least in its clearly defined and more dogmatic forms, is of comparatively modern growth. Historical facts were adduced, which tended to show that man did not ascend first from fetichism to pantheism, but sank to it

_{Recapitulation.}

[1] Introduction.

from pure monotheism, after he had forsaken God.[1] For obvious reasons, Benedict Spinoza was selected as the representative of this system. He had been a pupil of Descartes at the outset; but it was only the philosophical method, not the Christian faith, of his master that he accepted. I undertook to show, so far as required by my more immediate purpose, what the leading doctrine of Spinoza was; as also how that doctrine might be legitimately reached from the premises of Descartes.[2] The development of pantheism in philosophy was then briefly sketched, especially in the school of German transcendentalism, beginning with Kant and ending with Hegel.[3] In immediate connection with this, the Tübingen school of criticism, as represented by Strauss and Baur, was examined with a view to make clear its pantheistic spirit.[4] Thus the way was open for what seemed to me to enter more directly into my main undertaking; namely, a survey of the development of pantheism in literature, — especially in the widely-read works of Goethe, Carlyle, Emerson, and Theodore Parker.[5] It is in the treatment of these popular authors, whose influence Christianity more manifestly meets in its progress, that I have aimed to be thorough, and at the same time accurate and candid. I have allowed them to state their own views, as far as possible, adding my personal comments mainly to elucidate the current of their thinking.

It would be easy to extend this list of names in the domain of letters; though no others have occurred to me as deserving to be classed with leaders in pantheistic

---

[1] Lecture I.   [2] Lecture II.   [3] Lecture III.
[4] Lecture IV.   [5] Lectures V., VI., VII., VIII.

doctrine. Very likely something might be gathered from almost every great author, which, by itself alone, seems to be in sympathy with pantheism. But each writer, I hold, is to be judged by his main spirit and tendencies, together with his open attitude towards Christianity, rather than by the utterances he makes here and there when his feelings and imagination happen to be strongly excited. I do not think it at all necessary to the completeness of my undertaking, to trace the particulars in which the writings of Swedenborg seem to reproduce those of Spinoza: Pantheism may be the logical ultimate of his doctrines, and of the church founded on them, as one ingenious critic has tried to prove;[1] but I am content to leave that question untouched, having laid down the tests by which every student of Swedenborg may decide it for himself. I have already quoted lines from Pope which are pantheistic in sentiment, and might have added others of similar import from the same author. But just how much weight should be given to these, as decisive of Pope's speculative views in religion, is uncertain; for he has written much, the sentiment of which is opposite to this; nor does it appear that he ever declared himself the foe of Christian theism. Willis, in his Life, Correspondence, and Ethics of Spinoza, adopts the conclusion already referred to, that Swedenborg was a Spinozist; but he also puts many others into the same category, by what seems to me a very unfair method of criticism. Even the writers of the

Authors excluded from this survey.

---

[1] This critic is the late General Hitchcock, of the United States army, who, in 1846, published a work entitled "The Doctrines of Spinoza and Swedenborg identified, in so far as they claim a Scientific Ground."

Bible do not escape his classification; and authors so wholly unlike as the poet Tennyson and the naturalist Darwin are named among pantheists. To Wordsworth a prominent place is assigned. Undoubtedly this poet, in common with many others not pantheistic, has written passages which, taken by themselves, have a savor of Spinozism. There are lines in the Ode on Immortality which carry the doctrine of Plato to the very verge of pantheism. Also, in the Ode on Tintern Abbey, Wordsworth speaks of

"A presence that disturbs us with a joy
Of elevated thoughts, a sense sublime
Of something interfused
Whose dwelling is the light of setting suns,
And the round ocean, and the living air,
And the blue sky, and fills the mind of man —
A motion and a spirit that impels
All thinking things, all objects of all thought,
And rolls through all things."

But these lines must be explained by others, and by the well-known religious views of the author. Wordsworth never professed any creed which would warrant us in giving his poetry a pantheistic construction; he never assumed an attitude of hostility or attack towards the Christian religion. But far more surprising than Willis is an English clergyman, — Hunt by name, — whose work has just fallen under my notice.[1] This critic, in an extended treatise on the general subject, finds pantheism not only in the writers now named, but in Augustine,

[1] An Essay on Pantheism, by Rev. John Hunt. 8vo. pp. 382 (London, 1866).

Anselm, Leibnitz, Sir William Hamilton, Mansel. Wesley, and Cowper, and Bryant, as truly as Goethe and Shelley, are to him poets of pantheism. He finds the doctrine of Spinoza in Milton and Toplady no less than in Emerson. Frederick Robertson, as judged by him, is a pantheist of the same class as Theodore Parker. But such criticism cannot be allowed. It is wholesale and indiscriminate. We are left to infer from it that pantheism is a wholly innocent thing, into which even Christian writers must be expected to fall at times. There is, as it seems to me that I have successfully shown, a vast difference between most of these writers and those whom I have classified as pantheists. Undoubtedly I have not named all; but it will be found, I think, that those not named are either disciples of one or the other of those I have examined, or indeterminate in their views, so as to preclude all claim to any separate or special treatment. If there are around us free-thinkers, and propagandists of free religion, even they are substantially answered in the reply to Emerson and Parker. Either this, or they do not fall within the limits of a treatise on a-priori thinking, but belong to the school of empirical thought, and must be reserved for treatment under the general head of Positivism.

Refutation of pantheism.

It was stated, in the Introduction, that something in the way of refutation might be expected at the close of this survey of pantheism. To that concluding work we have now come; and I prefer to entitle it a statement both of *the strength and the weakness* of pantheism, rather than a precise refutation. I do this for two reasons. In the first place, I have sought to make the refutation go along side by side with the exposition of the doctrine. The overthrow of this, and of all forms of religious error, as was maintained in the latter part of the Introduction, depends more on the practical fidelity and broad generosity of Christians, than on any arguments addressed to the understanding. Yet such arguments must not be thrown aside as valueless. It behooves us to overturn pantheism from the position of philosophy; to show that the clear head disowns it, as truly as the pure and tender heart. This work I have tried to do, in some measure, at each point of our progress. Nor did the doing it require much break or diversion in our line of treatment. The premise on which pantheism rests is so simple, that only a brief hint, or turn of a phrase or sentence, was needed, for the most part, to guard against any plausible aspect of the doctrine which met us from time to time in the course of our inquiry. It is at the risk of repeating myself that I proceed to notice some of those suggestions more distinctly. Besides, as I have said in the course of the investigation, the best refutation of a religious error is the clear statement of it. Such a statement of pantheism I have endeavored to give,—recognizing it as a half truth, and presenting its comely features together with the repulsive, in the various authors passed in review. The fact that it is not unmixed error in its origin, that it arises out of a blending of the false with the true in philosophy, would seem to require that something should be said for it, however adverse the final decision in estimating it thoroughly. But whether I speak of its strength or

This went along with the exposition.

The clear statement of error its best refutation.

weakness, I shall still feel, as I thus far have, that every mind which goes along with me will see its utter untenableness,—judging it in the light of those necessary and immutable convictions of our nature which never fail to pronounce it false when its essential meaning is brought clearly to view.

In the second place, I do not here pretend to any exact refutation of pantheism, because there is something in almost every author treated which might, in that case, seem to require a special reply. The gross doctrine which Theodore Parker calls pantheism, as if to divert attention from the real thing, is too unphilosophical to deserve a particular answer. It may draw an odious name from his "theism," when offered to minds which do not discriminate; but to attack it would be investing it with a dignity it cannot claim. And there are reasons why the recognized masters of pantheism need not be answered separately. Though there is something distinctive in each one of them perhaps, yet their main position is so essentially the same, that what thoroughly refutes any one is a substantial refutation of them all. In one form or another they make consciousness the organ and the criterion of truth. " I think, therefore I am," is the point from which Spinoza sets out, but which he seems to me to abandon quite as unwarrantably as Descartes. Consciousness is the mind's knowledge of what it does as being its own acts. It is therefore always a particular and determined knowledge, never universal and absolute. Its sphere is psychology; nor can it, by any possibility, transcend this limit so as to include ontology. It has

Every pantheist has something peculiar to himself.

Wherein they agree.

nothing to do with being in general, but is always shut up to being in particular. Hence Spinoza, to be consistent, cannot affirm an absolute reality, of which he is the fleeting manifestation; for on his own premise, and by his own method, he himself, as known in consciousness, is the only reality. Spinoza's method cannot reach ontology.

The reasoning of Fichte also is defective, and in the same way as that of Spinoza. He cannot pass from the finite ego to the Infinite Ego in consciousness. That step must be taken by an inference, or through a conviction which carries one beyond the province to which consciousness is shut up. In like manner, Emerson may say that his soul is a conditioned image of the unconditioned over-soul, but he abandons the so-called philosophy of consciousness in thus affirming. He utters an ontological doctrine, to which his consciousness can never attain. And he certainly is one of the most consistent of pantheists when he intrenches himself within the sphere of psychology, declaring that he is God and nature, and that he knows no reality save the subjective self. Same fault in the reasoning of Fichte and Emerson.

Some of the later pantheists, as if hoping to escape this fatal defect in their reasoning, have given a new definition of consciousness.[1] They arbitrarily enlarge its function; say that it is not limited to subjective knowledge, but includes that which is objective and infinite. They define it as a knowing not only with one's self, but with the universal whole. Is there, however, anything in human experience answering to such a definition? Manifestly it is not real, but only verbal. An objective consciousness is an absurdity. It does not Function of consciousness mistaken.

See North American Review, Article "Hegel" (April, 1868).

24

even seem to lay a path out from the conditioned to
the unconditioned. It is a phrase without a meaning, for
there is no corresponding fact in our experience. What
these pantheists call "consciousness" is more properly
suggestion. Spinoza's finite thinking suggests an infinite
thinking. Fichte's particular ego suggests a universal
ego. Emerson's my-self suggests an other-self. Hegel's
being suggests its opposite, which is non-being. But these
contraries are not united in the human consciousness.
There is another and more royal faculty of the human
mind, which holds them together. As soon as we duly
examine this nobler power, we find that it renders pantheism forever impossible. The proper office of this power is
to furnish us with our primary beliefs, — with those convictions respecting ourselves and the world,
which are universal and necessary. It is properly named the intuitional faculty. This faculty
it is, however designated, which gives us a sure passage
out into the ontological world. We may, thoughtlessly or
for the sake of convenience, call it consciousness; but it is
not such a power as to imply, in its workings, that we are
part and parcel of all which we know. It leaves us eternally distinct from the external universe with which it
acquaints us. We can never grant to the pantheist that
he has found the absolute, the unconditioned, in his own
consciousness. It is in the exercise of this other, our
noblest and divinest faculty, — by the intuition of objective
and necessary truths, — that we leap "the flaming walls of
the world," and stand face to face with the Father of our
spirits. The only consistent form of pantheism is that
idealism by which a man denies all reality save the thought-

Differs from the faculty of intuition.

process of which he is conscious. It is not objective, but purely subjective. It is not absolute, but forever cast in the mould of his particular being.

We are obliged, therefore, at the very outset, to grant the pantheist a position he cannot legitimately reach, in order to consider some of the more general arguments on which he relies. *What is granted for argument's sake.* We will allow that he has planted his foot in the world of unconditioned thought, not forcing him to explain the process by which he reached that position. Having conceded this much, the way is open for us to look at the arguments with which he seeks to fortify himself, that we may know what weight or want of weight there is in them.

It is sometimes said that pantheism follows from the truth, admitted by all theists, that God is an infinite being. This is the point at which Parker especially stumbles. *The infinity of God said to involve pantheism.* He fears to clothe God with personality, lest God should thereby be unclothed of his infinity. To make him personal — so runs the argument — is to make him finite. He must be impersonal in order to be infinite. Personality involves limitation; but God is unlimited; therefore God is impersonal. This sounds quite conclusive; is, in form at least, unanswerable. But let us look at it. Has the major premise been proved? What human intellect has discovered that personality, always and necessarily, involves limitation? Let us see the proof that there is a whit more difficulty in the idea of an infinite, than of a finite person. No such evidence can be found. The syllogism is therefore baseless, and the whole argument sinks into a fallacious assertion. Personality is properly but another name for determinateness; and as the amount of being is greater in any case, the demand for this is not less, but more. "In reality there is no contradiction," says Julius Müller, "between determinateness and infinity. Infinity not only implies determinateness, but positively requires it.; it demands a fulness of determinations in no way limited from without by any other being, nor from within by one another."[1] But by what right do pantheists say that God must be impersonal because he is infinite? They deny all personality. Man, to their view, is essentially impersonal; a person only a personification.

This argument assumes what the pantheist has denied.

Upon this theory simple reality, quite as necessarily as infinity, excludes personality. Persons are the images of our own dream. We flatter ourselves with the illusion of personality, in this phenomenal and unreal life; but we shall awake from this fantasy at length, — shall be absorbed back, that is, into the impersonal substance, whose bright shadows we are. Turning from this argument, which so remarkably defeats itself, we say that the seat of personality is in the will. It is not bound up with the idea of a given amount of being, whether less or more; but is essential to the idea of freedom, liberty, independent choice. There can be no personality in the material world; for that is without the determining power, it is the realm of fate. According to the pantheist there cannot be personality anywhere, for he lifts the iron sceptre of necessity over all things. But we know that we are free. Nothing can

The essence of personality is free-will.

[1] Christian Doctrine of Sin, Book III., Pt. I., Chap. IV.

uproot this conviction, or stand against it. In the freedom thus vouched for is the citadel of our personality, of all personality. To affirm that God is impersonal, is therefore to degrade him below man; is to teach that he can never have the sublime sense of liberty which we all have; is to affirm that he must come out of the sphere of the infinite, and be as one of his finite creatures, in order to feel that he has the power of doing as he will. It is not the personality of God, but of man, that is imperfect. Our will is overborne by temptation. It is weak, owing to the finiteness of the circle of being in which it acts. But God's being is not limited. Its centre is everywhere, its circumference nowhere. Hence he is immeasurably above us, in all that goes to constitute him a person. He is infinite in his being, and therefore as a person he is absolutely perfect. *God the only perfect person.*

Another argument, equally high-sounding and equally hollow, is founded on the ambiguous postulate that the mind cannot act excepting where it is. Hence it is inferred, by the pantheist, that all truth lies within the compass of the mind; and that we can have knowledge of nature, or of any other objective thing, only as our minds, in the last analysis, are identical with it. In all our acquisitions of truth we are mistaken, if we suppose that our researches pertain to external facts; for that which we regard as outward is only a shadow of the inward, while, spider-like, we spin our theories of God and the world out of our own dream. But in reply to this argument we have only to bring those principles of the common-sense philosophy, so clearly enunciated by Reid *The assertion that the mind can act only where it is.* *Contradicted by our necessary beliefs.*

and Hamilton, and to which I have already referred as there was occasion. It is a fundamental belief with us — a persuasion beforehand, which we bring with us to every problem in science — that we are independent entities, separate from nature; and that it is not through consciousness as an organ of discovery, but by immediate cognitions, that we get our knowledge of the external world. These cognitions are inexplicable, yet are they irresistible; and we find ourselves always naturally believing what they declare. Now we must insist

Whatever else fails, must insist on these beliefs.

that this fundamental belief in the separate existence of the subject knowing and the object known is true, until the pantheist proves it to be false; for if it be shown that this our necessary conviction is deceptive, then no one of our faculties is any longer trustworthy, and all knowledge of truth, even that of which the pantheist makes his boast, is forever at an end. There is no point short of absolute scepticism, wild, dark, terrible beyond all we can imagine, at which logically to stop, the moment we swing loose from our faith that the mind may hold converse with objects outside of itself. If we know anything, we know that the human spirit is a royal child. It can act upon realities external to itself. Consciousness is no prison, in which that spirit must remain shut away from the knowledge of objective truth. The everlasting doors of consciousness are lifted up, and through them the soul is constantly looking forth on a universe without, sure that what it sees is not "the vision of its dream," but a revelation of God's glory in the works of his hand, which it may evermore study, and admire, and subdue to its royal control.

One great service which mental science owes to Christianity is a thorough investigation of the fundamental beliefs of the soul. They are the armory to which we never go in vain for weapons; weapons mighty to the pulling down of the strongholds of pantheism; of that pantheism which would draw all reality into the maelstrom of consciousness, and give us its own thought-process, at last, as the only universe and the only God. These necessary convictions cannot be too much studied in the colleges and all other schools where youthful intellect is trained; for they are the golden links in a chain which is the only chain that binds the conditioned world to the unconditioned. They are the pontoons which the advancing soul throws out over the swollen streams of scepticism, making for itself a way into the regions of absolute truth, along which it moves with assured step, conquering and to conquer. God is in heaven, and we on the earth. Yet the Father may commune with his children while we behold these angels, faithful messengers between the two worlds, ascending and descending along the ladder let down for them.

The duty of mental science to clear up these first truths.

Pantheists urge, as one of the strong arguments for their doctrine, its capabilities as a system of philosophy. It deduces all reality from consciousness, on mathematical principles. This is thought to be eminently satisfactory to the philosophical thinker. All things — mind, matter, church, state, society, the Bible, the Koran, Jesus, Confucius, Zoroaster — are analyzed back into an eternal nature-process. In this solution, we are told, is comprehensiveness; everything

The claim of comprehensiveness.

covered by a single formula; perfect unity, and perfect demonstration. But we say, in reply to this boasted strength, that it is a glaring and fatal weakness. The claim of comprehensiveness cannot be made good; is just the opposite of the actual state of the case. So far from being all-inclusive, pantheism is a system of exclusion. It begins with leaving out some of the most important data of a perfect philosophy. There are within us certain convictions, which are as inevitable as consciousness, though not in their origin a part of it. We have, for instance, an unconquerable faith in the freedom of our will; in the power, whatever choice we make at any time, to make either that or some other choice. This persuasion is as truly a certainty to us, as the thinking of which we are conscious. But the pantheist has no place for this intuition in his system. He excludes it. His fatalism represents it as purely a chimera. Not only does pantheism deny the possibility of this freedom; it rejects other intuitions of the reason, which are bound up with the action of all our mental faculties. Men know that they commit sin, and they feel guilty for it. But on the theory of the pantheist that feeling of guilt is an illusion, for the sin itself is impossible. We are as thoroughly persuaded, also, of the distinctions of right and wrong as that we think. Yet pantheism, by resolving all things into a chain of necessity, makes these distinctions impossible. Our thoughts are compelled either to accuse or else excuse one another. How, then, can we accept, as at all adequate to the facts of our nature, a philosophy which denies that there is anything praiseworthy or

This claim cannot be made good.

Important truths which pantheism excludes.

blameworthy in human conduct? Its optimism is flatly contradicted by a voice in our conscience which we cannot disown. If consciousness be all-inclusive, and its contents are evolved under fixed laws of fate, it is absurd to speak of gratitude, blame, remorse, the approval or disapproval of one's own or another's life. For there can be no such thing as good or ill desert. Nothing can be otherwise than it is; and we should take everything as it comes, thanking no one and condemning no one. But pantheism is not founded on anything as inevitable as these same feelings of gratitude, remorse, censure, praise. They are true if anything is true. And yet the temple which the pantheist builds allows them no entrance within its doors. The alleged capacity of the system for including and unifying all truth, is therefore a hollow pretence. Its foundation is not broad enough for the facts of the soul. It leaves out, and makes war upon, one whole department of the soul's activities; namely, the moral and religious. It allows room for the thinking faculty alone; affirms that all truth lies within the conscious action of this single power; and on so narrow, so insufficient a basis, it attempts to construct a philosophy of the universe and of God.

And this favoritism, it should also be remarked, is shown for an inferior department of our humanity. The city which John saw gave no entrance to the unclean, but only to the pure, within its pearly gates; but the New Jerusalem of the pantheist reverses this action, excluding what is noblest, and admitting that which maketh a lie. The weeds are cherished in his paradise, and the flowers thrown over the

Gives precedence to an inferior faculty.

walls. Our highest capacity, that in which the most important of all truths are revealed to us, is the ethical and religious; the capacity in virtue of which we have to do with the right, with God, with immortality. This supreme power of the soul is conscience, the seat of the moral sentiments; and it should ever take precedence of mere intellect. Both are worthy of recognition.

All the faculties of the mind should be recognized. The true philosophy assigns a niche to each one in its temple; but the place of honor belongs, evermore, not to that which moves only within the sphere of natural law, but to that which spurns the dominion of fate, — which bears the soul upward on tireless wing, into communion with the holy, the uncaused, the self-directed, the divine. Conscience and the understanding should not be put asunder; and in joining them together, conscience should be assigned to the uppermost seat. Hers is of right the throne and the sceptre. The faculty which aids us

Precedence should be given to the moral faculty.

chiefly in acquiring unreligious and conditioned knowledge must not command her, much less attempt to usurp her kingdom. Its duty is both to admit her, and to obey the voice she utters. This was conceded by Kant, in his Critique of the Practical Reason, where he shows that bare thinking, the basis on which the pantheist tries to build, is too narrow to sustain the most vital truths of philosophy. Buckle, whose positivism is at one with pantheism in this particular, rejects the teaching of the sage of Königsberg. He puts knowledge in advance of goodness; welcomes the data of the senses and understanding, and out of them constructs a so-called history of civilization. But he pays no regard to the categories of man's moral nature, excepting to class them with the superstitions of a theological and metaphysical age. The reception his work has met with shows the repugnance of his doctrine to the convictions of wise and good men.

It is not theology and metaphysics, but human nature, which demands that supreme deference be shown to the dictates of the moral faculty, — which forever takes man out of the province of necessary law, and makes him the free and responsible child of God. That which sees God, and opens to us the book of eternal truth, is not the mighty intellect, but the pure heart. Behind our inmost thought, coming out of the depths of our spirits, far beneath the subtlest play of consciousness, there is a thrill upward through all the soul's action, confirming and re-echoing the sentence, that it pleases the Father to hide from the wise and prudent things which he reveals to babes. This vision of moral truth is within the veil, in the holy of holies of the human spirit. In that inner sanctuary we find the true glory of man. And that character is worthiest, that life mightiest, that philosophy most surely grounded, which lays here the beams of its chambers. To turn away from this shekinah, is to miss the brightness in which forevermore is the hiding of its power. Virtue is greater than intelligence. Without holiness there can be no clear understanding. Only as he fears the Lord and departs from evil, is either the statesman wise, or the orator eloquent, or the poet inspired. The essence of foolishness is wickedness, and moral perfection is the only foundation of a perfect philosophy. There is in every man a voice which gladly responds to these simple state-

<small>The emphasis of the soul demands this.</small>

ments. And it is a voice of authority, no less than of gladness. It speaks out in indignant tones of threatening, when this order of things is reversed — when the crown which innocency should wear is made to deck the brow of guilty power. It forces us to cry shame, and covers us with blushes, when we see a thoughtless public showering honors upon a corrupt man, however grand his mental proportions. To our moral nature, which looks from between the cherubim, the aspiring politician is often dwarfed to insignificance beside the poor husband, wife, or son; the dashing warrior eclipsed by some pale-faced girl, toiling alone to support the mother she loves. And if gratitude were not so often "a lively sense of favors expected," — if we could make up our minds to act out our inmost and most sacred judgments, — that suffering child of penury, not the great man whose trumpet is blown before him, would receive from us the statue and the eulogy.

Every honest nature welcomes it.

A main source of the charm of pantheism, for many minds, is its doctrine of the divine immanency. It is this doctrine which gives to the writings of Theodore Parker nearly all their beauty and power. He seemed to dwell in an ocean of deity. Whichever way he turned, he met the divine in all things. The apotheosis of nature was celebrated in his sermons, and especially in his prayers. Thus he transfigured the whole world to the imaginations of his disciples; they mistook poetry for philosophy, the enchantment of their own minds for religion. The fascination of Goethe arises in the same way. He did not distinguish between the divine and the simply natural. He animated

The doctrine of the divine immanency said to be a source of power.

nature with God. All the world, under his handling, was made to take on a strange beauty; every highest and every lowest thing was idealized, and painted as a part of the universal whole, till it carried away the reader in an ecstasy of nature-worship. If we watch our minds while following Emerson through his pages which delight us most, we shall see that the secret of his power over us is the same. He pours floods of divinity all through the world; and this sorcery of the imagination, boldly practised where angels fear to approach, so captivates us that we are tempted to believe in it as the exact and unvarnished truth. Yet this charm is dissolved when we come to apply the doctrine of God's imma- *Proves too much.* nency in all its bearings. If everything is divine, then are even the vices and crimes of men a part of the life of God. These, as we have had occasion to notice in several of the authors reviewed, may claim our worship as really as that which seems to us most innocent and pure. Thus it is that the doctrine, by its very thoroughness and consistency, breaks the spell it had thrown around us. Its power becomes weak. Our minds are disenchanted. The moral sentiments utter their strong protest. We behold, with clear eye, that he who makes God identical with all reality, deals in fancies rather than fact; he is a poet simply, not a teacher of religion or its true philosophy.

Even the Christian poet, therefore, has every advantage which the pantheist may claim, and at the same time may keep his pages pure. He knows that God is not *The real power not* really the same thing as the world; and hence, *limited to this doctrine.* while painting nature as divine, he may avoid all those objects which are in their essence base, and give us only such as are fit emblems of a character infinite in holiness and truth. Bryant, for instance, does not claim to be a philosopher, but only to utter poetic fancies quickened by faith in a personal God, when he says, —

"Thou art in the soft winds
That run along the summit of these trees
In music. Thou art in the cooler breath
That in the inmost darkness of this place
Comes scarcely felt — the barky trunks, the ground,
The moist, fresh ground, all are instinct with thee."

Thomson. Nor have we reason to infer that Thomson would confound the Creator with his works, though he, in the fervor of poetic contemplation, could say, —

"These, as they change, Almighty Father! these
Are but the varied God. The rolling year
Is full of thee. Forth in the pleasing Spring
Thy beauty walks, thy tenderness and love.
Wide flush the fields; the softening air is balm;
Echo the mountains round; the forest smiles;
And every sense and every heart is joy."

The first lines of this description would be as baldly pantheistic as anything in Emerson, were we *These have as much poetical vantage-ground as Emerson.* forced to read them in the light of Emerson's philosophy; and did not the personification of Spring, the fields, the mountains, and the forests, which immediately follows, show that the whole passage only gives voice to a poetic reverie. We must interpret the words of "the Concord Sage" more strictly in his May Day and other poems, where he confounds natural forces with the attributes of God. He declares that he is looking into the real substance of things, and expounding them in exact terms, when he says, —

> "Thou seekest in globe and galaxy;
> He hides in pure transparency.
> Thou askest in fountains and fires;
> He is the essence that inquires.
> He is the axis of the star;
> He is the sparkle of the spar;
> He is the heart of every creature;
> He is the meaning of every feature;
> And his mind is the sky,
> Than all it holds more deep, more high."

All those features of modern literature which are repulsive to our moral sense, whether found in the novels of Charles Reade or the Poems of Swinburne and Walt Whitman, can find no apology short of pantheism. Whatever may be the speculative views of the writers, they are simply vulgar, save as they go back to the doctrine which Goethe and Carlyle drew from Spinoza. Those who take pleasure in the poetry of Byron and Shelley thereby reveal the grossness of their tastes, or betray a sympathy with that philosophy to which even sin is divine and beautiful. This disregard of the moral imperative, which so abounds in a class of popular works, has its primary source, no doubt, partly in the wish to please sordid minds for the sake of notoriety or gain, partly in the eagerness of writers to indulge a feeling of unrestrained freedom, and partly in

Source of immorality in literature.

efforts to imitate the great masters of this species of literature; but its only claim to respect, or even to toleration among people of pure tastes, is through the favor of that system which transfigures all things into deity. Even the freshness and originality of Joaquin Miller, his sympathy with nature in her wildest and loveliest moods, his brilliant word-painting, which makes the wonders of tropical life pass before us so vividly, should not blind us to the moral defects of his poetry. Describing the filibuster Walker and his fellow-criminals, he calls them —

<small>Joaquin Miller.</small>

> " Men strangely brave and fiercely true,
> Who dared the West when giants were,
> Who erred, yet bravely dared to err.
>   .   .   .   .
> With iron will and bated breath,
> Their hands against their fellow-man,
> They rode — each man an Ishmaelite.
>   .   .   .   .
> I did not question, did not care
>   To know the right or wrong. I saw
> That savage freedom had a spell,
> And loved it more than I can tell,
>   And snapped my fingers at the law."

This love of "savage freedom," and painting it as the ideal of human enjoyment, should be more careful to discriminate. Among Christians, and in the teachings of the pulpit, there is danger, unless we have a wise care, that views will be held which cannot stand before conscience; danger lest our hatred of artificial life, and the joy we take in unrestrained liberty, should drive us upon ground where Spinozism will be the

<small>Good men exposed to peril.</small>

only reason we can give for the faith which is in us. That is the shelter of respectability, under which everything immoral, or gross, or lawless and wicked, may gather. It is a shelter which may be stretched out over all that is fair and charming; but it is equally hos- *The doctrine of the* pitable to base and repulsive things. This want *divine immanency a* of discrimination, disregard of moral differences, *weakness of pantheism.* confusing the good with the bad, is a fatal weakness. Pantheism must be judged, not by the pure things for which it claims to make room, but by the impure things which fly to it for protection.

Another source of power in pantheism, to which multitudes of men are especially susceptible, is the intellectual eminence, and in some instances the moral purity, of its masters. The argument is, that a *The argument from* doctrine held by such persons should be pre- *great men.* sumed to be true. But let us see what becomes of this argument, when we examine and discriminate. The masters of pantheism have never been first-rate, but at the best only second-rate thinkers. Descartes was the teacher of Spinoza; discovered, by his transcendent genius, the data which Spinoza's logic carried out to their gloomy conclusion. So Fichte, Schelling, and Hegel are overshadowed by Kant, who was not a panthe- *Pantheism cannot claim these.* ist. Without him they could not have been. He is the great primary in the system of transcendental thought; and he remains such, while they wander into darkness. The power, therefore, is not in the pantheism, but in that spiritual philosophy which pantheism distorts and caricatures. The charm is in the Kantian metaphysics, in the transcendental philosophy. With this philosophy the greatest names of the race have been associated, and will be. Of all subjects of investigation it is the most difficult, and hence appeals only to the highest order of minds. It is subtle, profound, inexhaustible. There can be no other such intellectual gymnastic as it affords; for it taxes the attention, the reason, the imagination, the logical understanding, the power of expression, to their utmost, and ever more and more. Now those must be minds of more than the average rank, which are first attracted to this philosophy; nor can they escape the benefits of its discipline altogether, though not great enough to hold themselves back from the abysses of pantheism. It is their love of a-priori thought, of purely spiritual investigation, that proves them great; that some of them lose their balance, and drift into pantheism, is a proof of weakness. Life is a probation, a constant scene of trial; and that trial which affords the grandest discipline, offers at the same time the most fearful temptation. The exposures of the a-priori philosophy are very great; and the fact that some of the foremost thinkers of the race have slid from it into pantheism, but makes more conspicuous those who have stood firm on its slippery edge, — secured not so much by the grandeur of their intellect, as by their sublime faith in the Son of the Living God. The best philosophical fruit of the ages is ripened by that style of thought; yet as soon as the thought begins to be pantheistic, that ripe fruit becomes over ripe, and to the discriminating taste loathsome.

I cannot forbear to speak here of the growing disposition, in some quarters, to let scientific studies take precedence of metaphysics, at our colleges and universities. It seems to me to be one of the most serious mistakes of educators at the present day. Though it may be true that the spiritual philosophy will give us here and there a Spinoza, a Hegel, a Goethe, a Carlyle or Emerson, yet what are these to the spawn of an empirical philosophy? If the infidelities growing out of transcendentalism were even worse than those growing out of materialism, yet it has this signal advantage: it honors the soul; it emphasizes the spiritual nature of man; it trains our noblest mental faculties as material science never can. I would not pluck one honor from those who are extending our knowledge of nature; we owe them a great debt, but their pursuits do not give the discipline which most ennobles human minds. The names of great naturalists are spoken reverently; but where is the volume contributed by them to the literature of the ages, and living from generation to generation in the hearts of men? Their discoveries become, after a little, the tools of the craftsman and economist. To their honor be it said that all works of present utility owe them a vast debt; but where is the poem, the classic, the moral or religious volume, conceived in their minds, which lives on through time, and ennobles and inspires? In vain do we look to the future for an order of men who shall write our hymns, who shall enrich our literature, who shall elevate and refine the tone of thinking among the people, if we turn the minds of our students down from the ideal realm, to labor on that whose fashion is all the time passing away. " It is as the best gymnastic of the mind," says Sir William

Metaphysics in education.

Better than physical science.

Hamilton, "as a mean principally and almost exclusively conducive to the highest education of our noblest powers, that we would vindicate to metaphysical studies the necessity which has too frequently been denied them. By no other intellectual application, and least of all by physical pursuits, is the soul thus reflected on itself, and its faculties concentrated in such independent, vigorous, unwonted, and continuous energy. By none, therefore, are its best capacities so variously and intensely evolved. 'Where there is most life there is most victory.'"[1] If we look into the history of literature, we shall find that its most glorious eras have been illuminated by metaphysics; that its proudest achievements were the fair outgrowth and blossom of a spiritual philosophy. And on the other hand we shall find that its most barren periods, when the oracles were dumb and there was no open vision, when no monumental work was printed, when nothing was written which the world refuses to let die, have been times of the bondage of genius to empirical pursuits. The mind of the age ceased to have its conversation in heaven, and was led captive in the chains of the flesh. Thus it became weak, and groped in darkness; nor did it any longer have to do with the deep intuitions of humanity, but built hay, wood, and stubble into the walls which are from everlasting to everlasting.

But not one of the great benefits which result from the study of metaphysics is to be accredited to pantheism. These benefits have been secured in most transcendent measure where no pantheistic

[1] Philosophical Discussions, p. 30.

element mingles. They begin to be tainted as soon as that element appears. It changes insight to mysticism, largeness of view to vagueness, wealthy thought to corrupting dreams. It is only as the transcendentalist holds back from this extreme, not slipping down from the plane of high discipline into the state of mental lassitude, that he continues to be strong and to prevail. Nor is that purity of life, seen in such men as Spinoza and Emerson, any real support of their doctrine. It fascinates their disciples, and thus makes way for what they teach, but it is no fruit of their teaching. A thinker may be pure in life, while thinking out a system fearfully corrupting to others. He is too much absorbed in profound investigation to desire base indulgence. With him study is the pleasure which satisfies every craving; he has no other passion to be gratified. "Keep men thinking," says a late writer, "and it matters not what their doctrines or their philosophy may be; we know pretty well what their lives must be. A Spinoza gives as little trouble to the state as the Seraphic Doctor himself. All men absorbed in thinking have that which will keep them steady, as they pace the strange passage from birth to death."[1] It is only as the doctrines of these thinkers flow up from the fountains to the surface, and mix with social and every-day life, that we discover their true character. And here the weakness of pantheism is made overwhelmingly manifest; for the morals of communities brought under its influence will not bear even the most superficial scrutiny.

Purity of life in the teacher not a test of his doctrine.

A system of thinking cannot be true, which thus fails to

[1] "Thorndale."

endure the test of conscience. Our better nature forces us to turn from it to that which helps pure-hearted men and women in actual life. Their right impulses, which it is never unsafe to heed, demand a doctrine from which they can draw comfort in trouble; which arms them against temptation; which girds them for every good word and work. They are very unwise champions of Christianity, knowing but little of its blessed spirit, who cower in the presence of popular errors; who try to stretch their charity so as to take in every great philosopher, whatever his religious views, fearing that if he be left out, the gospel may fall into disrepute. Christianity is no client. Much less does it need the patronage of those who are slow to confess its excellency. If any of the so-called great men of the world find it in their hearts to disown Christ, the loss is all their own. It is they, not the Rock cut out of the mountain, that must be ground to powder.

The ethical criterion.

Christianity above all patronage.

We see, therefore, that the strength of pantheism turns to weakness when duly examined. It has no ground at all in strict reason. How, then, shall we account for its ascendency over minds of no mean order? We can explain this fact quite naturally. The system has been to such minds what Calypso's cave was to the hero of the Odyssey. In their search homeward for eternal truth, demanding of them tireless effort and caution, they have grown weary, and have allowed this charm to draw them out of their course. Worn out by the ceaseless strain, and no Star of Bethlehem rising

How men become pantheists.

on them, they have yielded to the enchantress. The soft fascination, half poetical and half philosophical, gradually overcame them. They were borne away on a delicious dream; grew averse to argument; vaguely believed their dream true — either because they wished it true, or through doubt of all other things. The system has lived, for the most part, in the minds of a few solitary thinkers. It has become popular only as it has enabled those holding it to voice forth some great feeling of the times. Thus, when everything was ripe for a revolution in Europe, the ruled rising up against their rulers in both church and state, pantheistic writers stepped forward, and led in the wide revolt. The practical import of their creed was, that every man should act out what might be in him to his utmost, regarding as sacred only the impulses of his own nature. Established forms were profane and unreal, over which the people might boldly ride, borne forward by the divine strength of their own desires. Thus did Goethe and others give the reins to malcontents, and apply the spur, raising a storm from which they were glad afterwards to hide their heads. It was not argument, but the discovery of something favorable to their revolutionary spirit, which brought the masses into love with pantheism. Here was a philosophy which legitimated disorder. They were willing to embrace, without careful study, a doctrine which encouraged them in overturning governments, guillotining monarchs, and sacking public treasuries. So more recently in England, and to some extent in America. If pantheistic teachings have spread among our people, it is because lawless desire had

Times in which pantheism may be popular.

Legitimates disorder.

paved the way for theory. Enemies, not only of political wrongs, but of the Bible, the Sabbath, the church, the family, the state, wish some plausible premise from which to deduce their action. Champions of free love, and of a higher law found in their lower nature, know that the social chaos they invoke can never come, in a thoughtful community, save as they are able to show for it some ground of authority. Hence pantheism, more or less clearly defined, is their natural ally. From this their laxness of morals, and general irregularity of life, may be legitimately reached by a chain of practical logic. It is the fruitful root out of which all their disorder and corruption can be made to grow. It gives them the license they crave, and at the same time invests their libertinism with the air and grandeur of philosophy.

The pantheism which has poisoned so much of our popular literature for a generation past, seems now to be in its decadence. Should its reign be hereafter restored, let us at least hope that it may not be ushered in through the gateway of man's lower passions. What we know of the English, and especially of the Puritan stock, persuades us that such is not the first danger. Our danger seems to me to arise rather from that worship of intellectual greatness which is so natural to our people. This was the source in which the stream of German pantheism began. The race of which we come is largely Teutonic. Its dispersed members, like those of the fatherland, are too much inclined to exalt sheer mental power. The honor they yield it is sometimes a homage not due to the creature, but only to the Creator. That which we idolize, to which we burn incense, is not

Our exposure to the peril.

simple moral worth, but natural genius, refined by scholarly culture. In this habit lies our special peril. It makes us too willing to be influenced by men of commanding intellect, without regard to the moral principles they teach, and it may be also practise. This habit shuts our eye to the higher and nobler part of man's nature. It prepares us to accept doctrines which may poison our character, simply because they are held, and urged upon our attention, by some imperial thinker.

I would not discredit mental activity. Let it continue to distinguish the English-speaking races, and especially the people of America. In the future, more than in the past, let ours be the land of teachers, lecturers, authors, scholars. But let us not worship intellectual eminence. Let us insist on some other and diviner quality in the man whom we accept as truly great. Let us demand of every leader, and of every volume that asks our favorable verdict, fidelity to conscience, moral purity in tendency as well as tone. Let us bid the new comer stand afar off, as an infected and deadly thing, if it only stimulates the thinking faculty, and does not lift the soul nearer to God. If it would escape this quarantine, and sail into the harbor of our faith and love, let it bring, besides and above everything else, an influence which shall cleanse and exalt the natural affections; which shall guard the sanctuary of the heart; which shall build broader and higher, instead of stealthily undermining, that wall of instinctive delicacy which keeps the honor and happiness of our firesides.

Our defence.

Then there will be no stock on which pantheism may ingraft itself among us. Our ideal of the true man, and of the true woman, will continue to be grander than anything of which Spinoza dreamed. And so we shall not exchange, for this monster which devours up all things, the one only living and true God. We shall not exchange, for this hideous nightmare of the absolute being which is nothing, our sweet faith and instinctive trust in the Father of our spirits. The peace passing all understanding shall still be ours; even the peace which comes of the assurance that he is with us, and that we are his children, whom no power can pluck from his hand. He draws about us the savor of his companionship, and undertakes with us, while we are toiling downward after the lost and vile. He covers us with the shield of his presence, and reënforces our strength with his own almighty power, when we march forth to fight against iniquity and outstanding wrongs. It is unto a personal God, who knows our frame, that we lift up our cry out of weakness and troubles; and we are sure that he is attentive to our prayer. Whether living or dying, we are his. We go to our graves, even, trustfully and in blessed hope. For it is he who bids us depart; and we hear his whisper, in fatherly mercy, saying to us that after the natural cometh the spiritual, and that we shall be satisfied with beholding his face, when we awake in that nearer fellowship to which his love invites us.

Something better than pantheism offers.

Of the subjects considered in this course of lectures, we now take our leave. I have endeavored as a companion, and in some sense as a guide, to go with others through the depths and windings of pantheistic thinking. If our incursion into that realm has

Conclusion.

reminded any of scenes described in the Sixth Book of the Æneid, I trust they have not lacked, throughout, a charm more potent than Virgil makes his hero carry. It is from the Tree of Life that we must pluck a branch, if we would walk unharmed in the shadow-land of scepticism. What the adored Beatrice was to Dante, in his Inferno, while he passed through circle after circle of the deepening abyss, the Spirit of Truth must be to us in the underworld of religious error. I am relieved A feeling of relief. even to gladness, coming up as I now do out of this investigation, into a realm where I may again breathe the upper air and see the sweet light of the Christian faith. It is as though one were awaking at length from a long and fearful dream. Notwithstanding the mighty intellects which pantheism may claim, and though I have tried to recognize the grandeur of the literary works of its disciples, I yet experience a refluent joy and peace in standing once more amid the radiance of Christian ideas, and hearkening to the voice of the Living God, my Father and Friend, speaking to me with the accents of a personal and tender love. This experience, coming after so much groping in the regions of darkness, recalls what Richter so graphically describes as happening to him one summer evening, while he lay on the hill-side and slept.

He dreamed that he was in the parish church, and that he saw the dead leave their graves and gather about him. " The shadows stood congregated near the altar; and in all the breast throbbed and trembled in place of a heart. One, which had just been buried in the church, lay still upon its pillow, and its breast heaved not, while upon its smiling countenance lay a happy Richter's Dream.

dream; but on the entrance of one of the living he awoke, and smiled no more. A lofty, noble form, having the expression of a never-ending sorrow, now sank down upon the altar, and all the dead exclaimed, 'Christ, is there no God?' And he answered, 'There is none! I traversed the worlds. I ascended into the suns, and flew with the milky ways through the wildernesses of the heavens, but there is no God! I descended as far as being throws its shadow, and gazed down into the abyss, and cried aloud, " Father, where art thou?" but I heard nothing but the eternal storm which no one rules; and when I looked up to the inmeasurable void for the divine eye, it glared upon me from an empty, bottomless socket, and eternity lay brooding upon chaos.' Then there arose, and came into the temple, the dead children who had awakened in the churchyard; and they cast themselves before the lofty form on the altar, and said, 'Jesus, have we no Father?' And he answered with streaming eyes, 'We are all orphans, I and you; we are without a Father.' And as I fell down and gazed into the gleaming fabric of worlds, I beheld the raised rings of the giant serpent of eternity, and she enfolded the universe doubly. Then she wound herself in a thousand folds around nature, and crushed the worlds together; and all became narrow, dark, and fearful, and a bell-hammer, stretched out to infinity, was about to strike the last hour of time, and split the universe asunder, when I awoke. My soul wept for joy that it could again worship God; and the joy, and the tears, and the belief in him were the prayer. And when I arose, the sun gleamed deeply behind the full, purple ears of corn, and peacefully threw the reflection of its evening blushes on the little moon, which was rising in the east without an aurora. And between the heaven and the earth a glad, fleeting world stretched out its short wings, and lived, like myself, in the presence of the Infinite Father; and from all nature round me flowed sweet, peaceful tones, as from evening bells."

There are expressions in the writings of Richter which indicate that even he did not wholly escape the pantheistic virus. It may have been hatred of atheism, rather than of Spinozism, which moved him to utter these words. Yet are they applicable to the latter, in some respects, more than to the former. I am willing to take the passage as declarative of strong faith in a personal God; for such it certainly is, at least in form. Whatever Richter's speculative belief may have been, therefore, we may adopt his Dream as illustrative of the workings of our Christian faith in view of pantheism. Thus viewing it, the chord of gladness within us, which vibrates responsively to its closing words, is deeper than any pantheistic doctrine can ever reach. Nor has Goethe, the illustrious friend of Schiller, written anything so reverent and touching as the prayer which Schiller's father, an unlearned but pious man, offered up for his infant son: "O God, that knowest my poverty in good gifts for my son's inheritance, graciously permit that even as the want of bread, to thy Son's hunger-stricken flock in the wilderness, became the pledge of overflowing abundance, so likewise my darkness may, in its sad extremity, carry with it the measure of thy unfathomable light; and because I, thy worm, cannot give to my son the least of blessings,

Pantheism cannot reach what is best in us.

The prayer of Schiller's father surpasses anything in Goethe.

do thou give the greatest; because in my hands there is
not anything, do thou from thine pour out all things; and
that temple of a new-born spirit, which I cannot adorn
even with earthly ornaments of dust and ashes, do thou
irradiate with the celestial adornments of thy presence,
and finally with that peace which passeth all understanding." We search in vain, throughout the pantheistic
literature of Germany, for anything so sublime as this faith
in a personal God, or which so stirs the pure heart. What
is there coming from the renowned Spinoza himself, or
from his most famous disciple, which can awake the sweet-
est and holiest emotions of our souls like the
twenty-third Psalm? As long as we believe
that what is noblest in us is most trustworthy,
as long as the purest impulses of our nature are any guide
to the truth, so long must we bow to the instinctive yearning for a personal God, and say, in calm defiance of the
wisdom which bewilders, "THE LORD IS MY SHEPHERD;
I SHALL NOT WANT. HE MAKETH ME TO LIE DOWN IN
GREEN PASTURES; HE LEADETH ME BESIDE THE STILL
WATERS. HE RESTORETH MY SOUL; HE LEADETH ME
IN THE PATHS OF RIGHTEOUSNESS FOR HIS NAME'S
SAKE. YEA, THOUGH I WALK THROUGH THE VALLEY
OF THE SHADOW OF DEATH, I WILL FEAR NO EVIL;
FOR THOU ART WITH ME; THY ROD AND THY STAFF
THEY COMFORT ME."

www.ingramcontent.com/pod-product-compliance
Lightning Source LLC
Chambersburg PA
CBHW022118290426
44112CB00008B/718